The Al Jazeera Phenomenon

Critical Perspectives on New Arab Media

Edited by

Mohamed Zayani

Paradigm Publishers
BOULDER

Published in the United States by Paradigm Publishers
3360 Mitchell Lane, Boulder, CO 80301 USA

Paradigm Publishers is the trade name of Birkenkamp & Company, LLC, Dean Birkenkamp, President and Publisher.

First published in the United Kingdom by Pluto Press
345 Archway Road, London N6 5AA

Copyright © Mohamed Zayani 2005

Library of Congress Cataloging-in-Publication Data has been applied for.

ISBN (hbk.: 1-59451-125-X alk. paper)
ISBN (pbk.: 1-59451-126-8 alk. paper)

Printed and bound in Canada on acid-free paper that meets the standards of the American National Standard for Permanence of Paper for Printed Library Materials.

09 08 07 06 05
 5 4 3 2 1

The Al Jazeera Phenomenon

Contents

Acknowledgments

This book would not have been possible without the support and encouragement of a great many individuals and institutions. I am particularly grateful to Sharifa Al Rawi, Nahawand Al Khaderi, Richard Bukholder, Sofiane Sahraoui, Abdelkader Daghfous, Mohamed Krichene, Mariam Wessam Al Dabbagh, Suzanne Gyeszly, Karen Peterson, Muhammad Ayish, Julie Stoll, Robert Webb, Laura Harrison, Jihad Ali Ballout, Anthony Collins, Khaled Al Hroub, Ann Lesch, Nidhal Guessoum, Ahmed Guessoum, William Gallois and Ronald Sheen.

I would like also to express my thanks and gratitude to the Social Science Research Council for supporting this project and for providing the framework within which international collaboration can thrive. Special thanks go to Graig Calhoun, Seteney Shami, Mary Ann Riad, Laleh Behbehanian, and Nazli Parvizi from the SSRC. Particular thanks are also due to the American University of Sharjah for granting me release time to complete this project.

Finally, my deepest appreciation is to Sonia for her support and patience during the time I was working on this project. I dedicate this book to her, to Aymen, and to my parents.

1
Introduction—Al Jazeera and the Vicissitudes of the New Arab Mediascape

Mohamed Zayani

Few phenomena in the Arab world are arguably more intriguing than Al Jazeera—a pan-Arab 24-hour satellite news and discussion channel beamed out of the tiny Gulf peninsula of Qatar. Its immediate success took the Arab media scene aback and even stunned Al Jazeera itself. Advertising itself as a forum for diverse views, focusing on issues of broad Arab concern and broaching controversial subjects, Al Jazeera has in no time managed to acquire a leading role in the Arab media scene. According to a 2002 report on Middle East communication published by Spotbeam Communications, "Al Jazeera is center-stage in the modernization of Arab-language broadcasting."[1] Not only has the network left a permanent mark on broadcasting in the Arab world, but it is also developing the potential to influence Arab public opinion and Arab politics. At the same time, Al Jazeera is highly controversial. Both inside and outside the Arab world, the network's coverage has been regarded with skepticism. In official Arab circles, Al Jazeera has acquired a maverick image and even prompted diplomatic crises. Since it catapulted to international prominence during the war in Afghanistan, the network has sparked a much publicized controversy, garnered much loathing and attracted considerable criticism. Away from the enthusiasm of those who champion it and the bitterness of those who criticize it, Al Jazeera remains not only a phenomenon that is worthy of exploration, but also one which begs for a better understanding.

AL JAZEERA'S NEW JOURNALISM

Al Jazeera is a relatively free channel operating in what many observers perceive as one of the regions that are less inclined toward freedom of expression. What made this venture possible was the initiative of Qatar to liberalize the press and do away with censorship, an initiative which gave Al Jazeera a free hand to operate more than it had an enduring effect on Qatari media as a whole. Upon taking power, the Emir of Qatar—who is keen not only on nurturing free speech but also on flirting with democracy—lifted censorship of the media by disbanding the Information Ministry, which was responsible for media censorship. Sheikh Hamad bin Thamer Al Thani, Chairman of the Board of Al Jazeera, explains the rationale: "The Ministry of Information ... is the Ministry that controls the news media, be it television, radio or newspaper ... We don't see that a Ministry of Information has any positive role to play in future media projects."[2] Seen from this vantage point, the key to the channel's success is the relative amount of freedom available to the people who work at Al Jazeera.[3] As such, Al Jazeera enjoys an unprecedented margin of freedom which makes it a haven for free speech in the Arab world. In fact, it is popular precisely because it openly discusses sensitive topics and tackles controversial issues. It ventures into a realm of open discussion rarely attempted by other broadcasters in the region. Its talk shows unabashedly tackle such unmentionables as government corruption, the human rights record of Arab regimes, the persecution of political dissenters, Islamic law (or Sharia), the (in)compatibility of Islam and democracy, and Islamic fundamentalism.

To some extent, Al Jazeera fills not only a media void but also a political void. In the absence of political will and political pluralism in the Arab world, Al Jazeera serves as a *de facto* pan-Arab opposition and a forum for resistance. It provides a voice for Arab opposing views and a high-profile platform for political dissidents many of whom live abroad. In a way, Al Jazeera has instituted the right to have access to the media for representatives of the region's myriad opposition groups. This has branded the network as one which questions authority and challenges the common political discourse. Projecting an unspoken reformist agenda, Al Jazeera does not shy away from covering political and social issues over which Arab governments prefer to keep quiet. In some of its programs, Al Jazeera tactfully welcomes criticism of governments and the hosts of its talk shows often challenge their guests if they are apologetic for their governments. Al Jazeera has also led the way in exposing Arab power abuses and giving an outlet to a pervading disenchantment with non-democratic and autocratic governing systems in the region. In doing so, it has instilled what may be loosely described as a culture of accountability. Leading figures and policy-makers have suddenly become accountable and answerable to their public.

It should come as no surprise that the network's frankness has angered most if not all Arab governments. Accordingly, the Arab States Broadcasting Union has denied Al Jazeera—the odd man out—access to the Pact of Arab Honor for not abiding by the "code of honor" which promotes brotherhood between Arab nations. While theoretically this move is impelled by the urge to meet standards of broadcasting propriety, in reality it is politically motivated. Al Jazeera is deemed a threat to the very hegemony and ideology of Arab regimes whose "survival instincts ... continue to pre-empt any liberalizing impulse of satellite TV."[4] The rhetoric of the network has, indeed, rankled some Arab governments who are unaccustomed to opposition. Naturally, Al Jazeera has been regarded with suspicion by Arab governments who complain that its programs bruise their sensitivities and threaten the stability of their regimes. For a few Arab statesmen and leaders, Al Jazeera is out there to undermine the reverence with which they are treated in their own media, criticize them, challenge their wisdom and undermine the very legitimacy of their regimes.[5]

Sure enough, Al Jazeera's insistence on challenging the culture of political restraint and showing little inhibition in its broadcasting about Arab states has prompted reprisals. In fact, some governments have denied Al Jazeera permission to open a bureau or closed its bureaus temporarily. While some Arab states have rebuked the network, others have banned its reporters or refused them visas. Even in Palestine, the Ramallah office of Al Jazeera was closed after Al Jazeera broadcast an unflattering image of Chairman Yasser Arafat in a promotional trailer for a documentary on the 1975–90 Lebanese Civil War, showing a demonstrator holding a pair of shoes over a picture of the Palestinian leader in a sign of contempt, thus silencing a media outlet that had provided extensive coverage for the Palestinian intifada against Israel and has helped put the Palestinian issue on the front burner.[6] Likewise, Arab states—including so-called moderate governments—have complained to the Qatari foreign ministry about Al Jazeera. Qatar's relationship with some of the Gulf states, namely Saudi Arabia and Kuwait, has been strained because of what the channel telecasts. Other countries such as Jordan and Egypt have either broken or threatened to break diplomatic relations with Qatar at times for being criticized by Al Jazeera, thus causing occasional diplomatic crises. But the Emir of Qatar has resisted pressure from Arab leaders to bring back Al Jazeera to the straight and narrow of the region's conformist tradition—and that has made a difference. According to the aforementioned Spotbeam Communications report on Middle East communication, Al Jazeera's "strength is that it is not cowered into self censorship."[7]

THE SPECIFICITY OF AL JAZEERA

Interestingly enough, the official stand toward Al Jazeera does not match its popularity with a large segment of Arab viewers. The network has gained as much popularity among Arab viewers as it has garnered loathing and attracted criticism from Arab governments. According to a 2002 Gallup poll on the Arab and Islamic world conducted in nine countries, Al Jazeera is widely watched—albeit with interesting nuances between regions.[8] In the Persian Gulf region and in Jordan, Al Jazeera is by far the preferred station for news (56 per cent in Kuwait and 47 per cent in Saudi Arabia); in the Levant, viewership of the network is relatively high (44 per cent in Jordan and 37 per cent in Lebanon where it vies for first place with a Lebanese channel); and in the Maghreb, Al Jazeera is fairly popular although not the preferred channel (20 per cent in Morocco, with two local channels faring slightly better).[9] The poll's findings that viewers in such countries as Kuwait, Saudi Arabia, Jordan and Lebanon are most likely to turn to Al Jazeera first to catch up on world events suggest that, by and large, Al Jazeera is regarded positively in the Arab world.[10]

The poll attributes the success of the network to a variety of factors. A high percentage of the viewers included in the poll turn to Al Jazeera because they feel it is always on the site of events, which in turn gives it direct and instant access to information and an instinct for airing breaking news. Not only does Al Jazeera pursue aggressive field reporting, but it also has come to claim a unique access to information—information which may not otherwise be available. For instance, during the so-called War on Terrorism, Al Jazeera has been a vital source of information, providing news and reports from Afghanistan and Iraq. Many tapes have found their way to the network featuring figures ranging from Osama bin Laden to Saddam Hussein, to Palestinian activists. Although access to such material raises questions about the significance of Al Jazeera's trustworthiness in the eyes of groups like Al Qaeda, the Taliban, Saddam Hussein's regime and various Islamic "opposition" groups, Al Jazeera has proven to be a window on a part of the world that is all too often alien to the West.[11] Over the years, Al Jazeera has come to provide comprehensive coverage of news and events that matter to the Arab and Muslim world. Part of the appeal of Al Jazeera according to the Gallup poll is its commitment to daring live unedited news as well as its tendency to broadcast uncut, live pictures. Particularly in times of turmoil, viewers are subjected to live feeds and unfiltered news on Al Jazeera. Likewise, its current affairs and talk show programs are aired live without screening out embarrassing questions or controversial statements. Viewers are drawn to Al Jazeera also because it offers intrepid reporting, candid talk, timely debates and vivid commentaries. Last but not least, the poll suggests that Al Jazeera is valued for the honesty and fairness of its reporting. As such, it aims at journalistic objectivity by presenting news and balancing it through a narrative and/or by inviting guests who represent different perspectives.

While such an opinion poll is suggestive, it does not capture the rich dynamics Al Jazeera sets up in their full complexity. Beyond the findings of this Gallup poll, one can venture a number of explanations for the relatively wide appeal of Al Jazeera. The network is popular partly because it is attentive to political news and caters to an audience that is politically conscious, that cherishes reliable political news and that craves intelligent political debates. Naturally, the geo-political situation of the Middle East has made politics an important component of media programs. Regional developments, tensions, crises and wars over the past few decades have enhanced such an interest. Being a major component of TV programs, political news has done much to develop the Arab viewers' political instinct. In fact, the media coverage of politics has contributed further to what Muhammad Ayish calls "the politicization of Arab viewers."[12] Al Jazeera has capitalized on that, providing food for an audience that is hungry for credible news and serious political analysis. One of the aims of Al Jazeera, as its former managing director Mohammed Jassim Al Ali explains, is "to bring the Arab audience back to trusting the Arab media, especially the news … We treat them as an intelligent audience, rather than the conventional idea that they will take whatever you give them."[13] Al Jazeera is popular partly because it takes the viewers seriously with its content and programming. In the not so distant past, large audiences received programs but were unable to make direct responses or participate in vigorous discussions. However, the viewers' expectations of media have changed. Arab viewers are no longer seen as consumers in a one-way communication stream. Through interactive debates with live phone-ins,

Al Jazeera has helped initiate a new kind of viewer experience. The kind of debate championed by Al Jazeera is something new in the Arab world where public political debate is considered subversive. What is particularly interesting about Al Jazeera is its ability to expand what people in the Arab world can talk about.

The advent of Al Jazeera has not only changed the viewers' expectations, but also altered some media practices in the Arab world. Overall, Al Jazeera has instilled a competitive drive in some mainstream Arab media and accelerated the institutionalization of new trends in programming. Certain programs, or at least program formats, which are typical of Al Jazeera have been injected into many Arab satellite channels in bandwagon fashion as is the case with talk shows with viewer call-ins. Al Jazeera is also nudging competitors toward live interviews and is pushing some channels to display a new savvy for finding stories. Some Arab satellite channels such as Abu Dhabi TV have tried to emulate Al Jazeera's free style in news broadcasting. Recently, the Arab media scene has also seen the proliferation of news channels, the most prominent being the Dubai-based Al Arabiya. Even state media establishments can no longer ignore what pan-Arab stations like Al Jazeera are doing and have, indeed, become more aware of the need for more appropriate programming. Al Jazeera's programming has challenged the restrained coverage available on state media which has no other choice than to follow suit and even send reporters to the scene for fear of losing audiences. Not only have Al Jazeera's professional standards informed many other channels, but the mobility of some of the network's staff has also helped dissipate such journalistic practices. In February 2004, the network set up a Media Center for Training and Development aimed at instilling its journalistic values into journalists and media institutions throughout the region.[14]

AL JAZEERA AS A PAN-ARAB CHANNEL

Al Jazeera distinguished itself by its attempt to reach out to a large Arab audience, discussing issues that are pressing in the Arab and Muslim world, in general, and the conflict-ridden Middle East, in particular. Dealing with a wide range of issues that touch the Arab world—such as the Anglo-American bombing of Baghdad in operation Desert Fox, the plight of the Iraqi people under the decade-long sanctions, the Palestinian intifada, the war in Afghanistan and the invasion of Iraq—Al Jazeera has managed to carve a niche for itself.

Not only are Arab issues prominent on the network's news and discussion programs, but the very issue of Arabness is paramount. According to Suleiman Al Shammari, Al Jazeera plays off and even feeds an Arab nationalist trend in its viewers. Through some of its programs and talk shows, "the channel promotes an Arab nationalist discourse wrapped in a democratic style which makes it easy for viewers to palate."[15] But Al Jazeera is no Sawt Al Arab. It may be vaguely reminiscent of the heyday of Nasser's Arab nationalism but, as David Hirst rightly points out, it is very different for "neither in style nor content can Al Jazeera be compared to Cairo's Voice of the Arabs ... but some regard it as its closest successor."[16] The pan-Arab overtones are not only subtle, but different and less contrived. Al Jazeera has come to play an important role in broadening pan-Arab interaction. As such, it projects an inclusive identity which crosses national boundaries.

This new notion of Arabism manifests itself to a certain degree in the very image the network projects of itself—its staff, its language, its name, and its location. Al Jazeera employs people from various Arab nations. Its staff, some of whom came out of the BBC Arabic service, are Arabs from almost every corner of the Arab world, with no apparent domination of any single group. Although there is no deliberate policy of diversification when it comes to personnel decisions, the network has an exceptionally diverse workforce. Naturally, the lack of a dominant group gives the network a pan-Arab ring. Equally important is the language factor. Al Jazeera, which broadcasts exclusively in modern standard Arabic, has gone a long way to creating a kind of connectivity between Arab viewers. Likewise, the name of the network has pan-Arab overtones. In Arabic, the term "Al Jazeera," which literally means "island," is closely associated with and even connotes the word "peninsula"— the likely allusion in the minds of most Arab viewers being not so much to the peninsula of Qatar itself, the home country, as much as it is to the Arabian Peninsula (Shebh Al Jazeera Al Arabiya).[17] The location of the network is also not without meaning. Al Jazeera may not have been the first private channel to appeal to a pan-Arab public, but it has represented a turning point in Arab broadcasting in so far as it operates from within the Gulf region. In so doing, it is closer to its core audience, breaking away from the previous experiences of offshore media democracy and the myth that one of the conditions for establishing a free media is its location outside the Arab world.

Being close to the events in the region, Al Jazeera has acquired substantial clout in the Arab world by bringing conflicts and issues right into the living rooms of its predominantly Arab audience. In many ways, Al Jazeera has reinvigorated a sense of common destiny in the Arab world and is even encouraging Arab unity, so much so that pan-Arabism is being reinvented on this channel.[18] As a pan-Arab satellite broadcaster, Al Jazeera caters to a transnational regional audience that may be heterogeneous in some ways, but is nonetheless bound by language, culture, history, and to a lesser extent religion and geography.[19] If anything, Al Jazeera has been at the forefront of Arab satellite channels which have brought about "a pan-Arab consciousness"[20] or a pan-Arab "imagined community," to borrow Benedict Anderson's term, comprised of individuals who have a sense of belonging to and affinity with other people they have never met and who actually speak the same language but are not geographically limited.

Al Jazeera also helps nurture a sense of community among the Arab diaspora. It does so in two ways: by tapping into Arab figures outside the Arab world and by appealing to Arab viewers outside their home countries. In a number of its programs, Al Jazeera has invited Arab intellectual figures and journalists who live in Europe for instance and political figures in exile. Because its coverage of Middle East issues has more depth and provides a different spin from that of Western networks, Al Jazeera has also attracted viewers outside the Arab world. In doing so, it has enhanced the cultural connection between its Arab viewers overseas and Arab culture. The network is one among many transnational channel which brings Arab countries and their diaspora into an ongoing public argument about timely Arab issues. This is not without consequences. In Europe, for instance, where there is a large Arab immigrant community that is keen on following Arab news, there is an increasing fear that satellite channels like Al Jazeera constitute a serious challenge to Europe's policy of culturally assimilating immigrant communities.[21]

Tapping into the Arab identity during times marked by Arab disunity, Al Jazeera has emerged as a key opinion maker. For Poniwozik, it is one of three institutions that have the power to influence people: "Among all the major influences on Arab Public opinion— the mosque, the press, the schools—the newest and perhaps most revolutionary is Al Jazeera."[22] In a way, Al Jazeera is a channel that appeals to the masses and has an overt populist orientation. Naturally, it has acquired some legitimacy through the Arab street.

It has developed the potential to shape public opinion in the Arab world. Arabs all over the world can now have instant access to what is happening in the Arab and Muslim community. Such exposure has helped develop a sense of political awareness among ordinary viewers. Occasionally, this awareness translates into popular pressure on Arab governments to step up their efforts to act on certain issues and to alter their tame policy. In some instances, Al Jazeera has sparked student demonstrations and inflamed public opinion and as a result some Arab governments are finding it more and more pressing to keep pace with popular opinion.

Faced with the discontent and occasional agitation of Arab public opinion—which it contributes to and fuels in some ways—Al Jazeera, much like some other alternative channels, opens up the waves so that viewers can call in and participate live thus venting some of the anger they have. The call-in segments of its talk shows allow viewers to openly criticize certain policies, give their views and express anxieties. Seen from this perspective, Al Jazeera becomes interesting because of what it can do in terms of diffusing—and not just inciting—public opinion. To a certain extent, Al Jazeera can be said to have a cathartic effect, and some of its viewers come to be content with the relief of expressing themselves. If, as Jon Anderson and Dale Eikelman put it, "free expression at the margins provides a safety valve and a new way of keeping tabs on opponents,"[23] then one may argue that Al Jazeera plays a role, jejune as it may be, in the pacification of Arab public opinion. At times, the channel acts as a window through which many muted ordinary Arabs can vent their anger, offering an Arabic and Islamic perspective that can be seen as a shock-buffer between reality and the viewers. To put this somewhat differently, Al Jazeera occasionally plays the role of a preventative medium and an outlet for the disenfranchised public, thus providing a safety valve in what may be described as a suffocating atmosphere in Arab countries. Thus, in some ways, the kind of pan-Arab consciousness Al Jazeera can be said to project and foster is what may be termed, after Bassam Tibi, a "rhetorical pan-Arabism" which does not go beyond such proclaimed themes as harmony and brotherhood.[24]

THE POLITICS OF AL JAZEERA

In spite of the inroads Al Jazeera has made, the freedom of speech this network enjoys is not without constraints. Al Jazeera is suspiciously silent on Qatar; it offers a sparing coverage of its host country and is careful not to criticize it. Although in a few instances Qatari issues have been covered and although the Minister of Foreign Affairs was, on more than one occasion, given a rough ride on Ahmad Mansour's prominent show *Without Borders* (*Bila Hudud*) on issues some of which pertain to Qatar and Al Jazeera, overall, the channel's programs steer clear of issues that bear on Qatar itself. The network, as its critics point out, "is under the thumb of the Qatari royal family, whose policies [it] never criticizes."[25] Jon Alterman concurs: "Qatari issues such as the power struggle between the current Emir and his father, whom he displaced, do not find an outlet on Al Jazeera, nor do critiques of Qatari foreign policy."[26] Furthermore, in spite of the political rows Al Jazeera has caused, it has strangely enough not had an impact on the domestic politics of the host country. It is as if Al Jazeera were an offshore company or a free-zone venture. For some critics, Al Jazeera probes the affairs of other Arab countries to distract viewers from its host's own internal politics and its arrangements with the US—which has its largest military base in the region as well as its Central Command in Qatar. There is a perception that the Qatari political leadership subtly manipulates Al Jazeera for the purposes of controlling Qatari society by ignoring domestic issues[27]—although Qatar is no Egypt with a large population or Iraq with diverse and often conflicting ethnicities and religious sects. In fact, there are fewer than 200,000 native Qatari citizens and they are well provided for by their rich government.

The foregoing analysis leaves a number of questions unanswered: Has Al Jazeera really made the censorship of news and views pointless in the Arab world or is it simply a self-serving endeavor? Does Qatar genuinely believe in what Al Jazeera stands for, including freedom of speech, or is it just using Al Jazeera as a public relations tool to claim a space in the region and play a more important role? What are the politics and motives of Al Jazeera's host country? Is it possible to depoliticize the study of Al Jazeera? Why couldn't Al Jazeera have been a Kuwaiti project, for instance, or a Lebanese media outlet—for, according to William Rugh's classical typology of Arab media, both Kuwait and Lebanon have a "diverse press" characterized by a relative margin of freedom and a certain degree of independence which are conducive to more information and opinion for people to choose from?[28]

For some observers, Al Jazeera has worked a thin line between objectivity and subjectivity:

> Unofficially, Al Jazeera's output indicates that it has been given considerable scope. Its staff prioritize stories according to their newsworthiness, not their acceptability to local regimes, and much of Al Jazeera's material is broadcast live. Newsworthiness criteria, however, are subjective, and Al Jazeera's criteria may well reflect the Qatari leadership's agenda.[29]

Indeed, the international eminence of Al Jazeera has never been at the expense of its national identity. At least in the newscasts, the name of the network is constantly linked with the name of its host country as viewers are repeatedly reminded that the news of Al Jazeera is aired from Qatar. In spite of the pan-Arab current that runs through it, Al Jazeera is first and foremost a Qatari channel—one that is sponsored by and beamed from Qatar. Naturally, one would think that Al Jazeera was created to serve the interests of its host country in one way or another.

Qatar is a small emirate in the Persian Gulf region of 11,437 km^2 with around 700,000 inhabitants, the majority of whom are expatriates or guest workers, mainly from Pakistan, the Indian subcontinent and other Arab countries. The country has ample energy resources. It is true that Qatar is an oil-rich country with large oil fields, but its strength lies in its vast natural gas reserves, an asset which not only frees it from the chronic dependence on oil so characteristic of other Gulf Cooperation Council states, but also guarantees its economic prosperity beyond the twenty-first century. Since the mid 1990s, the country has witnessed an economic boom that has yielded one of the highest gross domestic product per capita incomes in the world.[30]

This relatively conservative and fairly devout tiny country is ruled by a "liberal" emir, Sheikh Hamad bin Khalifa Al Thani, who seized power from his father while the latter was vacationing outside the country in a bloodless coup in 1995. Since then, the Emir has been attempting to transform his country into a liberal constitutional monarchy. Qatar projects an image of a country that is keen on modernizing itself and the Emir has, in fact, brought about liberal reform which includes holding elections for a chamber of commerce, having municipal elections and allowing women to vote.[31] Al Jazeera falls in line with the image of the Emir as a modernizer and fits into his vision of political liberalization. When asked about the correlation between the establishment of Al Jazeera and the coming of age of civil society in its host country, Sheikh Hamad bin Thamer Al Thani commented that

> Al Jazeera is going in the same direction as the State of Qatar in its recent developments ... This direction corresponds with the direction of the media, be it Al Jazeera, or lifting censorship on local Qatari newspapers. The two go together in this state ... The direction of Al Jazeera is a natural one that corresponds with the strategy Qatar is taking at this phase.[32]

The Emir of Qatar himself has argued that before introducing free parliamentary elections in Qatar such a satellite channel is a necessary source of information. For people to be informed politically and otherwise, they must have access to an open medium. Seen from this perspective, Al Jazeera is a showpiece of the Emir of Qatar and a symbol of his resolve to modernize his country.

Al Jazeera also fits in with Qatar's attempt to play an active role in regional politics and to achieve regional influence. Thanks to satellite technology, transnational television flow has given this small country some influence. Qatar is trying to extend its regional influence and to have an impact. As satellite media is becoming more and more pervasive, major Arab countries cannot effectively dominate smaller ones. Traditionally, Saudi Arabia has had considerable influence on the Gulf countries. This influence, which can be seen in the political and religious spheres, has also been extended to the media sphere. Seeking to influence what is written about it in the Arab press, Saudi Arabia, as Boyd puts it, has succeeded in positioning itself as a *de facto* owner of foreign-based media outlets.[33] Through semi-private, technology-conscious, Western-oriented, foreign-based media ventures in Europe, Saudi Arabia has managed to claim considerable clout in the regional mediascape and to exert an influence on Arab media. The Kingdom has, in fact, created a whole media empire and acquired considerable weight in TV broadcasting. It sits on well-established media conglomerates such as Orbit Communications, Arab Radio and Television (ART), and the Middle East Broadcasting Corporation (MBC), which is part of ARA Group International, a media conglomerate that includes a number of radio and television companies beamed throughout the Arab world—not to mention print media, as Saudi Arabia puts out a plethora of publications, the most prominent of which are the London-based *Al-Sharq Al-Awsat* and *Al-Hayat*.[34]

Being neither a big country nor a regional power, Qatar naturally felt the supremacy of neighboring Saudi Arabia—"Gulf Big Brother," as David Hirst calls it[35]—in the region and was keen on getting out of its shadow. Under Sheikh Hamad, Qatar sought a somewhat independent voice. Thanks to the popularity and wide reach of Al Jazeera in the Arab world, Qatar managed to acquire an increasingly influential media force—at least one that is hard to ignore. The network helped to give Qatar prominence which is disproportionate to its size, military power and economic strength.

Yet the key to Qatar's newly-acquired status is not simply the country's sponsorship of Al Jazeera, but also its development of regional relations. Qatar has exercised active diplomacy primarily by playing a mediating role in regional disputes. For example, Qatar has been involved in mediating efforts in the civil war in Sudan as well as the dispute between Eritrea and Ethiopia. Qatar has also played a significant role in the attempted rapprochement between Iran and Arab states and between Iran and the United States. More recently, it has initiated talks between the United States and Libya and mediated the release of Moroccan prisoners of war who were held captive by the Polisario Front. Qatar has also been open on Israel. This is evident not only in the low-level trade ties Qatar has had since 1996 with Tel Aviv (namely the establishment of an Israeli trade mission in Doha), but also in the various talks it has been holding with Israeli officials at the highest levels and the prospects of raising the level of representation between the two countries.[36]

It is doubtful whether Qatar's diplomacy has achieved a great deal. Nor has Al Jazeera done much for its host country beyond giving it a limited diplomatic presence and heightening its regional and international profile. In fact, Al Jazeera's function as an instrument of Qatari foreign policy is hard to discern as Al Jazeera's political discourse is often incompatible or at least out of sync with Qatar's foreign policy. As Gary Gambill points out,

> decisions as to the content of the station's news coverage and the partici-
> pants in its televised political forums do not appear to be influenced by
> specific foreign policy objectives. If there is a cornerstone to Qatar's foreign
> policy, it is its development of friendly ties with all countries of the region
> (including Iraq, Iran and Israel), an objective that does not appear at first
> glance to be easily compatible with sponsoring a satellite news station that
> broadcasts interviews with their political dissidents, reports on their human
> rights abuses, and open debates on their religious practices.[37]

The hard-line approach one often senses in Al Jazeera is not compatible with the soft approach that characterizes Qatar's foreign policy; at the same time, it is not at odds with it. For Olivier Da Lage, the ensuing ambiguity is a calculated risk and a political strategy that serves the interests of Qatar well.[38]

THE POLITICAL ECONOMY OF AL JAZEERA

Tightly connected with the politics of Al Jazeera is its political economy. Al Jazeera has been financed with a yearly budget of $30 million. In 1995, the Emir of Qatar, Sheik Hamad Al Thani, signed a decree launching an independent news channel to be financed initially by the government. Accordingly, in 1996, the Qatari government provided Al Jazeera with a five-year $150 million loan which, theoretically, was due for repayment with Al Jazeera's fifth anniversary. Seen from a global perspective, there is nothing out of the ordinary about the ownership of Al Jazeera. If anything, the Emir's media venture corresponds with an interesting global trend favoring a marriage between media ownership and politics. For example, the Thai Prime Minister, Thaksin Shinawatra, is both a political figure and a telecommunications entrepreneur. Likewise, Silvio Berlusconi, Italy's Prime Minister, is a pioneer of commercial TV and publishing in Italy. In the Middle East, the Lebanese Prime Minister, business tycoon and media baron Rafiq Al Hariri, owns the satellite channel Future TV. Al Jazeera can be said to epitomize this new trend which is characterized by the politicization of media ownership.

At the same time, Al Jazeera fits in with a deep-seated regional tradition. In the Arab world, the media in general, and satellite channels in particular, operate under a patron who is either the government or some rich owner who in many cases is associated, in one way or another, with the ruling elite or the government. Most television systems in the Arab world are subsidized by the government partly because they need a great deal of money and partly because Arab governments have a stake in the media. Historically such monopolies go hand in hand with centralization; they help maintain a country's unity, preserve a centralized system of government and exercise control over the people. TV also serves as a propaganda tool, an extension of state power and a mouthpiece for state policies, and control of such an apparatus ensures that dissident voices do not have access to the public. Even though the effect and popularity of state TV are declining, governments have been reluctant to relinquish their influence on the media. In fact, some have sought to maintain such influence through partial government ownership (as in the case of Egypt) or private financing (as is the case with Saudi Arabia).[39]

Who owns what in the Arab media is an entangled issue and a subject of inquiry in itself.[40] Still, the patterns of media ownership in the Arab world point to some contradictions. On the one hand, governments are ideologically inclined to more commercialization and privatization; on the other hand, they still conceive of media as a state-controlled public service. The outcome is an interesting marriage of the two models: the public and the private, the ideological and the commercial. As it is, a network like Al Jazeera is both private and public. To overlook the interconnectedness of these two aspects is to ignore the specificity and complexity of the new patterns of ownership and financing in the realm of Arab media.

It goes without saying that the lifeline of any media outlet is advertising, which in turn depends on viewer numbers and profiles. Not so with Al Jazeera as advertising is tied with political considerations and succumbs to outside pressures. During the first few years of its existence, Al Jazeera did not get into the full swing of airing commercials. For one thing, big companies and potential large advertisers in the region have been wary of advertising on Al Jazeera partly because of the maverick image the channel has acquired among Arab and Middle Eastern governments. Many Arab marketers and companies have boycotted Al Jazeera for fear that dealing with a network which broadcasts sensitive programs and controversial material may trigger a backlash from governments in the region. Advertising agencies are indeed unwilling to lose advertising revenue in other Arab countries. The main pressure has come from neighboring Saudi Arabia which, given its size, is the major purchasing power in the area and has joint projects with international firms and multinational corporations who have been reluctant to advertise with Al Jazeera for fear of losing access to the media of Saudi Arabia, a country that represents an important market and controls most of the advertisement agencies in the Gulf region.

However, Al Jazeera seems to have survived this *de facto* commercial boycott. Anecdotal evidence credited to some officials in Al Jazeera suggests that the network is starting to break even thanks to its earnings from cable subscriptions, advertising, sales of programs and documentaries, and from renting equipment and selling satellite time to other networks.[41] Recently, the network has benefited from sales of rebroadcast rights of unique footage to Western networks especially during the war in Afghanistan and the invasion of Iraq. It is believed that the channel is close to or at least has the potential of being self-financed, but even so, only operational expenses are covered by its income from advertising, subscription fees outside the Arab world, sales of copyrights, and sales of programs and services.[42] The channel is still receiving financial assistance from the government to cover the cost incurred by capital investment, namely funding new projects, including an English language website, a documentary channel, a sports channel and an English language TV service.

But not all analysts are optimistic about Al Jazeera's financial prospects. Deprived of commercial autonomy—as more powerful governments in the region have bullied advertisers—and dependent on government handouts, Al Jazeera illustrates the fragility of some of the leading media outlets in the Arab world. At least in the Gulf, the willingness of states to provide funding for the media is tightly connected with oil prices. In times of crisis or when budgets are tightened, funding for the media will probably be the first to take a cut, although the argument is not readily applicable to Qatar, being one of the wealthiest countries and enjoying one of the highest gross domestic product per capita incomes in the world. Still, some observers find the financial picture far from encouraging and have doubts about Al Jazeera's ability to meet the big challenge of financial security, particularly in the light of its envisaged expansion. Judging by the paucity of advertising, Sharon Waxman believes that "the network is still quite far from achieving financial solvency."[43] Barbara Demick concurs. In her view, there is a sense that "imitators are likely to come along, perhaps better financed and equipped that might eventually drive Al Jazeera out of business."[44]

However, this type of business-oriented analysis misses the heart of the issue; in such a perspective media success means numbers, and in the case of Al Jazeera numbers do not add up. This is not to say that money and profit are not important considerations for the network, for, at least in its initial conception, Al Jazeera should eventually gain financial independence from the state of Qatar. Although relatively successful, Al Jazeera is not profitable. Al Jazeera claims that it would like to be profitable, but insists that profitability should not be at the expense of its *raison d'être*, which means that the financial stakes of Al Jazeera cannot be discussed independently of its goals, which in turn are intertwined with the politics of its host country.[45] So far, Al Jazeera depends on the Emir of Qatar financially but also politically. Being the pet project of the Emir, Al Jazeera is more of a one-man vision than a deep-seated institution, which in the words of Louay Bahry means that

> any serious domestic change in Qatar, such as instability in the ruling family or even change of government—though currently unexpected, always a possibility—would impact Al Jazeera. Without strong support from the Emir and political will to continue this media experiment, Al Jazeera could fall prey to external pressure to curtail its daring style. Over time, such pressure could leave it weakened, resulting in a loss of appeals to Arabs outside Qatar.[46]

SOME SHORTCOMINGS

Despite its funding from the state, Al Jazeera has been envisaged since its inception as an "autonomous" network with editorial independence. Of course, autonomy and independence are relative concepts for, after all, Al Jazeera is governed by a board of directors that is chaired by Sheikh Hamad bin Thamir Al Thani, a member of Qatar's ruling family. Still, the idea of a TV channel that is government-financed and yet independent is altogether new to the region. This independence and autonomy lend Al Jazeera a great deal of credibility and creativity. At least in the Arab world, it is perceived by many viewers as a credible source of news. It must be said that Al Jazeera provides a rare case of the funder not interfering with and intervening in editorial policy. Nonetheless, some find the link between this source of the news and the government somewhat uncomfortable. Al Jazeera may claim independence, but the network has only relative independence; it is not government-controlled, but is nonetheless government owned. To what extent state funding affects the independence and editorial decision-making of the network remains a pressing issue.

Even if the problem of independence is overlooked, Al Jazeera remains open to criticism. In the aforementioned Gallup poll, objectivity is perceived as the network's weakest area.[47] While in relative terms—that is, compared with the other channels included in the poll—Al Jazeera is ranked the highest channel with regards to objectivity, in absolute terms, it is perceived as lacking in objectivity. Only about half of the respondents associate Al Jazeera's coverage with objectivity, with the highest percentage being 54 per cent in Kuwait and the lowest 38 per cent in Saudi Arabia. Viewers and media commentators alike acknowledge that Al Jazeera has made a breakthrough but remain wary of its agenda and of the politicized discourse it fosters, although the network claims fairness of reporting and denies it has any political agenda—or at least any agenda other than presenting contrasting points of view. If Al Jazeera has become so popular, the network claims, it is not because it defends its theses and advances its agenda, but because it promotes and encourages various views on timely and important issues—in fact, because it has instituted a pluralistic media discourse. Upon the disjunction between what Al Jazeera believes it is producing and what it is perceived as producing there lies a more potent question pertaining to the very conception of objectivity and neutrality in media. For example, one cannot say that Al Jazeera is neutral in reporting the Palestinian–Israeli conflict. This raises the very question of whether and to what extent one can be truly objective when reporting from the Arab world about issues that matter to Arabs the most. The question is not specific to the Arab media.

The debate about the notion of embedded journalists—reporters embedded with American and allied troops, providing live coverage of the military actions during the Gulf War—further complicates the issue. In an episode of Ghassan bin Jeddou's weekly program *Open Dialogue*, which was occasioned by the seventh anniversary of the network, one of its investigative reporters, Asaad Taha, ventured a perspective that goes beyond the proclaimed motto of "the view and the opposite view." Criticized on grounds that what he presents is permeated with an agenda that smacks of certain beliefs, thoughts, politics and ideology, Taha—who acknowledged that he did not shy away from being inflammatory (*tahridhi*) on an episode of his documentary program *Correspondents* devoted to the Iraqi resistance— made it clear that he is "adamantly against the notion of neutrality. There is no such thing as a neutral journalist or a neutral media for that matter ... This is not to say, however, that one should not be objective. The journalist can be objective but not neutral ... In fact, he or she must be message-oriented and have an idea for or carry a message to a public that watches the channel and trusts it."[48] Seen from one perspective, this statement is not philosophically speaking different from the position some US media took in the same context and the statement some journalists made by wearing yellow ribbons on their lapels. Seen from another perspective, Taha's position, which is not all that uncommon in the Arab world, cannot be discussed outside the cultural specificity of Arab media, the lack of media tradition, and the very role Arab media envisages for itself. Still, for many viewers, Al Jazeera is far from being responsible. Sometimes, the network's reporting produces as much emotion and sentiment as it provides factual information.

For some observers, Al Jazeera is neither sober nor analytical and its impact is exaggerated. Indeed, Al Jazeera is not without excesses. There is a certain aggressiveness to the network that is hard to ignore. With instant access to world events, Al Jazeera broadcasts news around the clock. News is fed to the viewers as it comes in, beamed to millions of viewers at such a speed that one is left with too much political information to digest. To watch Al Jazeera is to experience an information overload or an infoglut. With Al Jazeera, one has the impression that too much is going on around the world. There is always something that just happened or something that is imminent and could happen at any time. The tone and direction of the news are constantly ascending. In its attempt to capture everything, Al Jazeera appears to be running away with itself. One often experiences a sense of excess that emanates from the disparate and disjoined aired bits and bites of information. Although some critics feel that with time it will not be hard for Al Jazeera to moderate its excesses, others point to deep-seated problems. For example, the channel does not seem capable of sufficiently removing itself from that which it is reporting—although this is symptomatic of a problem that is not specific to Al Jazeera, namely can an Arab channel reporting on Arab issues remove itself from its Arab perspective? The war in Afghanistan and the invasion of Iraq have made this a pressing issue, even for Western media with a long tradition of press freedom.

Beyond that, some of Al Jazeera's political talk shows are often combative leaning more toward sensationalism than toward what Habermas calls "a rational critical debate." For example, in a program like *The Opposite Direction* real debate risks receding in front of the show aspect—and in fact the debate entertained tends to be less rational than programs like *From Washington* (*Min Washington*) or *For Women Only* (*Lil Nissa Faqat*). Through such programs, the channel is often perceived as creating a controversy, which it then fiercely pursues. Others find fault with Al Jazeera on grounds that endless debates about the state of the Arab world deepen existing differences between Arabs. Furthermore, some of Al Jazeera's talk shows tend to overshadow and marginalize programs designed to provide an informative and constructive debate to the public. For example, there is a need for more investigative reporting or programs like *A Hot Spot* (*Nokta Saakhina*), *Once Upon a Time* (*Yuhka Anna*) and *Correspondents* (*Mouraseloun*). This requires considerable funds and is not easy to produce as it entails travel and research. Naturally channels, including Al Jazeera, fall into airing talk shows which are not expensive to produce and do not require as much work.[49]

There is no doubt that Al Jazeera has played a leading role in an environment marked by the lack of alternative voices and opposing views, earning it the reputation of an Arab parliament on the air. However, the network seems to have fallen into its own trap. In spite of its freshness, newness and alternative edge, the channel has at times had to increase its provocative tone and its oppositional stand, and these have became addictive. Viewers have often been caught in this frame too and supporters of a certain debate have called in to confirm a point made by guests and to deride their opponents. Not only has the channel on occasions slipped into sensationalism, it has also acquired a certain monotony as some of its scenarios become routine and many of its programs lend themselves to the same format. Likewise, a number of its guests keep reappearing with the same line of argument being advocated.

There is also the danger of vulgarizing the kinds of popular programs on which Al Jazeera thrives. Al Jazeera has a lot of responsibility on its shoulders not simply because it is widely watched and has the potential to influence public opinion but also because it has been a trendsetter. As Al Jazeera's journalism is copied on other channels, so are some of the problems that come with it. Channels have started to compete with each other over who invites the hottest guest and who raises the most controversial issue. While some see in the proliferation of talk shows a healthy development, others remain skeptical. They see in this new frenzy a vent for public opinion to reaffirm the status quo.

Furthermore, the quantum leap Al Jazeera has achieved, which set it apart from other Arab channels, has not been entirely beneficial to it as the lack of real competition, at least in the first few years of its existence, prevented it from evolving and moderating its excesses. In order to continue to be viable, Al Jazeera has to go beyond playing the role of the devil's advocate—being that which is oppositional, anti and critical. Al Jazeera will have to move away from discussions that verge on fighting. As it is, Al Jazeera gives the impression that it has outrun itself. Al Jazeera has to rejuvenate itself by envisaging a

new role, a new mentality for engaging with pertinent issues and setting up more nuanced objectives. In this sense, the proliferation of
new news channels in the Arab media scene such as the Dubai-based
Al Arabiya may be to Al Jazeera's advantage.

AL JAZEERA AND THE WEST

Interestingly enough, while attracting criticism from Arab governments, Al Jazeera attracted attention from and gained the respect
of the US as a unique and long-overdue experiment. In 1999, The
Harvard International Review took note of this pioneering network.[50]
In May 2001, Ed Bradley profiled Al Jazeera on *60 Minutes*.[51] In the
same year, *New York Times* columnist Thomas Friedman hailed it as
a beacon of freedom and the biggest media phenomenon to hit the
Arab world.[52]

However, the September 11 events were a turning point in the
history of the network. Virtually unheard of outside the Middle East
and North Africa, Al Jazeera caught the world by surprise during the
war in Afghanistan in 2001, being for some time the only foreign
news organization with reporters in Taliban-controlled Afghanistan.
With its logo aired everywhere in the world, it catapulted to international prominence to become a super-station. The broadcasting of
the bin Laden videotapes and the airing of graphic images made Al
Jazeera part of the news it covered. Al Jazeera's views and coverage
were not very welcome, and the American press adopted a more critical stance toward it. Even those who were not critical of Al Jazeera
were suspicious of its intentions. Overnight, the benign image of the
network as a promising one and a huge rock in a tepid media lagoon
was deconstructed as Al Jazeera started to infuriate Western democratic nations with a predilection for the freedom of the press. For Robert
Fisk, the change in perception is specious but hardly surprising: Al
Jazeera "is a phenomenon in the Arab world, a comparatively free,
bold initiative in journalism that was supported by the Americans—
until it became rather too free."[53]

But what is so jarring about Al Jazeera's tune? For a number of
Western viewers, Al Jazeera stands out for its irresponsible journalism and its lack of professionalism. Its programs are aggressive and
its discourse is politically incorrect. For Dan Williams, Al Jazeera has
nothing more than "an approximation of credibility," while for
former Downing Street media chief Alastair Campbell Al Jazeera airs
lies, plain and simple.[54] The network is derided for what is often

described as its partisan and biased coverage. It is often portrayed as "less than honest," being more in the business of making stories than getting them. In this sense, Al Jazeera is perceived as lacking in fairness and balance. For Fouad Ajami, "its credibility is hampered by slanted coverage and a tendency toward sensationalism" as it often engages in the "Hollywoodization of news."[55] It is keen on airing grisly footage and is never shy about presenting graphic imagery, which makes it little more than a tabloid:

> Equipped with state-of-the-art technology, the station has the feel of a cross between tabloid television and a student-run newspaper that can't resist the impulse to publish, irrespective of concerns for taste, under the slogan of "freedom of the press."[56]

While some dismiss Al Jazeera as tabloid journalism, others point to its excesses:

> its reporters are sometimes guilty of over-exuberance. For example, they are inclined to claim that one telegenic student demonstration is representative of a whole country's "street opinion." Even Al Jazeera's supporters say that its success with audiences has caused a strident and highly politicized tone to creep into some of its programming.[57]

Thomas Friedman has a similar take on the channel: "Sometimes, it goes over the edge and burns people unfairly because some of its broadcasters have their own agendas, and sometimes it hypes the fighting in the West Bank in inflammatory ways."[58]

Al Jazeera has also been demonized as a platform for demagoguery. There is a tendency to see in Al Jazeera a mouthpiece or a vehicle through which opponents of the West get their views across. Some find Al Jazeera's perspective and tone excessively critical of the US and of Israel. For the Bush administration, the network gives too much airtime to anti-American activists and people who are hostile to the US. The Bush administration frowns on the amount of airtime Al Jazeera gives to analysts expressing anti-American rhetoric or criticizing American foreign policy. When asked on CBS's *Face the Nation* whether he believed Al Jazeera is anything more than an Arab television station, Defense Secretary Donald Rumsfeld responded that

> it puts out television images in Arabic, in the Arabic language and I do not watch it carefully. People who do tell me that it has a pattern of being anti-US,

anti-West and I have also seen pieces of information that suggest that they're influenced by people like Saddam Hussein's regime ... It is unfortunate that people of the world don't see as open and accurate a set of images in Arabic as I think they might and anything that can be done about that is a good thing.[59]

In spite of the network's claim to unbiased news, and in spite of the "non-generic" character of its viewers—the latter being fairly well-informed and, compared with other news viewers, more open to the West according to a Gallup poll finding[60]—Al Jazeera, as some perceive it, tends to take the side of the underdog. Some critics argue that Al Jazeera is giving prominence to guests who are keen on chastising the West by toeing an Arab nationalist or Islamist line that is antagonistic to the US and to pro-American regimes in the Middle East. For Zev Chafets, "its occasional interviews with Western statesmen are designed to provide it with a fig leaf of objectivity."[61] Al Jazeera has also been accused of being a mouthpiece for Islamic fundamentalists. For Chafets, "it is the most potent weapon in the Islamic axis arsenal."[62] While some consider Al Jazeera a channel that is controlled by Islamic fundamentalists, others see in it an outlet for Arab nationalist demagogues. For Ajami,

Al Jazeera's reporters see themselves as "anti-imperialists." These men and women are convinced that the rulers of the Arab world have given in to American might; these are broadcasters who play to an Arab gallery whose political bitterness they share—and feed.[63]

Last but not least, Al Jazeera is criticized for galvanizing Arab radicalism. According to some critics, it is igniting the anger of Arabs and the fury of Muslims against the US and is inciting public demonstrations, fueling the passions of fundamentalists, and even causing more violence against Americans. The type of journalism the network engages in deliberately "fans the flames of Muslim outrage"[64] and insidiously "reinforces existing prejudices."[65] In fact, Al Jazeera is looked at by some as a maverick media outlet "moving the masses in uncontrolled ways."[66]

During the so-called War on Terrorism, Al Jazeera has particularly infuriated American officials. It came under close scrutiny and criticism from the US for its coverage of the war in Afghanistan and, later on, the invasion of Iraq. Overall, Al Jazeera was criticized for what was perceived as irresponsible journalism. Upon transmitting the famous post-September 11 Al Qaeda videotapes, Al Jazeera was accused of serving as a mouthpiece of Al Qaeda, glorifying bin Laden and presenting him as a romantic ideologue. US officials were also disturbed by Al Jazeera's replays of its exclusive 1998 interview with bin Laden. Al Jazeera was viewed to be allowing bin Laden to use the channel in order to spread his propaganda and providing him with a platform from which to preach Jihad on the West, in general, and the US, in particular. Accordingly, Al Jazeera was pressured to censor its output on grounds that bin Laden might be using his videotaped messages and Al Jazeera to incite anti-American sentiment and even provoke more attacks on the US. From an American standpoint, bin Laden should not be given the oxygen of publicity and appear unexpurgated in video again. Al Jazeera was also criticized for rushing to report unscreened material and airing raw footage with no reviewing safety net and no editing process—just to keep astride of the competition in news media.[67] What the US found objectionable was Al Jazeera's repeated showing of graphic pictures of dead children, wounded civilians and destroyed homes for no other reason than to "to drum up viewership or else to propagandize against the United States."[68]

Afraid of losing the information war, the US tried to muzzle Al Jazeera. American officials lobbied the Emir of Qatar to tone down the coverage of Al Jazeera, stop the airing of news the US considered unfavorable and curb the anti-American rhetoric; however, Qatar showed a reluctance to interfere in the editorial independence of the channel (although later it agreed to share with the Americans Al Qaeda taped messages before airing them). In the American press, the channel was demonized, so to speak, and there were even calls to eliminate it. Zev Chafets, for instance, argued: "Dealing with Al Jazeera is a job of the military. Shutting it down should be an immediate priority because, left alone, it has the power to poison the air more efficiently and lethally than anthrax ever could."[69] Sure enough, Al Jazeera has come under attack not only rhetorically, but also literally by the US as a missile destroyed its Kabul bureau. While the US denied that it deliberately targeted Al Jazeera and said that the attack was an accident, others believe that the Al Jazeera's office was meant to be hit, especially as the same scenario was repeated in Baghdad during the Third Gulf War, this time with a missile attack on Al Jazeera's office in Baghdad causing the death of Al Jazeera reporter Tarek Ayyoub.

However, this has only increased the popularity of Al Jazeera. According to Faisal Bodi,

> people are turning to [Al Jazeera] because the Western media coverage has been so poor. For although Doha is just a few miles away from Central Command, the view of events from here could not be more different. Of all the major global networks, Al Jazeera has been alone in proceeding from the premise that this war should be viewed as an illegal enterprise. It has broadcast the horror of the bombing campaign, the blown-out brains, the blood-spattered pavements, the screaming infants and the corpses. Its team of on-the-ground, unembedded correspondents has provided a corrective to the official line that the campaign is, barring occasional resistance, going to plan.[70]

Since Al Jazeera aired an interview with captured American prisoners of war in Iraq and showed bodies of dead soldiers, the American media has taken it to task. A string of events have followed: its website was hacked; the US host of the channel's website removed it from its service; its business correspondents were kicked out of the New York stock exchange; and its Managing Director was sacked and cast as a scapegoat. On a few occasions, its staff in Baghdad faced harassment and even detention, and its former correspondent in Afghanistan Tayseer Allouni has been detained for some time in Spain on grounds that he was serving not only Al Jazeera, but also Al Qaeda.

The US has been defensive because it felt it was losing the "on-air supremacy"[71] in the war of words or the so-called propaganda war; it has been particularly wary about the ways Al Jazeera's bold coverage of civilian victims can sway Arab and even international public opinion, loosen the coalition, and affect the public support that has been rallied. From the standpoint of Al Jazeera, it comes down to competition—by airing the controversial bin Laden tapes, showing civilian victims, and bringing in guests who are vocal in their opposition to American foreign policy, Al Jazeera is doing what many other news networks would have done in an age of cutthroat network rivalries in which networks fight for every possible advantage in news reporting. The network defended its practices when asked whether or not it was aware that what it airs may incite actions against the United States:

> We worry about how we treat the news. We don't just take any tape that comes to our offices or to the station and put it on air. Before that we have

a meeting to discuss how we should treat the news, and not be subject to the propaganda from a party or organization or group, Osama bin Laden or others. When we aired the tape of bin Laden spokesman Suleiman Abu Geith, directly after that we brought Edward Walker, former US Assistant Secretary of State for Near East Affairs, for his comments, and after that a Muslim cleric to talk from an Islamic perspective about bin Laden's statements, to raise points such as that Islam doesn't allow you to kill innocent people, that bin Laden will condemn American bombings but at the same time give orders to kill innocent Americans. To air the statements without any comments, without any opposing statements or view points or analysis, that's when it is propaganda.[72]

The channel has played down its links with bin Laden and vowed to resist pressure to alter its coverage and to stick to its editorial policy of respect for all opinions and airing of all perspectives. In a sense, the US's attempt to influence Al Jazeera has backfired. Washington's criticism of Al Jazeera has only increased its credibility. Not surprisingly, US officials have started to change their approach to Al Jazeera and decided to make themselves available for interviews on Al Jazeera. Chided by Arab reporters for not using Al Jazeera as a channel of communication with the Arab world, the United States has tried to capitalize on the network during the information war. Still, the sense of mistrust persists. With no immediate viable alternative, the Americans have opted to speak through Al Jazeera while launching their "anti-Al Jazeera Radio Sawa"[73] and setting up their own Arabic-speaking channel, Al Hurra, in an already media congested region.

For many observers, though, the Americans may have a hard time selling their new channel to the Arab world. According to Marwan Bishara, the US initiative is flawed to say the least: "the rationale behind Al Hurra is based on two erroneous assumptions: that satellite networks are responsible for the anti-Americanism in the Arab world and that once America is more clearly heard, it will be more appreciated."[74] At least so far, the US media strategy in the Middle East has not been all that successful in pulling the rug from underneath Al Jazeera. If anything, the United States is caught up in a somewhat ambiguous relationship with Al Jazeera, at times finding itself almost compelled to take heed of the network it took pains to discredit. This is particularly the case during the race for the White House. Just four days before the 2004 US presidential elections, Al Jazeera aired segments of the first video recording from bin Laden in nearly three years, addressing a message directly to the American people in what the *Guardian* described as a "twisted parody of an Oval Office address."[75] Segments of the tape, which Al Jazeera obtained in Pakistan, were also replayed on the major American networks with voice over, followed in many instances by commentary on the extent to which bin Laden's message can affect the outcome of the elections. Interestingly enough, it is scoops such as this one that have branded Al Jazeera as a "mouthpiece" for the Al Qaeda network. What would have previously been dismissed as pure propaganda and anti-American rhetoric has become, on the eve of the American elections, food for the media industry in the United States. Suddenly, the often-invoked fear that bin Laden's message might be a coded signal for terrorist action ceased to be a major concern. Notably, as Dana Milbank points out, "the administration raised no warnings about the tape's airing on television; in the past, the administration had warned that tapes might be used to activate sleeper cells in the United States."[76] The incident is not without significance. That the United States tolerated the Qatari network where in the past it was highly critical and utterly dismissive suggests that, as far as the media industry is concerned (including the American media), bin Laden sells. In a close race such as the one between George W. Bush and John Kerry, the tape Al Jazeera aired is not without effects. While for some commentators, bin Laden's speech was unlikely to have a major impact on voters' choices, for others, it served Bush well. By resurrecting people's fears of terrorism and reminding them of the grave threats still faced by the country, it presumably gave the incumbent president a boost.[77] Seen in light of the attention Al Jazeera has been getting all along, and especially considering how it positioned itself during the so-called information war, the most important outcome of this instance is probably the crystallization of a new media dynamics. With Al Jazeera, an added significance to the term "information globalization" is arguably heralded whereby relatively small media players introduce an element of contingency, for lack of a better term, in a traditionally structured and well defined environment where media and politics are entangled.

A NEW(S) MEDIA ORDER

The tug-of-war between Al Jazeera and the United States is significant partly because it strikes at the heart of what are often perceived as sacrosanct Western ideals and, in fact, puts into question a system of beliefs the universality of which is often taken for granted. The latter pertains to the perception about the freedom of the American press, the thinness of the liberal discourse on democracy and the assumed Western media hegemony. It also brings to light closely-related issues, namely the specificity of Arab media and the significance of Arab public opinion.

To start with, the attempt to silence Al Jazeera shatters the widely held perception about the freedom of the American press and plays havoc with the liberal discourse on democracy. The idealized role of the press, at least as promoted by the United States, namely covering the story and reporting the news in a fair and balanced way and telling the truth as it is, is subjected to a reality check. The viciousness with which Al Jazeera has been criticized both officially and institutionally—that is, by the American administration and the press, respectively—leads one to raise a brow when it comes from a nation that promotes free speech and cherishes independent journalism—in fact, one which touts itself as the symbol of the free democratic world. Perhaps not surprisingly, many journalists did not shy away from defending Al Jazeera's commitment to the freedom of expression and to the profession. According to Ann Cooper, "it is 'disheartening' to see US officials adopt 'similar tactics' to Arab regimes that have sought to influence the news station's coverage."[78] It is ironic that an Arab news channel would broadcast more freely than the American media. For Saleh Dabbakeh, "it is precarious that the same people on whose image Al Jazeera was built are now criticizing the station for sticking to their rules of the game."[79]

What is sobering about the controversy surrounding Al Jazeera's coverage of the war in Afghanistan and the invasion of Iraq is not only the thinness of the American discourse on the freedom of the press in particular, and liberal democracy in general, but also the questionability of what is perceived as the irreversible hegemony of the Western media. The flawed US foreign policy vis-à-vis the Arab world is an important part of the equation. Resentment towards the US runs deep in the Arab world, and the objection to its foreign policy has never been stronger. As some see it, Al Jazeera is often consumed by a populace harboring deep-rooted resentment toward the US for what is perceived as an anti-Muslim, anti-Arab foreign policy. Likewise, there is an increasingly vocal rejection of Western cultural values, although some feel the anti-Western ideological component that runs through the network is a reaction to American hegemony. The popularity of Al Jazeera reflects a frustration with the bias of the

Western media in general and American media in particular. In many ways, Al Jazeera presents a challenge to the Western media. For one thing, the network has put an end to the Western monopoly on both the global production of news and the global dissemination of information.[80] For the first time, America finds itself without a monopoly of live coverage of the war. In fact, networks in the United States and other Western countries have found themselves relying on the reporting of an obscure channel. The images seen on Al Jazeera may be far worse than those presented on Western news channels (whether in relation to the Palestinian intifada, the war in Afghanistan or the invasion of Iraq), but for many Arab viewers it is a viable alternative which offers coverage of the Arab world that has been distorted by the American news media.

It is true that Al Jazeera has a relatively short history and is creating a tradition that is far from being entrenched in the region, but this network has become a player to contend with in the entangled world of news media—one that was able to compete at some point with Cable News Network (CNN)—although Robert Fisk finds it "a lot keener to tell the truth than CNN."[81] It would be unfair to compare Al Jazeera to the American media partly because the latter, much like the society they serve, have their own specificity. Certainly, the American media are more seasoned and more sophisticated, and Al Jazeera, and the Arab media in general have a lot to learn from the American media experience. At the same time, it is important to remember that the American press has had two centuries to mature and that the process of maturity has been coterminous with the evolution of other institutions. Still, exploring the impact of CNN on the development of the Arab media is instructive.

The Second Gulf War in 1991 played a noteworthy role in changing the conception of TV broadcasting in the Arab world, Particularly in the Middle East. CNN established itself as *the* source of information, providing live coverage and around-the-clock news. Contributing to the success of CNN was the mushrooming of satellite dishes in the region, making it easy to transmit signals to a large and concerned Arab audience. As such, CNN provided alternative news coverage which changed media practices and audiences' expectations. Its extensive live coverage of the Second Gulf War made clear the power of satellite television to Arab viewers, who have since grown ever hungrier for live, unedited and uncensored news during times when state media have fed them stale news and provided them with a turgid coverage of regional events. CNN's exclusive coverage of the Second Gulf War, which gave people in the Arab world and beyond a sense of how powerful the media can be, galvanized the development of Arab satellite broadcasting. Over the next few years, Arab channels gradually took over the space traditionally occupied by Western media, beaming a wide variety of programs to Arab viewers who have come to crave more reliable news, uncensored credible information and better programs than those offered by the heavily regulated state media.[82] The legacy of CNN is evident in the institution of not only the genre of 24-hour news broadcasting, but also certain broadcasting practices and standards among Arab satellite channels. Not surprisingly, Al Jazeera's live coverage of the American bombing of Iraq during Operation Desert Fox kept pace with CNN's. In Afghanistan, Al Jazeera found itself playing the same role CNN was called upon to play in the Second Gulf War when Peter Arnett was the only Western correspondent covering the war in Baghdad. This pivotal role was no less important during the invasion of Iraq in 2003.

However, it would be reductive to see Al Jazeera as merely an Arab CNN. Part of what distinguishes Al Jazeera is its hybridity. Al Jazeera is a phenomenon in the sense that it finds itself caught up, for lack of a better term, between two trends. On the one hand, the channel uses the best technical skills and journalistic practices that the West has to offer. On the other hand, it uses these means and practices precisely to advance ideas and views that contradict and doubt the Western narrative and interpretation of events and issues that are increasingly bringing the Middle East to the center of the world's news attention. Often enough, Al Jazeera does not tell the same version of the story the American media broadcasts, and when it does, it gives it a different spin. These differences point to a complex relationship of attraction and repulsion whereby Al Jazeera often engages the West in opposition. Therein lies the network's politics of identity. At the heart of Al Jazeera is a hybridity which paradoxically constitutes its cultural specificity; it is a mixture of the Eastern and the Western, the leftist and the rightist, the religious and the secular, the tribal and the urban, and the local and the global.

Seen from this perspective, Al Jazeera can be said to mark a turning point, symbolic as it may be, in the history of information globalization. Although it airs in Arabic and is targeted primarily at Arab speaking viewers, it has a reach and even an impact outside the Arab world. Al Jazeera provides a counterweight to the images that the mainstream Western media has been feeding to viewers. It is a case of information flow reversal, whereby information is no longer beamed from the North to the South or from the Occident to the Orient, but the other way around. The West no longer has a monopoly on "credible and responsible media." The repatriation of some foreign-based Arab media organizations such as MBC from European capitals to Arab countries intended to bring them closer to their customer base, and concomitantly the mushrooming of media cities as production sites in the Arab world—from Cairo with its long tradition in the media and film industry to the fast-growing Dubai which is emerging as the technological hub of the Gulf region—in the wake of Al Jazeera's success further crystallize this modest trend of a partial reversal of the globalization process. Ali Bayramoglu argues this point at length:

> Al Jazeera has become famous not because it engages in professional jour-
> nalism, but because it is the sign of some type of a symbolic equilibrium
> between the Occident and Orient. Al Jazeera is a phenomenon insofar as it
> engenders a certain politicization across Muslim nations and rivals the
> Western media giants both technically and professionally ... The secret and
> power of Al Jazeera lie in a vision structured around a context of interna-
> tional Islamic identity. Al Jazeera reflects the on-going process of the politi-
> cization of an Islamic identity and in that sense points to the "Other." In fact,
> there are two polarities in this struggle. Both of them are caught in a
> process of globalization which risks becoming even more acute and more
> dangerous and may border on a more important polarization.[83]

Another significant realization ensuing from this controversy per-
tains to the emergence of an Arab perspective and, along with it, a growing awareness of the specificity of the Arab media. Al Jazeera has effectively put an end to an era marked by what may be described as a one-size-fits-all media. Issues now lend themselves to a different perspective—in fact an Arab perspective that has been absent. In this respect, the history or at least the coming to eminence of Al Jazeera is instructive. It is interesting that Al Jazeera enjoyed a privileged position in Afghanistan and earned a certain credibility with the Taliban movement particularly during a time when foreign reporters were expelled from Kabul. Al Jazeera had access to the war zone while other media outlets did not. For some time, it was the only station broadcasting and airing exclusive footage from within Taliban-controlled Afghanistan. Al Jazeera's exclusive images from Afghanistan, which were shown worldwide,

were in part the fruit of a decision, taken two years prior to the war, to open a news bureau in Kabul. CNN received the same offer but declined. The United States, and by extension CNN, lost interest in Afghanistan after the fall of communism and the breakdown of the Soviet Union. Not so with Al Jazeera which had an inherent interest in Afghanistan, at the time controlled by the Taliban, partly because it is a Muslim state in a strategic yet tumultuous region and partly because it continues to be the host of many "Arab freedom fighters," as they were called then. Before Afghanistan became the center of attention for the whole world, Al Jazeera had exclusive coverage of certain related events. In 1998, it conducted an exclusive interview with bin Laden. It also broadcast the wedding of bin Laden's son (in January 2001) and covered the Taliban's destruction of the colossal Bamiyan Buddhas (in March 2001). Again, Mohammed Jassim Al Ali is worth quoting at length:

> When we started the channel, we first concentrated on opening offices in Arab countries and Islamic countries. We started with Palestine and Iraq, because these were hot areas and there was news happening. So we opened an office in Jerusalem, with sub-offices in Gaza and Ramallah, and at the same time opened in Baghdad, then moved to other Arab countries. When these were in place, we moved to the other Islamic countries, first Iran and Pakistan, then we tried to get into Afghanistan. We got permission from the Taliban—and at the same time permission was granted to us, it was granted to CNN, Reuters, and APTN ... We opened two offices, in Kabul and Kandahar. The others didn't move in because they didn't consider it very important and didn't see much news coming out of there. But for us, it was important because it's an Islamic country ... They are looking through international angles. The difference between CNN and Al Jazeera is that they look first to international news, then maybe to Asian, Middle Eastern specific issues. We look first to Arab and Islamic issues in detail, and after that to international questions.[84]

In appealing to the sensibility of the Arab–Muslim world, Al Jazeera departed from the exclusive reliance on the Western news agencies. The media are becoming more diverse than ever, the news is no longer limited to that which Western media authenticates and the dominant perspective is no longer one that is Western in essence. A channel like Al Jazeera prides itself on reporting Arab news from the Arab world better than other international stations, which makes it appealing to the Arab–Muslim world.

AL JAZEERA AND THE PUBLIC SPHERE

Is Al Jazeera an agent of social change or is it just a news channel? Are the role and influence of this satellite TV overstated? People in the Arab world may be better informed because of channels like Al Jazeera; but does the increased awareness among the Arab public lead to political action? Can Al Jazeera be a vehicle of political change? Does a network like Al Jazeera enhance or eviscerate democracy? Can such a media outlet bring about real democratic change?

Many viewers perceive Al Jazeera as grappling with democracy and hail it as a herald of democratization. For example, Ibish and Abunimah point out that "Al Jazeera presents the best trends of openness and democratization in the Arab world. It is a long-overdue two-way street in the global flow of information and opinion. It should be celebrated and encouraged."[85] Likewise, in an interview with Nicholas Nesson, Mohammed Jassim Al Ali observes that

> what Arabs need is more freedom ... In this age, the powerful can no longer control the people ... Democracy is coming to the Middle East because of the communication revolution. You can no longer hide information, and must now tell the people the truth. If you don't, the people won't follow you, they won't support you, they won't obey you ... The opportunities for political reform are great ... but we have a history, a culture that you can't change overnight.[86]

However, the experiment of Al Jazeera is fraught with a number of difficulties, chief among which is the perception that the inroads made by alternative Arab media such as Al Jazeera will obfuscate the real need for change. The margin of freedom that some media networks enjoy gives the illusion of democracy and in doing so goes a long way toward postponing real political reform. According to Steven Wu, "if Al Jazeera continues to promote only empty controversy, it will give more authoritarian Middle Eastern governments an excuse to delay liberalization of the media by pointing to Al Jazeera's excesses."[87] So far, the Arab public seems to be content with satellite democracy. Added to this is yet another danger, and that is the increasing marginalization of the role of the media in development and modernization. The media discourse is increasingly embroiled in an oppositional ideological underpinning. Such an ideological underpinning seems to reproduce or at least to fall prey to such a dichotomous logic as "Us" versus "Them." Suffice it here to note that Al Jazeera hardly entertains discussions or produces programs that pertain to pressing issues that plague the Arab world outside *realpolitik* such as sustainable economic development in the Arab world, unemployment and education, to name but a few. In "Mass media in the Middle East," Kai Hafez prompts us to take a more cautious look at the consequences of the proliferation of TV channels on democracy and public participation in the region:

> one of the most important questions leading to prospects of political and societal change in the Middle East is whether old and new mass media of the Middle East will be politically and culturally liberalizing in the age of globalized media spaces. Although some positive aspects of this development are already visible, countertrends are also apparent. It is rather doubtful whether the new indigenous media allow for greater freedom of speech than the state media. The use of the media for participatory development and modernization is less important in current media debates than it was in previous decades. Instead, there is an inherent danger that the discourse on communication and mass media will become an integral part of new ideological debates about a supposed cultural gap between "the West" and "Islam".[88]

Part of the problem is that the technical modernization of the Arab mass media has outpaced constructive social roles for the media in modern Arab societies.[89] The media boom in the Arab world is facilitated by technological innovation which itself often provides the justification for such media hype. The media has capitalized on technological advancements but has not kept up with other institutional development. To treat Arab media as the fourth estate, and to say that TV leads to political changes is to look at the issue from a narrow perspective, namely that technology and the information revolution it brings about are unquestionably promising and emancipatory. This overstated faith in the impact of the communication revolution in the Middle East is common even among such seasoned media figures as NBC's Tom Brokaw who comments in a *New York Times* article, published on the eve of the Third Gulf War, that

> as a result of this widespread dissemination of information, the fundamental structure of Middle East politics has been altered, if not over-hauled. Today, political pressure develops quickly and independently from the ground up, not just from the top down, a dramatic difference from a decade ago.[90]

One should be skeptical about the often ambitious transformative claims for new media as well as the claims about its democratizing potential and its ability not just to increase and widen participation among the various social strata in the Arab world, but to transform social and political organization. Real change cannot be expected solely or mainly from the media sector. Democracy cannot emanate just from the media; the political systems and institutions themselves have to change, evolve and adapt. Short of that, our faith in new Arab media is misplaced.

A comparative perspective can further illustrate the point. In the West, the media are part of an institutional framework; the media evolved in tandem with the developments in various institutions which include politics, economics and the law. Broadly speaking, the role of journalism in Western liberal democracies is to help citizens learn about the world in which they take part, debate their responses to it, and have informed discussions about what action to take and what choices to make—to be able to act better in their capacity as voting citizens. In democratic societies, particularly in the West, media have the power to enhance the interconnectedness between citizens and their government, make the process of governing more transparent, open up the potential for direct democracy, promote citizen participation in government, contribute to the development of political institutions, lead to greater public awareness about and participation in public policy debates, decentralize power, help strengthen civil society, advance civil rights, and potentially project democratic values. This institutional framework within which Western media operate is quasi-absent in the Arab world. Seen from this perspective, it would probably be naive to place high hopes on such alternative media in the Arab world as Al Jazeera or to think that Al Jazeera can and will have immediate effects or lead to dramatic changes in the region. We should not be under the illusion that satellite TV can dramatically change society or revolutionize its institutions. In terms of democracy, the Arab media have so far had little impact on the Arab world, and the extent to which they can effectively introduce significant changes is questionable.

In "Mid-tech revolution," Jon B. Alterman provides a sober assessment of the potential impact of the information revolution in general and the media revolution in particular:

-

> one can be bolder in predicting the political effects of technological change, namely, that it is unlikely to force a deep restructuring of Middle Eastern

governance patterns. Authoritarianism has predominated in the region for decades and seems poised to continue to do so for years to come. The usual argument about information technology and authoritarianism is that the former undermines the latter by freeing the public from the rulers' grip. Such a notion, however, misunderstands the nature of authoritarianism in the Middle East. It is not merely a top-down system, and it has never been so. Every authoritarian government in the region has to maintain a watchful eye on public sentiment, and it has to balance coercion and cooption— albeit in different measures at different times in different places. Technological developments have made that balancing act more difficult because states lost some of the tools that have helped them lead public opinion—and thus, co-opt their populations—in the past. While most states still maintain an overwhelming advantage over any possible opponent in the public sphere, their ability to control what happens in that sphere is waning.[91]

Although the state media have been responsive to these new challenges by ceding public space to oppositional voices, the voices that gain access do not significantly threaten the regime, and ultimately such initiatives keep real changes at arm's length.

The fact that several influential Arab satellite TV networks remain under the sponsorship and control of Gulf states raises doubts about the likelihood of any imminent change in existing power structures. The new media are caught up in a conflictual identity in which a liberalizing apparatus feeds off a conservative instinct. It is unlikely that the rise of alternative media such as Al Jazeera will lead to a fundamental change in governance. For Christa Salamandra, the global flow of information is contributing to the construction of Arab localism, while the increasing imposition of new global information technology, including the internet and satellite TV, is producing parochialism. In her view, the new transnational Arab media are by and large inherently undemocratic: "satellite television has worked to strengthen rather than undermine existing regimes as new televisual media have been harnessed by Gulf ruling elites to support and enhance non-democratic power structures in the Gulf Cooperation Council states."[92]

Nonetheless, one cannot ignore the impact of satellite TV and its potential to influence its viewers beyond the intentions and politics of Arab governments which are heavily investing in the telecommunication industry. Seen from this perspective, it is what Jürgen Habermas calls "the public sphere,"[93] as the space within which issues are contested, and the impact of Al Jazeera on that sphere—rather than how media can bring about democratic changes—that need to be analyzed. One can point out symptoms of a real change. With Al Jazeera has come the growing realization that Arab public opinion matters—albeit a changing Arab public opinion. Until recently, there was an assumption at least that Arab public opinion does not matter because authoritarian regimes in the Middle East region can control their discontented masses. The new media is changing that perception. A channel like Al Jazeera is broadening the form, content and extent of public involvement. As there are more interactive programs, there are more people who call in to express their views and more viewers who are exposed to such a diversity of views.

Al Jazeera has also helped take the Arab media beyond the transmission view of communication to the ritual view of communication. The former is often equated with "imparting," "sending," and "transmitting" information for the purpose of control, the latter is usually associated with "sharing," "participation," "association," and with community and communion.[94] What new Arab media like Al Jazeera are producing cannot be reduced to the prevailing paradigm of media as a form of domination (in other words, media as a means of controlling or moving the masses). Viewers are developing interactive habits which make them more than mere passive recipients. This makes communication more problematic than we usually assume; the way the viewers make sense of Al Jazeera and even affect it becomes no less important than the presumed effect Al Jazeera might have on its viewers. To invert the relationship of communication is to assume that Al Jazeera's relation to its viewers is not one of power pure and simple, but one of a social drama and a complex reality in which a public sphere is constructed rather than being merely reflected. As Kai Hafez put it,

> the media's ability to influence or even manipulate society and politics should not be overstated. Contradictory and sometimes puzzling findings about media effects and media coverage are evident for the fact that the mass media are not omnipotent, but that their products are, in fact manipulated by audiences and the public.[95]

Such an engagement is not only multiplying the number of interactions and making communication a symbolic process in which reality is produced, negotiated and transformed, but also increasing what people can publicly talk about, particularly in a channel like Al Jazeera where there are few red lines and where the controversial nature of the discussed topics naturally generates a fair degree of involvement. The participation in interpretation that previously occurred in coffee houses and living rooms is now part of what is being broadcast in call-in shows.[96] "Al Jazeera TV's migration of debate-and-discussion formats from salons to the air," to use Jon Alterman's words,[97] facilitates and encourages participation in a public discourse. In turn, the aired debates spur even more debates within a public which considers watching TV a communal activity. In times of crisis, cafés become political saloons. This type of inter-action can only broaden the public sphere. More segments of soci-ety are now brought into public discourse.

For Marc Lynch, the significance of these changes does not lie in the sheer number of participants who call in to express their views; the new public sphere that is emerging goes beyond the category of the layperson, which is often implied in discussions about the Arab street.[98] What seems to matter more than the street today is an Arab public opinion shaped by "the consensus of elite and middle-class public opinion throughout the Arab world."[99] Many influential and articulate Arab intellectuals, newspaper editors and political fig-ures who may be described as opinion leaders are starting to claim a space on Al Jazeera, among other media outlets, and are actively shaping a public sphere that is thriving within the increasingly influential transnational media. These figures are not without agenda or allegiances, but the sheer variety of the discourse that is being aired on the network is creating a more potent public sphere with multiple interpretations, views and opinions on what is going on in the Arab and Islamic world. This sphere may have excesses—as the debates we see on some of Al Jazeera's programs are sometimes far from being what Habermas calls "rational critical debates"—but the very development of a media-mediated Arab public sphere may have a lasting effect on Arab political culture.

UNRAVELING THE AL JAZEERA PHENOMENON

This project, which is made all the more timely by the latest world developments and the pivotal role that the previously disenfran-chised Arab media have started to play regionally and internationally, is motivated partly by a genuine interest in alternative media in the Arab world and partly by the scarcity of academic research in this fast-changing area of inquiry. Existing studies about Al Jazeera, the bulk of which are journalistic in their thrust, are either dated, descriptive or lacking in depth. Although recently some interesting academic work has been produced, the Al Jazeera phenomenon has not been deeply analyzed, leaving much ground unexplored. Part of the problem is that the network is often either subjected to an idealistic view or seen from a dismissive standpoint. In other words, Al Jazeera is either adored and championed or vilified and bashed. The former view often emanates from an *amour propre* for what Al Jazeera stands for and what it is doing, while the latter view fails to see in the channel anything more than an evil force and a propaganda tool. Assuming that Al Jazeera, much like new Arab media which are going through a period of experimentation, has its merits and its drawbacks, its strengths and its weaknesses, its achievements and its limits, this project seeks to delve in some depth into some aspects of this network which have combined to make it a phenomenon that is worthy of exploration. It also seeks critically to probe the rich set of dynamics it sets in place in the Arab media scene and beyond.

The complexity of the topic at hand requires an interdisciplinary approach that transcends divisional lines and a collaborative endeavor. This work brings together the efforts of scholars with different disciplinary perspectives and various backgrounds. It is composed of nine essays by scholars from the Middle East, the United States and Europe from such varied disciplines as media studies, communication, journalism and political science. While they vary in focus, perspective and methodology, these essays contribute, each in its own way, to the unraveling of this media phenomenon.

The first section of the book is devoted to the politics of Al Jazeera, particularly as they relate to the question of the public sphere. Olivier Da Lage's essay sets the ground for other contributions by situating Al Jazeera squarely within the geo-political constraints of Qatar and its political entanglement within a fast-changing region. In his view, there is an inextricable though seemingly contradictory relationship between Qatar's foreign diplomacy and the role it envisages for itself in the region, on the one hand, and its media strategy, on the other hand. Da Lage argues that the pro-American foreign policy of Qatar and the anti-American editorial line of Al Jazeera are two sides of the same coin. Mohammed El Oifi's "Influence without Power: Al Jazeera and the Arab Public Sphere" takes the analysis further by exploring whether the influence Al Jazeera has acquired over the Arab mediascape is likely to give Qatar long-lasting political gains. For Oifi, Qatar's attempt to position itself in the Arab public sphere by aligning itself with Arab public opinion while at the same time serving its own interests and acquiring a soft power by aligning itself with the United States is a combination which may have unpredictable consequences. Focusing more on identity, Gloria Awad provides a semiotic analysis of Aljazeera.net in her essay "Al Jazeera.net: Identity Choices and the Logic of the Media." More specifically, she examines the cartography of space Aljazeera.net configures and its agenda setting function in an attempt to explore the ways in which the site constructs reality and represents identity.

The second section takes a close look at Al Jazeera's programs. It opens with Faisal Al Kasim's reflections on his own controversial program *The Opposite Direction* and how it changed the Arab mediascape. Set against Al Kasim's assessment of the contribution of his own program is Muhammad Ayish's essay "Media Brinksmanship in the Arab World: Al Jazeera's *The Opposite Direction* as a Fighting Arena." Ayish uses the concept of "brinksmanship" to probe the show critically and explore the ways it creates an effect of sensationalism and heightens the drama, and how such media practices contribute to the evisceration of a rational critical debate. Taking us away from the strident oppositional "crossfire" ethos that is the hallmark of Al Jazeera's prominent talk shows, Naomi Sakr takes a close look at an innovative weekly program on women's issues. Her essay "Women, Development and Al Jazeera: A Balance Sheet" explores the extent to which Al Jazeera's *For Women Only*, among other programs, contributes to overcoming the deficit in women's empowerment and affects the region Al Jazeera operates in and serves.

The last section of the book is devoted to Al Jazeera and regional crises. Ehab Bessaiso's "Al Jazeera and the War in Afghanistan" looks at Al Jazeera in the context of the other battle that took place in Afghanistan—the information war. Paying special attention to bin Laden's communication with Al Jazeera, Bessaiso examines whether Al Jazeera acted as a delivery system or as a mouthpiece for the Al Qaeda network. No less important is Al Jazeera's coverage of the Palestinian uprising. "Witnessing the Intifada: Al Jazeera's Coverage of the Palestinian–Israeli Conflict" looks at the extent to which Al Jazeera has helped put the Palestinian question on the front burner and the impact of its intense coverage on Arab viewers and Arab official circles. Extending the conversation, R.S. Zaharna explores the relationship between public diplomacy and media diplomacy. Her essay "Al Jazeera and American Public Diplomacy: A Dance of Intercultural (Mis-)Communication" is concerned with the role Al Jazeera has played in American public diplomacy in the Middle East during the information war, and how the Bush administration, which at various points perceived the network as promoting a negative image of the United States, used it as a tool in its public diplomacy initiative to win over the Arab public.

NOTES

1 "Middle East communications and internet via satellite" published by Spotbeam Communications Ltd., October 2002, <http://www.mindbranch.com/page/catalog/product/2e6a73703f706172746e65723d31303326636636f64653d523133312d30308.html>.

2 Sheikh Hamad bin Thamer Al Thani, Interview with Abdallah Schleifer and Sarah Sullivan, *Transnational Broadcasting Studies*, No. 7 (Fall/Winter 2001), <http://www.tbsjournal.com/Archives/Fall01/Jazeera_chairman. html>.

3 Naomi Sakr, "Optical illusion: television and censorship in the Arab World," *Transnational Broadcasting Studies*, No. 5 (Fall/Winter 2000), <www.tbsjournal.com/Archives/Fall00/sakr1.htm>. See also Mohammed El-Nawawy and Adel Iskander Farag, *Al Jazeera: How the Free Arab News Network Scooped the World and Changed the Middle East* (Boulder: Westview Press, 2002), pp. 83–90.

4 Sakr, "Optical illusion."

5 Mary-Denise Tabar, "Printing press to satellite: a historical case study of media and the Arab State" (Diss., Washington DC: Georgetown University, 2002), p. 57, <http://cct.georgetown.edu/thesis/MaryDeniseTabar.pdf>.

6 "Palestinians shut a West Bank TV office," *New York Times*, March 22, 2001, p. 3A, and Ibrahim Hazboun, "Palestinians urge Arafat to end ban on independent Arab TV station," *Independent*, March 23, 2001, p. 13.

7 "Middle East communications and internet via satellite."

8 Lydia Saad, "Al Jazeera: Arabs rate its objectivity," *Gallup Poll Tuesday Briefing*, April 23, 2002. Equally noteworthy is a poll conducted by the Qatari Daily *Al Watan* in 2002 which ranks Al Jazeera as the best Arab specialized channel (Al Jazeera 55 per cent, Abu Dhabi TV 25 per cent, MBC 11 per cent, and others 9 per cent). The same poll also shows Al Jazeera's news hour as the best political news hour (Al Jazeera 64 per cent, MBC 22 per cent, Abu Dhabi TV 9 per cent, and others 5 per cent). See Abdul Dayem Abdul Aziz, "Al Jazeera is the best specialized channel without a contestant," *Al Watan*, January 4, 2003, p. 5.

9 Saad, "Al Jazeera."

10 Richard Bukholder, "Arabs favor Al Jazeera over state-run channels for world news," *Gallup Poll Tuesday Briefing*, November 12, 2002.

11 "Why Al Jazeera matters to us," *New York Times*, March 30, 2003.

12 Muhammad Ayish, "Political communication on Arab world television: evolving patterns," *Political Communication*, Vol. 19 (2002), p. 151.

13 Mohammed Jassim Al Ali, Interview with Abdallah Schleifer and Sarah Sullivan, *Transnational Broadcasting Studies*, No. 7 (Fall/Winter 2001), <http://www.tbsjournal.com/Archives/Fall01/fall01.html>.

14   "Al Jazeera launches its Media Center for Training and Development,"
     <http://www.aljazeera.net/art_culture/2004/2/2-24-3.htm>.

15   See Suleiman Al Shammari, *The Arab Nationalist Dimension in Al Jazeera
     Satellite Channel: A Case Study of The Opposite Direction* (Doha: Dar Al
     Sharq, 1999), p. 45.

16   See David Hirst, "Qatar calling: Al Jazeera, the Arab TV channel that
     dares to shock," *Le Monde Diplomatique*, August 8, 2001.

17   It is interesting that MBC's newly launched news channel "Al Arabiya"
     derives its name from the other half of the Arabic term for "Arabian
     Peninsula." The geo-political consideration is important. Al Arabiya would
     not have been named so if the mother company, MBC, were still based in
     London.

18   Tabar, "Printing press to satellite."

19   It is important here to note, along with Lila Abu Lughod, the theoretical
     difficulties fraught with "the typifying of communities that results from
     thinking of them as 'cultures'." Although one can note trends when it
     comes to the politicization of Arab viewers, it would probably be an
     exaggeration to generalize such a trend and to consider the Arab viewer
     as a type a politicized viewer. See Lila Abu Lughod, "The interpretation
     of culture(s) after television," *Representations*, Vol. 59 (Summer 1997),
     pp. 109–43.

20   Mawan   M.   Kraidy,   "Arab   satellite   television   between
     regionalization and globalization," *Global Media Journal*, Vol. 2, No. 2
     (Spring 2003), pp. 10–11, <http://lass.calumet.purdue.edu/cca/gmj/
     SubmittedDocuments/Kraidy.htm>.

21   See Naomi Sakr, *Satellite Realms: Transnational Television, Globalization
     and the Middle East* (London: I.B. Tauris Publishers, 2001), p. 80; Paola
     Caridi and Emanuele Giordana, "A smaller Mediterranean: satellite TV
     channels and the Arab community in Italy," *Transnational Broadcasting
     News*, Vol. 9 (Fall 2000), <http://www.tbsjournal.com/Archives/Fall02/
     fall02.html>; Hassan Al Mohamadi, "A pioneering media study on Arab
     viewers of Al Jazeera in the US gets Qatar in the *World Press Encyclopedia*,"
     Al Watan, February 4, 2003, p. 6.

22   See James Poniwozik, "The battle for hearts and minds: even before bin
     Laden's tape, the US was losing the propaganda war in the Arab world,"
     Times Magazine, October 22, 2001, p. 65.

23   Jon Anderson and Dale Eickelman, "Media convergence and its conse-
     quences," *Middle East Insight*, Vol. 14, No. 2 (1999), pp. 59–61.

24   Bassam Tibi, "From pan-Arabism to community of sovereign Arab states:
     redefining the Arab and Arabism in the aftermath of the Second Gulf
     War," in Michael C. Hudson (ed.), *Middle East Dilemma: The Politics and
     Economics of Arab Integration* (New York: Columbia University Press,
     1999), p. 104.

25   Andrew Hammond, "Moving the masses," *Jerusalem Report*, January 15,
     2001, p. 22. See also Sara Daniel, "Al Jazira la voix des Arabes," *Le Nouvel
     Observateur*, February 13, 2003, <http://www.nouvelobs.com/articles/
     p1997/a120399.html>.

26   Jon Alterman, *New Media, New Politics: From Satellite Television to the
     Internet in the Arab World* (Washington DC: The Washington Institute for
     Near East Policy, 1998), p. 24.

27   See Khaled Al Dakheel, "The tension between Qatar and Saudi Arabia … is not caused by Al Jazeera," *Al Hayat*, October 6, 2002, p. 9; and Sakr, "Optical illusion."

28   William A. Rugh, *The Arab Press: News Media and Political Process in the Arab World* (Syracuse: Syracuse University Press, 1987).

29   Naomi Sakr, "Satellite television and development in the Middle East," *Middle East Report* (Spring 1999), <http://www.merip.org/merip.org/mer/mer210/210_sakr.html>.

30   For an assessment of Qatar's economic development, see Moin A. Siddiqi, "Qatar economic report: the tiny emirate of Qatar is on track to become the Gulf's new super energy power," *Middle East*, No. 332 (March 2003), pp. 46–9.

31   See El-Nawawy and Farag, *Al Jazeera*, pp. 140–2.

32   Al Thani, Interview with Abdallah Schleifer and Sarah Sullivan.

33   See Stephen Franklin, "The kingdom and the power," *Columbia Journalism Review*, Vol. 35, No. 4 (1996), pp. 49–51; Douglas Boyd, "Saudi Arabia's International Media Strategy: Influence through Multinational Ownership," in Kai Hafez (ed.), *Mass Media, Politics, and Society in the Middle East* (Cresskill: Hampton Press, 2001), pp. 56–7.

34   For a detailed account about Saudi print media, see Alterman, *New Media, New Politics*, pp. 8–12.

35   See Hirst, "Qatar calling."

36   For more on Qatar and regional diplomacy see Ehud Ya'ari, "The Al Jazeera revolution," *Jerusalem Report*, March 27, 2000, p. 42; Hammond, "Moving the masses"; and Gary C. Gambill, "Qatar's Al Jazeera TV: the power of free speech," *Middle East Intelligence Bulletin*, Vol. 2, No. 5 (2000), <http://www.meib.org/articles/0006_me2.htm>; "Israel holds talks with Qatar," BBC News Online, May 14, 2003, <http://news.bbc.co.uk/1/hi/world/middle_east/3027909.stm >.

37   See Gambill, "Qatar's Al Jazeera TV."

38   Olivier Da Lage, "La diplomatie de Doha: des yeux plus gros que le ventre," *Arabies* (May 2000), <http://mapage.noos.fr/odalage/autres/qat.html>.

39   Mamoun Fandy, "CyberResistance: Saudi opposition between globalization and localization," *Comparative Studies in Society and History*, Vol. 41, No. 1 (1999), pp. 124–7.

40   On this point, see Sakr, *Satellite Realms*, pp. 27–65.

41   See Daniel Pruzin, "Qatar-Based news channel hopes to gain financial independence from state," *Sunday Business*, October 14, 2001, and Davan Maharaj, "How tiny Qatar jars Arab media," *Los Angeles Times*, May 7, 2001, p. A1.

42   According to some estimates, 30 per cent of the income of the channel comes from subscriptions and commercials. See "Al Jazeera: une télé comme les autres?," *Le Kiosque Média*, October 22, 2001, <http://www.sciencepresse.qc.ca/kiosquemedias/bref221001.html>.

43   Sharon Waxman, "Arab TV's strong signal: the Al Jazeera Network offers news the Mideast never had before," *Washington Post*, December 4, 2001, p. C1.

44   Barbara Demick, "The CNN of the Arab world, Al Jazeera, attracts big audiences and official ire," *Inquirer*, March 5, 2000.

45   Jihad Ali Ballout, Interview with author, February 5, 2003. The issue also concerns other Arab satellite channels. Discussing the Egyptian case in *Satellite Realms*, p. 39, Naomi Sakr observes that "income from the channels themselves was not the chief motive behind them. They were linked instead to the ruling elite's determination to present an image of Egypt as a 'cohesive community' to viewers at home and abroad. The many components of the satellite project conceived and implemented in Cairo ... were geared to a particular official view of Egypt's role in the region and internationally, its ability to provide a counter weight to Saudi Arabia and its future economic development."

46   Louay Bahry, "The new Arab media phenomenon: Qatar's Al Jazeera," *Middle East Policy*, Vol. 8, No. 2 (2001), pp. 88–99.

47   See Saad, "Al Jazeera."

48   Ghassan bin Jeddou, *Open Dialogue*, Al Jazeera, November 1, 2003, <http://www.aljazeera.net/programs/open_dialog/articles/2003/11/11-6-1.htm>.

49   Souha Zineddine, "Asaad Taha: Arab satellite channels undergo a random growth," *Al Hayat*, April 7, 2003, p. 21.

50   Steven Wu, "This just in: Qatar satellite channel," *Harvard International Review*, Vol. 21, No. 4 (1999), pp. 14–15.

51   Ed Bradley, "Inside Al Jazeera," *60 Minutes*, CBS, May 2001, <http://www.cbsnews.com/stories/2001/10/10/60minutes/main314278.shtml>.

52   Thomas Friedman, "TV station beams beacon of freedom to Arab world," *Milwaukee Journal Sentinel*, February 28, 2001.

53   Robert Fisk, "Al Jazeera: a bold and original TV station," *Independent*, October 11, 2001, p. 4.

54   Julia Day, "Al Jazeera airs lies," *Guardian*, March 31, 2003, <http.media.guardian.co.uk/broadcast/story/0,7493,926292,00.html>.

55   Fouad Ajami, "What the Muslim world is watching," *New York Times*, November 18, 2001.

56   Carol Rosemberg, "Qatar's maverick Al Jazeera TV news network causing major stir arena," *Knight Ridder Washington Bureau*, October 10, 2001.

57   "Al Jazeera: explosive matchbox," *The Economist*, October 13, 2001, p. 46.

58   Friedman, "TV station beams beacon of freedom to Arab World," p. 31A.

59   "Defense Secretary Rumsfeld on CBS Face the Nation," *Face the Nation*, CBS, April 13, 2003, <http://www.usembassy-israel.org.il/publish/press/2003/april/041402.html>

60   Lydia Saad, "Al Jazeera viewers perceive the West differently," *Gallup Poll Tuesday Briefing*, April 23, 2002.

61   Zev Chafets, "Al Jazeera unmasked: an Arab propaganda machine in the guise of real journalism," *New York Daily News*, October 14, 2001, <www.nydailynews.com/2001-10-14/News_and_Views/opinion/a-128499.asp>, p. 37.

62   Ibid.

63   Ajami, "What the Muslim world is watching."

64   Ibid.

65   David Makovsky, "A voice from the heavens: Al Jazeera's satellite broadcasts inflame emotions across the Arab world," *US News & World Report*, May 14, 2001, pp. 26–8.

66 Hammond, "Moving the masses."
67 Howard Rosenburg, "Negative stereotyping distorts Arabs' image," *Los Angeles Times*, July 30, 2001.
68 Brit Hume, "Special report roundtable," *Fox News*, October 16, 2001.
69 Chafets, "Al Jazeera unmasked."
70 Faisal Bodi, "Al Jazeera tells the truth about the War," *Guardian*, March 28, 2003.
71 Stuart Wavell, "Victory for the voice of Arabia," *Sunday Times*, October 14, 2001.
72 Al Ali, Interview with Abdallah Schleifer and Sarah Sullivan.
73 "Radio Sawa: l'anti-Al Jazira," *Le Nouvel Observateur*, February 13, 2003.
74 Marwan Bishara, "Propaganda TV won't help the US," *International Herald Tribune*, February 23, 2004.
75 "Bin Laden's surprise," *Guardian*, November 1, 2004.
76 Dana Milbank, "Impact of tape on race is uncertain", *Washington Post*, October 30, 2004, p. A1.
77 Adam Nagourney, "Terrorist tape, political angst", *New York Times*, October 31, 2004. See also Dana Milbank, "Impact of tape on race is uncertain."
78 See Michael Dobbs, "Qatar TV station: a clear channel to Middle East," *Washington Post*, October 9, 2001, p. C01.
79 Saleh Dabbakeh, "Al Jazeera: winning the battle for Afghanistan," *Star*, October 16, 2001.
80 Hussein Ibish and Ali Abunimah, "The CNN of the Arab world deserves our respect," *Los Angeles Times*, October 22, 2001.
81 Fisk, "Al Jazeera: a bold and original TV station."
82 Nasser Husseini, "Beyond CNN: the proliferation of satellite channels," *Middle East Insight* (Spring 1999), p. 35.
83 Ali Bayramoglu, "Al Jazira: vecteur d'une globalization islamique," *Sabah*, October 9, 2001, <http://www.medea.be/files/medea/3.doc>.
84 Al Ali, Interview with Abdallah Schleifer and Sarah Sullivan.
85 Ibish and Abunimah, "The CNN of the Arab world deserves our respect."
86 Mohammed Jassim Al Ali, Interview with Nicholas Nesson, *Arabies Trends*, May 1, 2001.
87 Wu, "This just in."
88 Kai Hafez, "Mass media in the Middle East: patterns of political and societal change," in Hafez, *Mass Media, Politics and Society in the Middle East*, p. 4.
89 Muhammad Ayish, "The changing face of Arab communications," in Hafez, *Mass Media, Politics and Society in the Middle East*, p. 129.
90 Tom Brokaw, "The Arab world tunes in," *New York Times*, March 7, 2003.
91 Jon Alterman, "Mid-tech revolution," *Middle East Insight*, <www.mideastinsight.org/5_01/midtech.html>.
92 Christa Salamandra, "London's Arab media and the construction of Arabness," *Transnational Broadcasting Studies*, No. 10 Spring/Summer 2003), <http://www.tbsjournal.com/Archives/Spring03/salamandra_refrences.html>.
93 See Jürgen Habermas, *The Structural Transformation of the Public Sphere* (Cambridge: MIT Press, 1989).
94 James W. Carey, *Communication as Culture: Essays on Media and Society* (London: Routledge, 1992), pp. 15–20.

95 Kai Hafez, "In search for new global-local nexus," in Kai Hafez (ed.), *Islam and the West in the Mass Media: Fragmented Images in a Globalizing World* (Cresskill: Hampton Press, 2000), p. 13.

96 Jon W. Anderson, "Knowledge and technology," *International Institute for the Study of Islam in the Modern World Newsletter*, Vol. 5 (2000), <www.isim.nl/newsletter/5/>.

97 Jon B. Alterman, "The information technology and the Arab world," *MESA Bulletin*, Vol. 34, No. 1 (2000), pp. 21–2.

98 Marc Lynch, "Taking Arabs seriously," *Foreign Affairs*, Vol. 82, No. 6 (September/October 2003), <http://www.foreignaffairs.org/20030901faessay82506/marc-lynch/taking-arabs-seriously.html>; see also by the same author "Beyond the Arab street: Iraq and the Arab public sphere," *Politics and Society*, Vol. 31, No. 1 (2003), pp. 55–91; and "America is losing the battle for Arab opinion," *International Herald Tribune*, August 23, 2003.

99 Lynch, "Taking Arabs seriously." For more on Arab media and the public sphere, see also Mohamed Zayani, *Arab Satellite Channels and Politics in the Middle East* (Abu Dhabi: The Emirates Center for Strategic Studies and Research, 2004).

I

Al Jazeera, Regional Politics and the Public Sphere

2

The Politics of Al Jazeera or the Diplomacy of Doha

Olivier Da Lage

When the Kingdom of Saudi Arabia or Israel, among other countries, complains to the British Foreign Office about the content of a particular BBC program, the answer is invariably the same: the government of Her Majesty cannot intervene in the editorial policy of the BBC, the independence of which is provided for by the law. As a matter of fact, the Iraqi crisis, and most notably the Kelly affair, has amply demonstrated that the British government itself is not immune from this editorial independence. This was the case not only with Tony Blair during the Third Gulf War but also with Margaret Thatcher during the Falklands War. Still, the Saudi government, which was not successful in dissuading British public television from airing *Death of a Princess* in the early 1980s,[1] thus triggering a series of diplomatic crises between London and Riyadh, keeps complaining to Whitehall about the BBC's portrayal of the Kingdom of Saudi Arabia and demands the taming of the recalcitrant channel.

The same scenario seems to recur in the case of Qatar and Al Jazeera: each time a government complains about a particular program on Al Jazeera, Qatar consistently maintains that it cannot interfere because of the editorial independence of the channel. However, such a position is usually met with a general skepticism equally on the part of Arab governments and American officials. Unlike Great Britain, Qatar is not known for its democratic tradition, nor does it have a long history of free press. Not surprisingly, Al Jazeera has caused innumerable diplomatic crises.

Does Al Jazeera operate according to strictly journalistic criteria independently of Qatar? Or is it a subservient instrument of its diplomacy? Though seemingly contradictory, these two claims are not irreconcilable. While in the long run Al Jazeera serves the diplomatic interests of Qatar well, in the short run the channel's freedom and jarring tone often complicate the task of the diplomats of this small emirate.

THE GEO-POLITICAL CONSTRAINTS OF QATAR

In order to adequately assess the impact of Al Jazeera and to fully understand the ensuing changes in Qatar's relationship with its neighbors and, more generally, how it positions itself in the Middle East region, it is useful to highlight the main characteristics of this small country which did not gain its independence until 1971, as is the case with Bahrain and the Unites Arab Emirates. In terms of both its image and its regional status, Qatar has come a long way; what it has managed to achieve in a relatively short period of time is quite impressive. In 1995, when the sitting Emir Sheikh Hamad bin Khalifa Al Thani ousted his father, Sheikh Khalifa bin Hamad Al Thani, the country was perceived as a discrete satellite of Saudi Arabia.

With some 700,000 inhabitants, about 150,000 of whom are Qatari nationals, Qatar is the archetype of an oil monarchy with plenty of oil and a few locals living to a great extent on oil revenues. More importantly, Qatar is fortunate to be sitting on one of the largest gas reserves, discovered around the same time as the country's ascension to independence. Qatar has indeed the third largest gas reserve in the world.[2] While oil is expected to dry out in the course of the twenty-first century, gas is expected to provide Qatar with resources well beyond that. The problem, however, is that a large part of that reserve is offshore, reaching as far as the disputed zones that are contiguous with Bahrain and extending to the heart of the Persian Gulf, way beyond the maritime borders with Iran. These geological complexities rekindled the dispute dating back to the 1930s between Bahrain and Qatar over territorial sovereignty. They also prompted the latter to adopt a non-confrontational approach with Iran, which guarantees it the continuing exploitation of gas in the North Dome regardless of the tensions that may erupt between Iran and its neighbors or Iran and the United States.

At the heart of the dispute between Qatar and Bahrain is an old rivalry between two dynasties: the Al Thani of Qatar and the Al Khalifa of Bahrain. Partly because of the rivalry, the project of a large federation of emirates, which the British envisaged before their departure from the Gulf in 1971, failed to materialize. While the UAE opted for a federal system, Bahrain and Qatar decided to go their own way. The dispute over the isles of Hawar and the Fasht al Dibel rocks, which came close to degenerating into a military confrontation in 1986, paralyzed the activities of the Gulf Cooperation Council (GCC) between 1987 and 2001, to the extent that in

December 1990, during the summit which took place in Doha some three weeks prior to Operation Desert Storm which followed Iraq's invasion of Kuwait, a great deal of the debates revolved around the territorial dispute between Qatar and Bahrain.

Finally, one should not fail to note a significant characteristic of the Qatari identity. Like the majority of the Saudis, the native population of Qatar is Muslim Sunni following Wahhabi precepts which are rigorous and austere to say the least.

Overall, the Qatar which Sheikh Khalifa handed over—albeit involuntarily—to his son is the most discrete student of the GCC class. The only diplomatic fantasy it has probably allowed itself is to be Francophile rather than Anglophile. Nonetheless, this Qatar—the loyal little brother of Saudi Arabia who is also jealous of Bahrain—came to understand the value of maintaining good relations with Tehran. Qatar's politics have always been inextricably linked to these geo-political constraints.

However, the ascension to power of Sheikh Hamad was a turning point for Qatar. With the help of his close circle, most notably the Minister of Foreign Affairs, Hamad bin Jassim Al Thani, the Emir would make out of the pulls and contradictions that characterize the dynamics at play in Qatar the official policy of this emirate.

Qatar's ability to turn its weaknesses into strengths predates the reign of Sheikh Hamad. In spite of its low profile, Qatar was not to be underestimated, particularly when it came to its powerful neighbor Saudi Arabia. In 1974, the United Arab Emirates ceded to Saudi Arabia a portion of a territory that is adjacent to Qatar. Since then, Saudi Arabia has laid claim to a strip situated between the UAE and Qatar. During Iraq's invasion of Kuwait in 1990, Saudi Arabia requested permission from Qatar to deploy its forces on Qatari soil. Taking a cautious stand, Qatar denied Saudi forces access. To further assert its sovereignty on this fairly ill-defined zone, Qatar set up the Khafous frontier post. For its part, Saudi Arabia, which was building a naval base on Khor Obeid, enforced strict customs control on vehicles using the coastal highway which links Abu Dhabi and Qatar. Eventually, Saudi Arabia restricted access to this road, compelling vehicles to make a detour through Saudi territory and stepping up vexatious controls. To express its discontent to Riyadh, Qatar started flirting with Iran. By the end of 1991 and throughout 1992, Iranian ministers flocked to Doha while members of the Qatari government were dispatched to Tehran. The two countries even started to tease out the possibility for security and defense cooperation. As if this were not enough, Qatar sent back its ambassador to Iraq. If the purpose behind such moves was to irritate the Saudis, then Qatar can be said to have succeeded in its endeavors, for in Riyadh, the perception was that Qatar had become the Trojan horse of Iran. Throughout the Gulf, Qatar's diplomacy started to worry even those who do not have much sympathy for Saudi Arabia.

Such then is the background against which the Khafous frontier post incident took place on September 30, 1992, incurring two deaths (three according to Saudi sources). Certainly this was not the first incident in the region. However, and much to the surprise of the Saudis, Qatar gave it considerable publicity and even accused the Saudi forces of violating its territorial sovereignty and of penetrating a few kilometers into its territory. Soon thereafter, Qatar suspended its frontier agreements which go back to 1965—a move which was supported by Iran and Iraq. Qatar also decided to boycott future GCC meetings. Sheikh Khalifa bin Hamad Al Thani made it clear that he intended to boycott the meeting of Abu Dhabi at the end of December.

However, on the eve of the summit, Egyptian President Hosni Mubarak managed to get King Fahd and Sheikh Khalifa to iron out their differences, thus enabling the summit to go on as scheduled. "Even if the younger party is at fault," an Emirati diplomat pointed out, "it is up to big brother to make concessions." However, for Saudi Arabia, the concession it made was not without strings attached to it: Qatar had to stop behaving as if it were a country that is independent of its big neighbor. The then Crown Prince of Qatar, Sheikh Hamad bin Khalifa Al Thani, flew to Riyadh, knowing full well what was awaiting him.[3] Obviously, the lesson that Sheikh Hamad retained is not the one the Saudis had in mind. To the contrary, the Khafous incident had plainly convinced him that, with strong determination, it was possible to bend this powerful neighbor by virtue of the very disproportion of forces evoked above by the Emirati diplomat—namely, imposing the will of the weak on the strong.

Not long after his ascension to power, Sheikh Hamad sought to level the playing field in almost all political spheres. On the diplomatic front, the tension with Bahrain acquired a new dimension with Qatar taking the case to the International Court of Justice in the Hague. Having taken a hard-line approach when serving as Crown Prince and Minister of Defense, Sheikh Hamad was not all that lenient with Bahrain. As a ruler, though, he adopted a more diplomatic approach. At the same time, he exercised some public pressure in his relationship with some of the GCC members, allowing, for instance, Bahraini opposition figures, including a Bahraini Air Force pilot who was granted political asylum in Qatar, to convey their views on national TV. In a way, these practices seem to prefigure the editorial policy of Al Jazeera. Paradoxically enough, the ascension to power in Bahrain of Sheikh Hamad bin Isa Al Khalifa—who, as Crown Prince and Commander-in-Chief of the BDF, was firm in dealing with Qatar—helped break the deadlock. The relationship between the two countries stabilized with Solomon's judgment which the International Court of Justice pronounced on March 16, 2001 and which, by means of a *tour de force*, managed to satisfy both parties.

A close reading of Qatar's actions since 1992 and of the Khafous incident reveals a certain consistency in Qatar's diplomacy: doing everything possible to distinguish itself from its Saudi neighbor. This can be seen not only in Qatar's decision to resume diplomatic ties with Iraq, its rapprochement with Iran and its *de facto* normalization of relations with Israel, but also in its position vis-à-vis the civil war in Yemen—Qatar being the only country which took sides with the North, preventing the foreign ministers of the GCC countries from officially recognizing the separatist Southern government during their extraordinary meeting in Abha (June 4–5, 1994). After the coup d'état, Qatar did not miss the opportunity to boast that its position on the question of Yemen was what spared the GCC the humiliation of finding itself on the side of the loser.

Domestically, Qatar adopted a constitution which guarantees civil liberty as well as religious freedom. For example, the Emir authorized the construction of churches which up to then had been forbidden in Qatar and are still forbidden in the neighboring Wahhabi Kingdom. Another initiative taken by the Emir, in fact one which earned Qatar much praise from the Occident in general and the United States in particular, was to abolish the Ministry of Information and to repeal censorship. However, the new measures do not necessarily mean that journalists can write whatever they want. The main difference is that now, instead of knowing with certitude where the red lines are drawn, they have to guess. In practice, the banning of censorship has even proven to be a real headache for local journalists who are no longer sure where to draw the line.

In November 1996, a year and a half after the coup d'état, Qatar's policy of media openness culminated in the launching of Al Jazeera, a private satellite channel made possible by a generous 500 million Riyal loan from the state to be repaid over five years.

AL JAZEERA AND THE POLITICS OF QATAR

The Arab World

It is probable that the initiators of this media venture might have thought that, in time, it would be possible to attract investors who would be willing to finance the channel after its formative years. However, the five years have already lapsed without any business plan materializing. As it is, Al Jazeera is still subsidized. Part of the problem is the boycott campaign launched by the Kingdom of Saudi Arabia with Arab advertising agencies. Nevertheless, Al Jazeera's "private" model is not without a precedent—Radio Monte Carlo Moyen Orient (RMC-MO), which emerged in the mid 1970s at the French government's behest. Soon thereafter, President Pompidou split ORTF, the public organism of French Radio and Television. Accordingly, Arabic programs were made independent of the foreign programs in the public service, and a subsidiary of Radio Monte Carlo, a private commercial radio beamed out of Monaco, was set up to transmit its programs in Arabic from Cyprus. Overnight, the dynamic, free and modern tone, which was derived from European commercial radio, captured Arab audiences who started to abandon the propaganda-ridden state radio. The presence of advertising was reassuring because of the perception that commercial radio cannot be at the service of the state. This was indeed a shrewd initiative on the part of the French. Behind the fig leaf of commercial radio was a station financed by Sofirad, a holding which was fully owned by the French state and whose directors were nominated by the French president. Ironically, Arab listeners and often decision-makers were unknowingly tuning in to French state radio.

Other models come to mind. For instance, CNN is a private television network, but one which is informed by an American vision of the world. Likewise, Middle East Broadcasting Corporation (MBC), which was launched in 1991 in the aftermath of the Second Gulf War with Saudi capital, was conceived as the first Arab information channel and in fact wanted to be the CNN of the Arab world. However, with the launching of Al Jazeera in 1996 came the realization that the Arab world had never experienced something like that before either in television (as MBC's name is associated with

Saudi Arabia) or in radio (as RMC-MO had never dared to break a number of taboos which were in vigor in the Arab and Muslim world in the way Al Jazeera did). The margin of freedom Al Jazeera has enjoyed is such that no Arab government is immune from the channel's on-the-air criticism. The only exception is probably Qatar itself. By and large, Al Jazeera has a very skimpy coverage of its host country. For some, the channel's quasi-inexistent coverage of Qatar's affairs is a sign of independence since Al Jazeera spares the viewers long reports on the daily activities of the Emir of Qatar, which is a real change from what is usually aired on the overwhelming majority of Arab TV channels, including satellite channels. Others see in this "double standard" the price Al Jazeera has to pay for the freedom it enjoys. There is probably a bit of both. Although contradictory, these two views are not mutually exclusive.

Much like Bahrain, which built its reputation after gaining its independence by developing offshore banking, with financial institutions trading throughout the region but not within Bahrain itself, Qatar decided to set up offshore TV. The results were spectacular to say the least. For one thing, there was a huge market for such a venture. State TV had no credibility and was usually seen as an extension of the regimes in place. As for satellite channels, the Egyptian ones were uninteresting, MBC was too dependent on funding from Saudi Arabia which had a conservative approach to the news, while the Lebanese channels were too Lebanese.

Qatar knew how to market itself. Al Jazeera has become the symbol of the emirate as well as the source of its fame. In a sense, Al Jazeera is for Qatar what the casinos are for Monaco. Having in the past been ignored and even despised as a state by other Arab countries, Qatar has at last found a place for itself. In the eyes of Sheikh Hamad who wants his small emirate to be promoted to the major leagues,[4] Al Jazeera instantly found its place in the panoply of instruments designed to achieve such an objective. Sheikh Hamad, who does not miss the opportunity to shock the other heads of state either by walking away from a Gulf summit or by threatening to boycott another, knows how to play the game. The Emir's tendency to raise the stakes in order to gain a better bargaining position is far from being a matter of whim; to the contrary, it is a deliberate and well thought out strategy. In the beginning, the target was Saudi Arabia and Bahrain. In some instances, heads of state like President Mubarak and Sultan Qabous of Oman offered to mediate. Soon though, even those leaders who tolerated the "whims" of the new

Emir came to realize that no Arab regime is immune from the initiatives of his satellite channel. Except for Qatari dissidents, dissidents of all sorts are welcome in the studios of Al Jazeera. The channel has provided them with a platform they never dreamed of. In 1998, Saddam Hussein was quick to understand the value of granting exclusive interviews to a channel that is viewed by some 35 million Arab viewers.

Not surprisingly, Al Jazeera has angered many Arab governments. During the GCC summit which was held in Muscat in 2001, Saudi Crown Prince Abdullah strongly criticized the Qatari channel and accused it "of being a disgrace to the GCC countries, of defaming the members of the Saudi Royal family, of threatening the stability of the Arab world and of encouraging terrorism."[5] In 1998, Jordan closed down the Al Jazeera bureau in Amman for six months only to come up against another crisis in 2002. Similar scenarios took place in Kuwait, Algeria and Egypt, among Arab countries. In one way or another, most if not all Arab states have at some point complained about Al Jazeera or criticized Sheikh Hamad for his complacency. In 2002, Saudi Arabia recalled its ambassador in Qatar. However, thanks to the unfailing support of authorities in Doha, the management of the channel is so far holding out fairly well and looking forward to better days. The demand for Al Jazeera is such that few if any Arab governments seem to be capable of keeping the channel at bay. In the meantime, the government of Qatar looks the other way, claiming unconvincingly its disapproval of a particular controversial episode of a program while pursuing its hands-off policy.

Still, there is some merit to Qatar's rationale for refusing to interfere. Al Jazeera is not a mouthpiece for the diplomacy of Qatar; at the same time, it is not at odds with it either. Qatar plays on this ambiguity. At first sight, one may characterize the foreign policy of Qatar as being the opposite of that of Oman. Under Sultan Qabous, Oman has followed a political line that is linear, steady, smooth and unambiguous both in the short and long term. In contrast, one gets a sense that Sheikh Hamad has opted for an approach that is chaotic, unorganized and at times ambiguous. But this is only an impression. When seen in retrospect, the Emir's actions reveal constants in the politics of Qatar that have apparently been influenced by the Omani model: maintaining good relations with the United States, Iraq and Iran no matter what happens and establishing significant relations with Israel.

Israel

The case of Israel warrants more than cursory attention. No sooner had the Oslo Accords been signed than Qatar started to capitalize on the new dynamics in the Middle East. As early as 1994, Qatar acknowledged entering into official negotiations with Israel to provide the Hebrew state with natural gas. The deal in question pertains to a feasibility study that may be worth $1 billion. This project is only one small part of a mega project which Qatar is developing to become the principal provider of gas in Europe, including Turkey. However, in light of strong reservations from such Arab states as Saudi Arabia (as the pipeline is supposed to traverse its territory) and Egypt (which finds its revenues from the Suez Canal jeopardized) and in light of the derailment of the peace process, the authorities in Doha have tempered their zeal without necessarily giving up their project. In October 1995, the new Qatari Minister of Foreign Affairs, Sheikh Hamad bin Jassim, met in New York with his Israeli counterpart Shimon Peres. In September 1996, an Israeli trade office was established in Doha. In 1997, because of the participation of Israel, Syria and Egypt boycotted the US-backed Fourth Middle East and North Africa Economic Summit. In spite of such reactions, Qatar held out as it did later in the Islamic Conference Organization Summit in November 2000. Officially, Qatar claimed that it closed down the Israeli trade office in 2000, just before the Summit which Iran and Saudi Arabia threatened to boycott if the Israeli office were to remain operative. In practice, however, the two Israeli diplomats at the office did not leave Doha; they were operating from inside their hotel suite. The eccentricity of Qatar manifested itself further in the encounter between the Qatari and Israeli ministers of foreign affairs, Sheikh Hamad bin Jassim and Shimon Peres, in Paris in July 2002 in spite of the decision of Arab states to freeze political ties with Israel because of the latter's violent repression of the Palestinian intifada. More recently, Sheikh Hamad bin Jassim met once again with his Israeli counterpart—this time Silvan Shalom—in Paris on May 14, 2003. In this last encounter, Sheikh Hamad indicated his willingness "to seriously consider the possibility of increasing the level of diplomatic relations."[6]

In this context, one can understand how Al Jazeera's Ramallah office has been relatively spared the muzzle of Israeli authorities in spite of its intensive coverage of the clashes between the Israelis and the Palestinians, its unabashed broadcasting of the rawest images of the conflict, its around-the-clock airing of images of Palestinian victims and its transmitting of recorded video messages of so-called suicide bombers. For doing much less than this, other foreign TV agencies have suffered from Israeli censorship as is the case with Abu Dhabi TV which saw its accreditation revoked. It is true that the head of the Al Jazeera office, Walid Al Omari, is an Israeli citizen, but this detail hardly explains the leniency with which he has been treated, especially considering that his coverage of the conflict has been consistently and undeniably pro-Palestinian.

Equally telling is the way Al Jazeera has broken another taboo among Arab media by regularly inviting Israeli officials to express themselves live. The Prime Minister of Israel, Ariel Sharon, was invited to speak live on Al Jazeera on the eve of the Arab Summit held in Beirut in March 2002. However, the interview was canceled *in extremis* when the Al Jazeera crew was already in place in the office of the Prime Minister. Yielding to the pressures and added exigencies of some of his advisors—who were in principle against such a live appearance—not to take questions from Mohamed Krichene, Al Jazeera's anchor in the Doha studios, Sharon withdrew.[7] Could Israel's relative "tolerance" of a channel that incites particularly the Palestinians but the Arabs in general against Israel be the reward for the open diplomacy of Doha toward Israel? Or does it emanate out of the consideration that Al Jazeera, while hostile to Israel, is also the latter's only conduit to Arab public opinion? It is probably a bit of both, for although Al Jazeera was not originally designed to be a means of communication between the Arabs and the Israelis, the "media normalization" it has adopted—that is, inviting Israelis to appear in a space which previously was completely closed off to them—becomes a *de facto* form of communication between the Arab world and Israel. From the latter's standpoint, Al Jazeera's overt anti-Israeli rhetoric makes it an even more effective means of communication as it pulls the rug from underneath those who accuse the channel of being "a tool in the hands of the Zionists."

The United States

In February 2003, at the end of Organization of the Islamic Conference Summit which was held in Doha, even as Sheikh Hamad bin Jassim—the head of Qatari diplomacy and the spokesman of the summit—was reading the final communiqué which called on the member states to refrain from any action which may "affect the integrity and unity of the Iraqi territory," thousands of US troops stepped up their preparation in the bases of Al Odeid and As Sayliyah a few miles away with the active cooperation of Qatar. The latter has a defense treaty with the United States which goes back to 1992. Although in the mid 1990s there were only a few troops stationed in Qatar, at the turn of the century, the country became—with the exception of the Philippines—the most important base for the US outside its national territory. Al Odeid military base was built in 1996. Four years later, Qatar invited to the US to make use of it—an offer the latter could not resist after the September 11 attacks. With an eye on the air campaign against Afghanistan, the Americans started to operate from Al Odeid as early as September 29, 2001. In the meantime, the runway was extended to 4,500 meters, making it one of the longest in the world. Work on As Sayliyah ended in August 2002 and the base was used for US Central Command during the preparation for the invasion of Iraq in early 2003.

To fully understand the degree of Qatar's cooperation with the United States, it is useful to consider the circumstances of the family coup d'état which brought Sheikh Hamad to the throne in June 1995. There are speculations that the American authorities gave their blessing to this non-violent succession. It is worth noting that, in his book on the ambiguous relationships between the United States and Saudi Arabia, former CIA agent Robert Baer makes reference to a prominent member of the inner circle of the then Crown Prince with excellent ties with Washington, pointing out on more than one occasion, the amazing ease with which this figure had access to the White House, even without appointment, which suggests an uncommon familiarity with key decision-makers in the United States.[8]

There is no hard proof to substantiate the speculation that the changes in Qatar were backed by the Americans. What is established though is the swiftness with which Washington recognized the new government, outdoing everybody else, including the Gulf states. Equally noteworthy is the amount of praise the Americans have heaped on Qatar since 1995, which is all the more surprising given that the new Emir has chosen to maintain normal relations with Iran and Iraq—two states which are the object of the politics of "dual containment" the Clinton administration chose to pursue. What is even more intriguing is Sheikh Hamad's public call to the United States, during his first visit after seizing power, to re-establish ties with Tehran. This odd suggestion, which would have brought down on anybody else scorn from a superpower which is not inclined to take lessons from anybody, was nothing more than an amusing indulgence for its initiator. Similarly, Qatar's Foreign Minister often does not shy away from contradicting the Americans during press conferences in Doha either on the question of Iraq, the issue of Iran or the Palestinian–Israeli conflict without necessarily reaping the wrath of Washington.

What profoundly irritated the American administration though was Al Jazeera's coverage of the so-called War on Terrorism, and in particular the airing of the bin Laden tapes before, during and after the war in Afghanistan. In the latter case, Al Jazeera's office in Kabul was bombed. Likewise, during the fall of Baghdad, the office of Al Jazeera was the target of an American missile which claimed the life of Tarek Ayyoub, one of Al Jazeera's reporters. As in the case of Kabul two years earlier, the argument of the American officials that Al Jazeera's office was not targeted or deliberately bombed did not sell.

A few months earlier, when Secretary of State Colin Powell asked the Emir of Qatar to tone down his satellite channel, Sheikh Hamad reportedly pointed out that the first amendment of the American Constitution guaranteed the freedom of the press. Behind the scenes, though, a deal seems to have been struck between the US administration and Al Jazeera. Accordingly, the Americans can publicly claim that they know the content of bin Laden tapes before they are aired. Of course, intercepting the satellite feeds would have done the job, but that has not been necessary as the management of Al Jazeera has agreed to communicate to the Americans a copy of such tapes 48 hours before airing them. Furthermore, and since November 2001, Al Jazeera has systematically invited the Americans to comment on the broadcast tapes. In some instances, as was the case with Ambassador Christopher Ross, the guest spoke fluent Arabic. This same channel, which in the eyes of the Occident is often considered a mouthpiece of the Al Qaeda network, has also aired interviews with Condoleezza Rice, Colin Powell and Tony Blair among other political figures who, in spite of their extremely busy schedules, have made themselves available to Al Jazeera to address the Arab public.

One should not also fail to note that on April 3, 2003, in the midst of the war, a huge demonstration took place against the US and Israel with the participation of some 10,000 people headed by members of the municipality of Doha and the Advisory Council as well as the famous Egyptian cleric Sheikh Youssef Al Qaradawi who is yet another Al Jazeera star. This demonstration, which evidently was organized with the blessing of the authorities in Doha and which took place not far away from the US Embassy, was a peaceful event—and for that matter markedly different from the less peaceful demonstration which took place in Bahrain a few days later.

In spite of the apparent eccentricity of a government which gives an outlet to those who wish to criticize the United States—in fact, the very country Qatar strives to be its best ally—Washington has nothing to complain about when it comes to Doha. Surprising as Qatar's pursuit of a "politics of extremes" may be, the only signs of loyalty which matter are acts, and where these are concerned Sheikh Hamad has abundantly proven the extent of his loyalty to the US since his ascension to power. The outcome is a real political stability in this small emirate. Regionally, the American umbrella is a positive and encouraging sign for Qatar's economic partners. Suffice it here to note that the contracts for supplying natural gas which Qatar signed with Japan, India, South Korea and some European countries are long-term contracts, often extending to 25 years. American protection makes Qatar all the more attractive for companies specializing in country risk assessment and forecast. Eventually, such a stability could appeal even to a big energy consumer like the US itself.

A VOLUNTARY BUT CONTROLLED DEMOCRACY

Internally, Sheikh Hamad's initiative to start a democratization process even before his society demands it goes also a long way toward enhancing the stability of his regime. Thus on April 29, 2003, the same day US Defense Secretary Donald Rumsfeld announced in Saudi Arabia the planned departure of US forces from the Kingdom before the end of the year, Qatar—where these same forces were to be relocated—adopted by means of a referendum a constitution which makes the emirate a parliamentary monarchy. This text guarantees fundamental public liberties, the independence of judiciary power and the freedom of the press. It also introduces a form of *habeas corpus* and fixes the responsibilities of the executive and legislative branches. The latter is made up of elected representatives through universal suffrage, with the participation of women both as voters and as candidates.[9] In its letter and spirit, the constitution comes to complement the openness that started with the holding of municipal elections in 1999. One can of course question the effective implementation of the new constitutional dispositions.

Still, it is hard to deny that Qatar has embarked on a democratization process, the intricacy of which cannot be fully understood independently of regional dynamics. At least three factors contributed to the strategic choice Sheikh Hamad made not long after his ascension to power: the ardent desire to come out of the shadow of the Kingdom of Saudi Arabia; the disastrous experience of Bahrain, which fell prey to a Shiite uprising quelled by the government between 1994 and 1999 (the year Sheikh Isa passed away); and finally the keenness to please Washington and to answer the call for democratic reform and openness following the liberation of Kuwait in 1991.

Having drawn lessons from the stalemate Bahrain reached as a consequence of pursuing repression without envisaging a political alternative, the new Emir of Bahrain, Sheikh Hamad bin Isa Al Khalifa, has in turn set his country on a course of democratization. Upon coming to power, he issued a general amnesty to all political prisoners and opposition figures in exile, conducted a nationwide referendum in February 2001, and promulgated an amended constitution in February 2002 which preserves his power privileges as head of state (henceforth king) but at the same time institutes an advisory council which is partly elected through universal suffrage. These changes are in line with a regional version of democracy whereby political parties are in practice banned. Such is the case for instance in Kuwait, a country where women still do not have the right to vote. In the meantime, the Sultan of Oman has advocated, with a slow but steady pace, a slightly open system which promotes the participation of his subjects. As for the Kingdom of Saudi Arabia, having justified the establishment of a non-elected Advisory Council, it envisages holding municipal elections; it also appears that there is some prospect of electing in the Shura Council in the near future.

A summary of the chronology of reform in the region gives an idea about the interaction between Gulf societies and the ongoing process of democratization which the region has apparently embarked on: municipal elections in Bahrain in May 2002, followed by legislative elections; legislative elections in Kuwait in July 2003; elections of the Advisory Council in Oman in October 2003; and after the new Qatari constitution was approved by a referendum in April 2003, it was announced that legislative elections would take place in 2005.

While outlining this process of democratization, one should not lose sight of the specificity of each case. Civil society in Kuwait and

Bahrain is very demanding when it comes to real political participation. In Oman, Sultan Qabous, who has drawn lessons from the War of Dhafar, has taken some initiatives. In the United Arab Emirates, the demand is almost inexistent and so is the political initiative of the governments. In Qatar, the Emir has repeatedly explained that he is taking initiatives before social pressure impels him to do so. The effect of this regional contagion and the overlapping of the timing for political reform are hard to ignore. Each step influences and in some instances prompts similar steps in neighboring countries, leading to a virtuous circle which makes the sincerity of the leaders irrelevant in the face of their subjects' growing awareness of their citizenry.

There is no doubt that the programs of Al Jazeera have played an important role in these ongoing changes, particularly the current affairs and *Crossfire* type of programs. The airing of election campaigns in a particular Arab country has an undeniable impact on the viewers of neighboring states. More generally, such programs are contributing to the popularization of political debates and the elimination of walls of censorship in scores of Arab countries.

CONCLUSION

Up until the emergence of Al Jazeera, Arab leaders thought they could consolidate their power by controlling the media. Upon coming to power, Sheikh Hamad did exactly the opposite, and, at least so far, he has not lost his bet. Al Jazeera has in fact made it possible for Qatar to impose itself on the regional scene. It has helped reduce Saudi influence, giving Qatar the opportunity to emerge and, in fact, to become the privileged ally of the Americans in the Gulf, before even Saudi Arabia and Kuwait.

Now that Sheikh Hamad has fulfilled the objectives he set for his country, a natural temptation would be to consider that Al Jazeera has served its purpose and that the margin of freedom that has been accorded to it since its inception could be gradually reduced. This suggests one way of interpreting the dismissal of the manager of the channel Mohammed Jassim Al Ali who was sidelined after having been the architect of its success for some seven years or so. There is speculation that this measure was taken to please the Americans who were unhappy with Al Jazeera's coverage of the war in Iraq. But even so, the Emir no longer has free rein as his hands are tied with the very success of Al Jazeera. In fact, many channels have started to emulate Al Jazeera. For instance, Abu Dhabi TV and Al Arabiya (a Saudi-funded channel which broadcasts from Dubai) have adopted, with varying degrees, the professionalism and journalistic aggressiveness which made Al Jazeera a success. Seen from this perspective, taming Al Jazeera can only bring trouble to the Emir of Qatar without significantly receding the margin of freedom that has contributed to its existence.

Another possible reading is that the close alliance with Washington was the original sin of the regime of Sheikh Hamad, which has been forgiven because of the role Al Jazeera has played. Thus, Al Jazeera and the United States can be considered the twin pillars of Qatar's diplomacy, giving the country a lot of room for maneuver while ensuring its security and maintaining its stability. Qatar's rapprochement with the US notwithstanding, Al Jazeera has made it possible for this small Gulf emirate to be taken seriously. What the right hand does is more or less ignored by the left hand. In the final analysis, no one has actually succeeded; nor has anyone failed because each one has derived some form of satisfaction from the situation. As Olfa Lamloum points out, "Al Jazeera is perceived as a stabilizing factor for Qatar in the region. It is both an indicator of democratization and a sign of its uniqueness in the Gulf. Moreover, the Al Jazeera effect is a sort of screen which hides the strategic alliance of the Emirate with the United States."[10]

The foregoing analysis does not in anyway suggest a political schizophrenia; if anything, it is a case of *realpolitik*—and in fact it is this very contradiction which strengthens Qatar's position.

The small one has grown big.

Translated by Mohamed Zayani

NOTES

1   See Annabelle Sreberny-Mohammadi, "The media and democratization in the Middle East: the strange case of television," in Vicky Randall (ed.), *Democratization and the Media* (London: Frank Cass, 1998), p. 189.
2   A recent *Middle East* economic report provides even higher estimates. See Moin A. Siddiqi, "Qatar economic report: the tiny emirate of Qatar is on track to become the Gulf's new super energy power," *Middle East*, No. 332 (March 2003), pp. 46–9.
3   Olivier Da Lage, "Regain d'activisme dans le Golfe: illusoire sécurité collective sans l'Irak et l'Iran," *Le Monde Diplomatique* (February 1993), pp. 4–5.

4 Olivier Da Lage, "La diplomatie de Doha: des yeux plus gros que le ventre," *Arabies* (May 2000), <http://mapage.noos.fr/odalage/autres/qat.html>.

5 AFP dispatch, January 17, 2002. See also Habib Trabelsi, "Crise larvée entre Ryad et Doha," AFP dispatch, July 24, 2002.

6 Fayçal Baatout, "Le Qatar lie des relations avec Israël à des progrès au proche-Orient," AFP dispatch, May 5, 2003. See also "Qatar ready to boost ties with Israel is Mideast peace process accelerates," *Jordan Times* May 16, 2003.

7 Walid Al Omari, Interview with author, September 23, 2003.

8 Robert Baer, *Sleeping with the Devil: How Washington Sold our Soul for Saudi Crude* (New York: Crown Publishers, 2003), *passim*.

9 For the text and interpretation of the constitution, see *Maghreb-Machrek*, No. 176 (2003).

10 Olfa Lamloum (ed.), *Irak: les médias en guerre* (Paris: Sindbad/Actes Sud, 2003), pp. 199–236.

3

Influence without Power: Al Jazeera and the Arab Public Sphere

Mohammed El Oifi

During the 1990s, the Arab media scene underwent momentous changes.[1] One of the outcomes of these changes was the emergence of a media coverage of political events that is relatively free from government control in the region. The autonomy of the media narrative and its relative independence vis-à-vis what is considered the official truth are enhanced by the pre-eminence of the non-official reading, being the prevailing interpretation of news the various players use as a point of reference or a standard against which the truthfulness of the official version of the news is measured. This reading is presumably internalized by a collective memory which gives rise to an enduring historical narrative and even defines the realm of the possible.

Al Jazeera Satellite Channel has played a central role in liberalizing the Arab media discourse.[2] Its pre-eminence in the nascent Arab public sphere has put an end to media control by Arab regimes, particularly when it comes to foreign policy.[3] In fact, Al Jazeera has triggered a profound shift in the way the Arab mediascape functions which may potentially contribute to the reconfiguration of the political systems in the Middle East region.

The factors that explain the demise of the official truth are as numerous as the implications in power relations within and between Arab states. Playing public opinion against the solidarity of Arab diplomacy in an explicit and strategic way,[4] Qatar has managed to disturb in irremediable ways the nature and logic of Arab relationships.[5] By following a strategy of addressing directly the Arab people and stirring them up against their own governments, Al Jazeera has placed the question of the gap between people's sentiments and governments' policies at the heart of both the Arab and international political debates, most notably in the United States. If anything, the growing interest in "what Arabs think" emanates from the conviction that Arab governments have lost the power to impose on their subjects a particular reading of events or explanation of actions concerning internal matters and foreign policies. The loss of control and the end of certain states' domination over their societies are the result of an authoritarian system of governance marked by flagrant inefficiency in such vital fields as the economy, education and security. However, the inability to preserve a national sovereignty acquired after decades of colonial domination has cost many rulers of the region their sacred aura.

Currently, special attention is given to interpretations coming from non-government actors who are supposed to translate more faithfully peoples' voices and reflect ideological streams to which people subscribe, and which give an outlet to their political aspirations.[6] It is from this perspective that one should understand the growing interest in Al Jazeera when analyzing the Middle East crises. Although sometimes contested, Al Jazeera's news coverage remains to a large extent an essential vector of social communication in the region. With all its weaknesses and contradictions, this satellite TV channel reflects the turbulences of a region in transition and often the impromptu choices of the foreign policy of Qatar—a country with little or no diplomatic tradition. Stunned as they may be by the resounding success of this news network, the Qatari leadership know full well that their country cannot resist pressures exerted by the various political actors in the region. The durability of this diplomatic activism is contingent on the permanent American military presence on its soil. At the same time, however, this indispensable resource for Qatar is also a form of constraint which may prove to be difficult to manage.

If Al Jazeera has managed to revolutionize the Arab and even international mediascape by giving rise to a new "Arab voice," it is partly because of a long twofold maturation process which started at the beginning of the twentieth century and resulted in the emergence of an Arab public sphere and the crystallization of an Arab public opinion. However, the influence Al Jazeera has acquired over the Arab mediascape is unlikely to give Qatar long-lasting political advantages. As it is, Qatar may acquire some influence but is unlikely to have power as it lacks the basic elements of power.

THE INCEPTION OF A PAN-ARAB TV CHANNEL

From Geo-political Deadlock to Media Openness

The motives behind the launching of Al Jazeera are varied. According to the initiators of this media venture, the channel is a manifest expression of the willingness of Qatar's "liberal Emir," who overthrew his father in 1995, to open up the country and to promote non-censored media in the region—media that can operate freely outside the tutelage of the government. Naturally, the emergence of Al Jazeera goes hand in hand with the abolition of the Qatari Ministry of Information.

Al Jazeera is also a "gift" to Arab viewers, providing access to uncensored news broadcasting in Arabic, by Arabs and for Arabs who, for decades, have been under the domination of foreign media broadcasters,[7] mainly the BBC and more recently CNN.[8] Al Jazeera's implicit criticism of other censored Arab media networks is in many ways lined with a desire to win over Arab viewers whom it perceives as allies against Arab regimes hostile to the Emir who dared to put an end to his own father's reign.

But Al Jazeera is not without critics. For some, this all Arab news channel is part of the global mediascape created by the American administration to contain the hostility of people in the Middle East against American hegemony and to legitimize the setting of American troops in the Gulf. In this sense, political modernization and media liberalization are the American answer to the heated rhetoric against the US presence in the region. The pursuit of pluralism, even when confined to media, is believed to lead to political moderation, particularly when it comes to foreign policy. The media front makes it possible to counter the predominant perception that the US is the enemy of the people in the Middle East and the supporter of unelected incompetent authoritarian regimes against the will of the people. This strategy was so desperately needed that Arab regimes, especially those under the umbrella of the United States, did not hesitate to use this popular feeling in order to conceal their failures or blackmail the American administration for whom they have become important. Partly because of the extent of "anti-American feelings" among Arab people,[9] some of these regimes receive financial aid and diplomatic and political support in return for which they are expected to prevent any hostile acts against the symbols of American domination. Advertising itself as a channel that presents the opinion and the other opinion, Al Jazeera seems to be part of the American recipe for a media liberalism that is capable of producing political moderation.

However, the foregoing thesis, which attributes the paternity of this satellite TV channel to the American administration, loses its poignancy when we consider the way Al Jazeera treats the American policy in the Middle East region. Al Jazeera, is in fact, the principal vector and the most efficient critic of the US policy. Despite the United States' hold over Qatar, which is no news, it is hard to give to the creation of Al Jazeera a purely exogenous explanation. Its launching obeys a logic that is specific to Qatar and is part of Qatar's regional environment, particularly its relationship with neighboring Saudi Arabia. Since the 1991 Gulf War, the little Persian Gulf emirates, which essentially owe their existence to the British presence in the region for some two centuries,[10] have become more than at anytime before aware of their fragility.[11] Iraq's invasion of Kuwait awakened in the Qataris' memories the specter of Saudi domination.[12] The border incidents which took place in the early 1990s between the two countries were instrumental in convincing the Emir of Qatar that his country needed a protector. The natural choice was to resort to the most powerful, namely the United States. The alliance between the two countries was consolidated over a period of a decade or so and culminated in the establishment of US Central Command near Doha.

Seen from this perspective, it does not make much sense to read Qatar's foreign policy according to the classical categories of foreign policy analysis.[13] In this case, the concept of national sovereignty does not mean much. In the absence of state structures or a nation *per se*, the nation-state becomes more of a fiction or, better yet, a rhetorical effect than a reality. In understanding Al Jazeera, then, one should not lose sight of important aspects which a classical angle of analysis cannot unravel, namely the identity of Al Jazeera, its underlying assumptions, its national mission (in consolidating the Qatari regime), its regional positioning (vis-à-vis neighbors like Saudi Arabia) and its international aspirations (namely gaining international and especially American recognition).

Al Jazeera emerged in an uncertain geo-political context in which the controversial ideology of the nation-state is receding in front of the more prominent trend toward transnational identities. To legitimate its very existence—which is often viewed with bitterness by Arab nationalists who consider it as a historical mistake and a sign of the weakness of the Arab nation—Qatar has tapped into these transnational sentiments, whether they be pan-Arab or pan-Islamic, and it has capitalized on them to serve its own interests. Its ostensible purpose is to strengthen and legitimize its national identity which remains highly illusory.

Monopoly Strategy versus Distinction Strategy

In its attempt to establish its transnational sense of identity which draws Arabs together, Qatar finds itself clashing with a powerful rival—the Kingdom of Saudi Arabia. Traumatized by the propaganda of Egyptian President Nasser in the 1950s and 1960s through the radio station Voice of the Arabs,[14] and wary of the influence that the discourse of Arab nationalism might have on its subjects,[15] Saudi Arabia has been more than ever convinced of the need to have some control over the Arab mediascape. Accordingly, the Kingdom has been pursuing a monopoly strategy which enables it either to claim or to own the bulk of Arab newspapers, magazines and Arab satellite channels which are likely to contribute to forming and informing Arab public opinion in an attempt to absorb any criticism of the Saudi regime. After the 1991 Gulf War, this strategy took phenomenal proportions,[16] so much so that the only pan-Arab medium with some influence that escaped this net was the London daily *Al Quds Al Arabi*, which is edited by the Palestinian journalist Abdel Barri Atwan.

Al Jazeera is important partly because it managed to disrupt the seamlessness of the Saudi media strategy thanks to its journalistic practices and editorial choices. Through Al Jazeera, Qatar has in fact changed the way the Arab mediascape functions at all levels. Qatar's media strategy reveals a fundamental concern—distinguishing itself from neighboring Saudi Arabia, a country with which it shares the same vital approach, namely American favoritism. Accordingly, Al Jazeera has been keen to distinguish itself from the Saudi media style, particularly when it comes to three important considerations: location, personnel and ideology.

If today the implantation of Al Jazeera in Qatar is taken for granted, when put in context, the choice of the location of the channel is ingenious. In fact, before the emergence of Al Jazeera in November 1996 in an Arab territory, the dominant belief was that location outside the Arab world, particularly in Europe, was the *sine qua non* for a free Arab media.[17] Not surprisingly, the Saudi media empire was erected in such European capitals as London and Rome. The emigration of some of the Lebanese media to Europe after the breakout of the Civil War in 1975 lent more pertinence to this thesis. The imposing presence of Arab and especially Lebanese journalists in Europe has facilitated the alliance between Lebanese journalists and the Saudi emirs who came to control much of Arab media. The massive transfer of Arab assets from Beirut to London and the heavy investments required by the media sector further consolidated the presumptions about the impossibility of having a free press in the Arab world. Such an operation had yet another objective—that of legitimizing the transfer of Arab funds abroad and facilitating the collaboration of Arab journalists with Saudi investors. Gradually, a large number of Arab journalists, most notably Lebanese journalists, turned into "mercenaries," so to speak, at the disposal of Saudi princes.[18] Being set up in Qatar, Al Jazeera has put an end to the perception that Arab media cannot thrive within the Arab world. The example of Al Jazeera shows that Arab media implemented in an Arab country can, in fact, have a large margin of freedom. As a consequence, Saudi media in Europe has gradually started to come back to the Middle East region, albeit to the UAE and not to Saudi Arabia.

Concomitant with the initiative of the conceivers of Al Jazeera to implement the new network on Arab soil was their decision to opt for the sociological diversification of its Arab journalists, thus putting an end to the Lebanese pre-eminence in the media sector. To encourage viewer loyalty, the conceivers of Al Jazeera pursued a practice which ensured that the recruitment of their staff is representative of Arab nationalities. Al Jazeera's pan-Arab recruitment policies and practices are noteworthy because they represent a clear break from the Saudi tradition in the press and media industry, which is often characterized by an informal alliance between Saudi money and Lebanese know-how. By providing an alternative model that is quite distinct from the Saudi recipe, Al Jazeera has effectively put an end to Saudi–Lebanese domination over pan-Arab media. Escaping the Lebanese influence—in which confessional pluralism gains pre-eminence over ideological pluralism[19]—Al Jazeera has legitimated other viewpoints and minimized the importance of confessionalism as a way of playing off political pluralism in the Arab world.[20]

Interestingly enough, the urge to diversify the pool of Arab journalists was also in the minds of the managers of the BBC Arabic Services when recruiting the journalists and staff who later came to constitute the core of Al Jazeera's staff. In 1994, the BBC World Service deployed its know-how and its international reputation to the service of Orbit, a private Saudi TV channel, in order to create an Arabic language TV channel. After about a year and a half, broadcasting was discontinued due to a disagreement on the editorial line of the channel, particularly in relation to the treatment of Saudi news. Following the intervention in a program devoted to human rights in Saudi Arabia of London-based opposition figures, the short-lived partnership between the two came to an end. Al Jazeera management seized this opportunity to recruit the most eminent journalists in this TV channel, including Faisal Al Kasim, Sami Haddad, Jameel Azer and Mohamed Krichene. These journalists brought the professionalism, rigor and tradition of the BBC to an environment that is characterized by more freedom and where the conditions for a commitment to Arab viewers are more favorable.

Three Conflictual Ideologies

For a number of years, the Arab world has seen a winner-less confrontation between three main ideological tendencies, the conflictual coexistence of which can be seen on Al Jazeera's screen. A close reading of the ideological orientation and editorial line of Al Jazeera in light of the programs it offers, the subjects it emphasizes and the allegiances its leading figures have reveals a subtle balance between three trends: the Arabist, the Islamic and the liberal.

To start with, Arab nationalism is very prominent as a unifying sentiment on the channel.[21] This is evident not only in the terminology that is used and the issues that are discussed but also in the tendency of Al Jazeera journalists to identify themselves first and foremost as Arabs. Arab nationalism has in some ways become the basis of a sharp critique of the politics of Arab rulers who have come to favor the fragmentation of the Arab public sphere, sacrificing thereby the ideal of Arab unity. This rhetoric is prominent in the weekly program of the Syrian journalist Faisal Al Kasim, *The Opposite Direction*. Here, advocates of Arab nationalism are regularly invited, slogans referring to the Arab nation or Arab solidarity are often invoked, and images which suggest the nationalists' struggle against colonialism or Zionism are frequently evoked.

Often overtly hostile to Nasserism and representing the Islamist trend on the channel is the Egyptian journalist Ahmad Mansour, a former host of the weekly religious program *Islamic Law and Life* who currently presents the weekly program *Without Borders*. The Egyptian (Qatari by naturalization) Sheikh Youssef Al Qaradawi, one of the most respected Muslim clerks, is a regular guest on Al Jazeera's *Islamic Law and Life*, which has been hosted by Khadija bin Ganna after the sudden death of the Palestinian journalist Maher Abdullah. The Islamic referent which is part of the identity of Al Jazeera and which is clearly assumed by the channel's management and journalists imposes itself as a universal code and goes down well with viewers in the Arab world and elsewhere.

At the forefront of the liberal line is the Jordanian Sami Haddad, host of the weekly program *More Than One Opinion*. The program consists of a debate in which at least three personalities with different political views and ideological orientations are set against each other. What this liberal discourse shares with the other two tendencies, the Arabist and the Islamist, are a radical and often sarcastic critique of Arab regimes and a commitment to both democratic claims and national sovereignty, all of which contribute to the success of Al Jazeera.

A CHAOTIC ARAB PUBLIC SPHERE

After the fall of the Ottoman Empire, European colonial forces played a key role in drawing the borders of an Arab territory that had long subsided under the Ottoman tutelage. The legacy of the mandating forces can be noted in what may be described as a constant tension between national and transnational levels in a region that is relatively homogeneous from the linguistic and cultural point of view, but certainly fragmented from the political standpoint into a number of nation-states. Along with collective aspirations and ideologies, language, as a common denominator and a unifying force, has enhanced the communication process[22] and facilitated transnational mobilizations which are often at odds with the logic of Arab states keen on forging national identities and political cultures. As early as the nineteenth century, the foundation of the Egyptian press by Syrian and Lebanese journalists and its promulgation in the Middle East showed the ease with which Arab media can operate transnationally.[23] From 1939 to 1967, the BBC Arabic Service was the principal source of information in the region.[24] The undisputed success of the Egyptian radio station Voice of the Arabs suggests that there is an existing Arab public sphere. Due to the intensification of transnational communication, this public sphere has become a space where various interpretations of events shaking the Arab world are contested. Afraid of losing control over their own informational space, several Arab states have engaged in a fierce battle to control this Arab public sphere.

This competition between Arab states, particularly oil producing countries, to control the Arab public sphere explains the Gulf states' heavy investment in the field of media and the proliferation of Arab satellite TV channels since the beginning of the 1990s.[25] Within this competitive environment, Al Jazeera has managed to position itself in such a way as to gain an edge over the other Arab channels. Setting itself in counterdistinction to the Saudi media empire, Al Jazeera has helped expose the limits of Saudi media: the tendency to be politically conservative, the pre-eminence of entertainment over news and the omnipresence of Lebanese journalists to the detriment of other Arab nationalities. However, what have really made the success of Al Jazeera are two important factors: the channel's tendency to deal with issues that are often considered taboo, including the radical critique of Arab rulers, and above all the channel's notable tendency to align itself with public opinion.

THE EMERGENCE OF AN ARAB PUBLIC OPINION

The terminology used to describe the manifestation of citizens in the Arab public sphere has changed significantly over the past few decades. In the post independence era and during the 1960s and the 1970s, the most common term was "the Arab masses." This Marxist term, which connotes class struggle and economic inequalities between the North and the South, soon gave way to "the Arab street." The powerful images of Iranians expressing their joy after the fall of the regime of the Shah and cheering the homecoming of Ayatollah Khomeini at the airport of Tehran made people more aware of the power the fanatic masses can have.[26] After the 1991 Gulf War, a number of elections were held in the Arab world. The main purpose behind these elections was to bestow some legitimacy on a power that was strongly contested by the Islamist parties.[27] It is in the framework of this "transition towards democracy" that the term "public opinion" acquired a particular pertinence, giving the illusion that citizens can choose among several competing projects in society and that they do play a role in a process which in reality aims at depriving them from their will.

The progressive emergence of an independent Arab public opinion thrived within the context of a number of phenomena. To start with, the Arab world has witnessed social changes which have made communication and the diffusion of ideas more efficient.[28] In fact, urbanization,[29] literacy and politicization have reached a critical threshold allowing society to resist the official political discourse of governments while at the same time being socially and politically mobilized so as not to seem indifferent to political questions.

Contributing to the formation of what may be described as an autonomous public opinion is the poverty of the concept of the nation-state as a modality for rationalizing political spaces. Rather than provide a strong popular legitimacy,[30] the durability of state apparatuses[31] and the affirmation of the nation-state ideology[32] (*al quotriya*) in the Arab world put these states in a vulnerable position that allows opponents of the regimes in place to contest them in the name of larger identity claims. Writings that question the legitimacy of the nation-state in the region abound particularly among independent Arab authors who are not co-opted by the system.[33] The widely held concept of the nation-state in the Arab world has become a historical trap leading this region to paralysis and further reinforcing submission to superpowers. The necessity for governments to legitimate a nation-state which is often contested as a center of power entangles them in an endless endeavor to distinguish themselves from neighboring states.[34] At the same time, these governments have proven incapable of developing a somewhat independent political culture or even handling the ensuing contradictions (such as border disputes or issues of nationality).

Contributing further to the demise of the notion of the nation-state is the information revolution in the Arab world and particularly in the Gulf region.[35] Broadly speaking, Arab satellite channels have introduced viewers to the culture of public debate between various Arab figures. "Common problems and common solutions" was the informal philosophy underlying the intensification of communication in the Arab world. The breathlessness of official truth imposed and defended by governments led to the emergence of a chaotic participation by different actors in endless debates, resulting in rational though negotiated compromises in the public sphere. It is in such a context, marked by the consolidation and legitimization of the Arab public sphere and the concrete manifestation of Arab public opinion, that Al Jazeera emerged. Being quick to notice this structural change in Arab societies, Qatar fully understood the need to envisage an adequate media framework which could engage the ongoing critical debate and at the same time serve its own interests.

INFLUENCE WITHOUT POWER

Al Jazeera is considered one of the biggest successes for Qatar in terms of publicity and political communication.[36] Prior to the launching of Al Jazeera in 1996, Qatar was very little known in the

Arab world and internationally. Today, it claims a central place among the Gulf states. More than any other Arab state, Qatar has arguably developed the potential to impose on Arab viewers a particular reading of world events.[37] It is affecting not only how diplomacy is effected,[38] but also the American administration's preferences in the region. For the US, Qatar is no less important an ally than Egypt or Saudi Arabia. Qatari diplomacy has managed, with a sharp sense of opportunism, to keep up with the evolution of the American strategic doctrine, while at the same time maintaining the credibility of Al Jazeera in the Arab world as well as internationally.

Qatar's intimidating use of the media keeps upsetting the United States' allies in the Arab world. Not surprisingly, the Arab press is full of articles on the claws of this small emirate.[39] Al Jazeera has become a weapon to contend with and a source of influence at the disposal of a tiny country[40] which does not possess any of the classical elements of power—it has no large population, no sizeable army and no big industry.[41] The soft power Al Jazeera puts in the hands of Qatar inescapably makes the latter part of the Arab political game. Ignoring Qatar has a cost which Arab leaders can make as insignificant as possible, but cannot escape altogether. This extraordinary shift of power—in fact, the revenge of the micro state over Arab countries that have a weight in the region—points to momentous changes or imbalances which are shrewdly exploited by the American administration.

QATAR: SLAVE OF TWO MASTERS

Still, the media and diplomatic success of the state of Qatar remains fragile, to say the least, because this country remains the slave of two antagonistic masters whose interests in the long term are bound to diverge: the American administration and Arab public opinion.

In a way, the relations between Qatar and the United States are of a neocolonial type. Qatar allied itself with the US in return for security. This unequal relationship reduces drastically the Emir of Qatar's room for maneuver. Having in a way subordinated national sovereignty, he is left only with media sovereignty. Although Al Jazeera is sometimes used as an arm of dissuasion against the United States, most if not all observers believe that it is the American army that has the upper hand. This seemingly comfortable situation might turn out to be problematic in the long run.

In order to counterbalance its image of a country that is "entirely subjected to the US," Qatar has to satisfy its other master—Arab public opinion. The diplomatic influence of Qatar is due exclusively to the popularity and credibility of its satellite channel in the Arab world and in the rest of the world today. To maintain its credibility, Al Jazeera finds itself compelled to be in line with the political sentiments and preferences it deems dominant in the Arab world. Thus, the bigger the concessions to the Americans are, the fiercer the critics to pro-American Arab regimes will be. In order to "disguise" its contribution to American hegemony in the Gulf region, Qatar has played a crucial role in promoting freedom of expression in the Arab world. By presenting itself as the champion of media and political pluralism, Qatar tries to rebuff the accusations of being agent to the US but also to Israel in the Gulf. In spite of the compromises it has made to the Israelis and the Americans, Qatar is relatively spared the criticism of Arab intellectuals many of whom praise Al Jazeera's endeavors to unveil the disfunctional state of the Arab political system. By adopting transparency as an ideology (which tends to apply less to Qatar than it does to other Arab states), Qatar has done much to expose the actions of Arab leaders to the critical public opinion. Taking into consideration public opinion in political decision-making is a structural change constituting henceforth a constraint which both local and international actors have to handle with extreme care lest they have their policies contested.

Translated by Mohamed Zayani and Rana Raddawi

NOTES

1 Kai Hafez (ed.), *Mass Media, Politics and Society in the Middle East* (Cresskill: Hampton Press, 2001); *The Information Revolution in the Arab World: Its Impact on State and Society* (Abu Dhabi: ECSSR, 1998); Edmund Ghareeb, "New media and the information revolution in the Arab world: an assessment," *Middle East Journal*, Vol. 54, No. 3 (Summer 2000); Hussein Y. Amin and Douglas A. Boyd, "The development of direct broadcast television to and within the Middle East," *Journal of South Asian and the Middle Eastern Studies*, Vol. 18, No. 2 (Winter 1994).

2 Mohammed El-Nawawy and Adel Iskander Farag, *Al Jazeera: How the Free Arab News Network Scooped the World and Changed the Middle East* (Boulder: Westview Press, 2002).

3 Peter Dahlgren, "L'espace public et les médias: une nouvelle ère," *Hermes*, Vols 13–14 (1994); Hans Verstraeten, "The media and the transformation of the public sphere: a contribution for a critical political economy of the

public sphere," *European Journal of Communication*, Vol. 11, No. 3 (September 1996).

4   Haydar Badawi Sadek, *The Future of Diplomacy in the New Media and Communication Reality: The Arab Dimension* (Abu Dhabi: ECSSR, 1996).

5   For an account on the logic of inter-Arab relations, see Michael C. Hudson, *Arab Politics: The Search for Legitimacy* (New Haven: Yale University Press, 1977).

6   Thomas Risse-Kappen, *Bringing the Transnational Relations Back In: Non-State Actors, Domestic Structures and International Institutions* (Cambridge: Cambridge University Press, 1995).

7   Douglas A. Boyd, *Broadcasting in the Arab World: A Survey of the Electronic Media in the Middle East* (Ames: Iowa State University, 1993); N. Barbour, "Broadcasting to the Arab world: Arabic transmissions from the BBC and other non-Arab stations," *The Middle East Journal*, Vol. 5, No. 1 (Winter 1951).

8   Peter Partner, *Arab Voices: The BBC Arabic Services, 1938–1988* (London: BBC External Services, 1988).

9   Barry M. Rubin, "The real roots of Arab anti-Americanism," *Foreign Affairs*, Vol. 81, No. 6 (2002), pp. 73–85.

10   John C. Wilkinson, *Arabia's Frontiers: The Story of Britain's Boundary Drawing in the Desert* (London: I.B. Tauris, 1991).

11   Mohammed Ahmed Al Hamed, *Gulf Security and its Implications for GCC Member States* (Abu Dhabi: ECSSR, 1997).

12   Rosemarie Said Zahlan, *The Creation of Qatar* (New York: Croom Helm, 1979).

13   Marie-Claude Smouts, "Que reste-il des politiques étrangères?," *Pouvoirs*, No. 88 (1999).

14   Noor Ahmad Baba, "Nasser's pan-Arab radicalism and the Saudi drive for Islamic solidarity: a response for security," *India Quarterly*, Nos 1–2 (January–June 1992).

15   F. Gregory Gause III, "The foreign policy of Saudi Arabia," in Raymond Hinnebusch and Anoushiravan Ehteshami (eds), *The Foreign Policies of Middle East States* (Boulder: Lynne Reinner Publishers, 2002).

16   Farouk Loqman, *Hishem and Mohamed Ali Hafez: The Internationalization of the Arab Press* (Cairo: Al Ahram, 1997).

17   Farouk Abou Zayd, *The Expatriate Arab Press* (Cairo: Alam Al Kutub, 1993).

18   Nassereddine Al Nachachibi, *Hadrat al Zumala' al Muhtaramin* (Jerusalem: Dar Akhbar Al Balad, 1996); Bayssouni Ibrahim Hamada, "Relations between journalists and politicians in the Arab world," *Alam al Fikr* (September–December 1994).

19   Hilal Khashan, *Inside the Lebanese Confessional Mind* (Lanham: University Press of America, 1992); Illiya Harik, "Rethinking civil society: pluralism in the Arab world," *Journal of Democracy*, Vol. 5, No. 3 (July 1994).

20   R.D. MacLaurin, *The Political Role of Minority Groups in the Middle East* (Westport, CT: Praeger, 1979); Mordecahi Nisan, *Minorities in the Middle East: A History of Struggle and the Self-Expression* (Jefferson, NC: McFarland & Company, 1991).

21   Suleiman Al Shammari, *The Arab Nationalist Dimension in Al Jazeera Satellite Channel: A Case Study of The Opposite Direction* (Doha: Dar Al Sharq, 1999).
22   Karl W. Deutsh, *Nationalism and Social Communication: An Inquiry into the Foundations of Nationality* (Cambridge: MIT Press, 1966).
23   For an account of the domination of the Egyptian press by Syria and Lebanon and the subsequent decline of such an influence, see Thomas Philipp, *The Syrians in Egypt, 1725–1975* (Stuttgart: Franz Steiner Verlag, 1985).
24   Partner, *Arab Voices*; Boyd, *Broadcasting in the Arab World*.
25   Ayad Chaker Al Badri, *Satellite Television War* (Jordan: Dar Al Shourouq, 1999).
26   David Pollock, *The Arab Street?: Public Opinion in the Arab World* (Washington DC: The Washington Institute for Near East Policy, 1992).
27   Ghassan Salamé, *Démocraties sans democrats: politique d'ouverture dans le monde Arabe et Islamique* (Paris: Fayard, 1994).
28   Deutsh, *Nationalism and Social Communication*.
29   Philippe Fargues, *Générations Arabes: alchimie du nombre* (Paris: Fayard, 2000).
30   Hudson, *Arab Politics*.
31   Dawisha Abeed and Zartman Ira William, *Beyond Coercion: The Durability of the Arab State* (London: Croom Helm, 1988).
32   George Tarabichi, *The Nation-State and Pan-Arabism* (Beirut: Dar Atalia'a, 1982).
33   Idriss Hani, *The Arabs and the Occident* (Beirut: Dar Atalia'a, 1998); Khaldoun Hassan Al Naquib, *Perspectives on Regression* (London: Dar Al Saqi, 2002); Mohammed Tareq Qa'biya *The Pillars of Arab Nationalism* (Beirut: Dar Atalia'a, 2001).
34   Fred Haliday, *Arabia without Sultans* (London: Penguin, 1974).
35   *The Information Revolution in the Arab World*.
36   Piers Robinson, "Theorizing the influence of media on world politics: models of media influence on foreign policy," *European Journal of Communication*, Vol. 16, No. 4 (December 2001).
37   Robert O. Keohane and Joseph S. Nye, "Power and interdependence in the information age," *Foreign Affairs*, Vol. 77, No. 5 (September–October 1998).
38   Nathalie La Balme, "Opinion publique et politique étrangère: l'évolution d'un débat," in Frédéric Charillon (ed.), *Politique Etrangère: Nouveaux Regards* (Paris: Presses de Sciences Po, 2002).
39   Sadek, *The Future of Diplomacy*.
40   Efraïm Inbar and Gabriel Sheffer (eds), *The National Security of Small States in a Changing World* (London: BESA Studies in International Security, 1997).
41   Kapiszewsky Andrzy, *Nationals and Expatriates: Population and Labour Dilemmas of the GCC States* (Ithaca: Ithaca Press, 2001).

4

Aljazeera.net: Identity Choices and the Logic of the Media

Gloria Awad

Journalism has the particularity of representing identity and its other. The logic of the media induces the presentation of models proposed for identification.[1] Journalism also opens the door to otherness by describing situations that permit one to penetrate the attitude and the experience of the other.[2] Being a game in space and time—which goes back to the early days of the printed word, but certainly extends to the virtual world of the web—the media constructs symbolic spatio-temporal nexuses of communion.[3] According to the rules of proxemics—which studies the relations between spatial distance, culture and communication—the communitarian link reveals a psychological distance and not merely a proxemics of concrete space.

How does Aljazeera.net treat war reporting and the polemics of conflict and violent death which engage the social group? What images and which protagonists does the site promote? Finally, how does this medium participate in culture and in the ongoing construction of reality?

Attempting to answer these questions requires a cartography of space which the website configures through its links, its headings and its discussion forums based on the principle that space built by information is based on representations and on schemas of reality. Equally worthy of study and examination is the depiction of the problematic of the moment, which could be termed "agenda setting,"[4] and which consists of selecting, forming into a hierarchy, organizing and legitimating information which attracts the attention of the receiving public to the detriment of other news. Such an analysis also calls for a full review of the physical and symbolic representation of the various actors which figure in the "contents" of the site.

THE NEW MEDIA ECOLOGY

During its short history, Aljazeera.net has established itself as a popular source of news for Arab-speaking audiences throughout the world. Launched in January 2001, Aljazeera.net claimed 161 million hits for the year 2002 originating mainly from the Middle East (54 per cent), Europe and United States (39 per cent). The site has been ranked among the top five most visited sites.[5] The surge in information requests about a region such as the Middle East should come as no surprise. The war against Iraq has propelled Aljazeera.net to the forefront of online information. Traffic on Aljazeera.net was considerable well before the war against Iraq was launched on March 20, 2003. The September 11 attacks, followed by the American bombing of Afghanistan, resulted in about 120 million hits with 40 per cent originating from the US, followed by Europe and then the Arab world.[6] In its third year of existence, Aljazeera.net had over a billion hits.[7]

Like other interactive electronic publishing media, Aljazeera.net has identified itself in relation to a recognized media, Al Jazeera Satellite Channel. In the beginning, the continuous Arabic-speaking news channel was hailed by Western media as a "window to democratic expression" or "the CNN of the Arab world." However, after the September 11 attacks, it was labelled by the Americans as "the Taliban channel," partly because it aired exclusive recorded messages of Osama bin Laden.

Taking into account the relationship between this new media (the website) and the old one (the satellite channel), and before going further into the analysis, it would be useful to provide a short history of the channel and its online version so as to place them in their media, political and social environment. To consider media in its ecology is of utter importance since there is an interdependence between media and its environment.[8] This ecology of media consists in raising the question of the role that the media plays, first as a meaning, then as a means controlled by those who filter its access and organize its contents to transmit it to its public, and finally as a means among others, competing with similar outlets.

Television was already pervasive in the Arab world when Al Jazeera was launched in 1996. The stream of images is propagated according to a marketing logic combined with high-tech satellite systems, cable networks and radio relay systems. Technical innovation is the support of media space internationalization, particularly with respect to television, which abolishes the fence enclosing the various spaces of society and opens society to other communication streams. Information and the world now erupt in the private space in a straightforward manner without the need for a political power detour. Information fills the gap created by state-controlled national televisions. This new televisual effect is multiplied tenfold as media outlets are forced to compete for new market shares in a new cross-border market. Public and private regional channels—whether they be Saudi, Egyptian or Lebanese—broadcast beyond their national space. Images are now goods sold in return for public rights of access. In turn, the public is turned into potential consumers for the advertiser's publicity campaigns.

Information broadcast by Al Jazeera is part of a worldwide transmission and distribution network, organized as much by states as by transnational commercial cultural industries to mesh with the new international commercial communication space. At the same time, Al Jazeera marks a rupture, and doubly so.

First, it marks a rupture with brutal state propaganda and with the journalism of opinion. Through information, state propaganda and the journalism of opinion bind the sphere of action and the sphere of power, with the aim of causing and controlling the echo in the public sphere,[9] first instituted by the press and then developed by the other media, open to all publicly expressed speech. Al Jazeera adopts the rhetoric of objectivity,[10] which puts the principle of "the relation to the truth" between the journalistic speech and democratic transparency against the opacity of the secret and the propaganda of authoritarianism. The channel also uses the principles of the news show, a characteristic of audio-visual media. Thus, Al Jazeera engages its public in the information era, which began more than a century ago in Western countries with the end of censorship and the emergence of political and literary journalism, the depoliticization of the press and the diversification of its content, the spectacularization and the commercialization of information, sold to the largest number of people with the lowest price:

> Al Jazeera Satellite Channel is the only Arabic satellite channel broadcasting news updates every 60 minutes with four main news a day offering high standards of independent journalism and unmatchable coverage of correspondents throughout the world. Al Jazeera is practising an overwhelming extent of freedom of speech making itself the first independent Arabic news and information channel in the world.[11]

Second, Al Jazeera marks a rupture with the immense process of hetero-assignment that the media engage in while producing and refracting representations and stereotypes of the other in a global-ized world where news circulates faster than people, rebalancing the scales of the near and the far. News is the entertainment of the world. Through news, the media organize people's calendars and retrace their sensory borders, morals and identities. Insignificant, free and natural as it should be, the news, which has a tendency to confound itself with its referent, reveals its character built in the war, the exception that strips the rule.[12] The establishment of Al Jazeera followed the Gulf War which did not take place.[13] It was a surgical war, a worldwide live TV coverage, zero death and video game pictures whose unique source was CNN.[14] The launch of the continuous news channel must be viewed in relation to the events of the early 1990s, particularly the Gulf War which demonstrated Anglo-Saxon domination of international news and especially the supremacy of CNN as an image provider. Euronews, the European continuous news TV channel, was launched in the same context and with the same objective in 1993.[15]

After September 11, Al Jazeera exercised the same monopoly on images from the zones under the coalition's bombardments which CNN had during the Second Gulf War. Furthermore, the channel had the sole rights on Al Qaeda's chief messages. Al Jazeera's jour-nalists, many of whom graduated from the BBC school, applied the principles of the "news show," a characteristic item of the popular press destined for the largest number of people and amplified with televisual information. Its executives put forward the information market rules—taking a high added value product, selling it to other networks and promoting it to advertisers through the ever-climbing audience share:

> One of the policies of Al Jazeera TV is neutrality, so we do our best to avoid any position toward the events or to add any colours to it or any judge-ment. According to this policy, we used the word "attack" to [refer to] the terror attacks on New York and Washington. Also we used the same word to [refer to the] U.S. strikes on civilian targets in Afghanistan. To take another example, we used the word "assassinate" when the Israeli forces killed the Palestinian leader Abu Ali Mustafa, and we used the same word when a Palestinian killed the Israeli Minister Rehavam Zeevi.[16]

Arabic is the language in which the channel fulfills and transports the modifications in the news intended for its public inside and outside Arab countries. However, a language establishes an invisible border, different from that of the territory and the ethnic group, but one which is nonetheless a fundamental attribute of self-awareness[17] and auto-definition, or better yet an imagined community. "Al Jazeera provides Arab news from an Arab perspective," is the slogan of the satellite channel that positions itself thus in the stream culture,[18] joining by this perspectivism the offer of the transmitter to the expectation of the receiver in the stupendous acceleration and multiplication of information in our time.

ALJAZEERA.NET: INFORMATION SITE AND COMMUNAL MEDIA

The launch of Al Jazeera's online information website in 2001 was a step forward by the channel to invest in a new socio-technical device. The objective of the presence on the web for an old media is visibility and accessibility, which in turn help keep pace with world information market transformations, while helping to generate new income via new services enabled by this new media. Like many similar sites, Aljazeera.net was initially designed as an internal electronic archiving system to support the TV broadcasting needs. Later on, however, it became an information website available to many Arab subscribers throughout the world, before being widely open and free of charge. Today, the site has four main sections: (1) continuous information for press agencies and channel correspondents, (2) live broadcast, (3) archived broadcasts distributed by Al Jazeera, and (4) interactive services:

> Aljazeera.net is the electronic version of Al Jazeera Satellite Channel. It is part of the same organisation, using the same resources for news and information, but we are in a different type of media with new technologies and new methodology ... .When we planned for the website, we specified that our audience [would be] the Arabic-language speakers everywhere in the world.[19]

Every media is an entity in space and time that links a speech isolated from its referent to a context made of a place, a moment and a given receptor. The website goes beyond the television channel; its public is no longer regional. It is now accessible in the most remote locations worldwide, and those who choose to visit the site can react instantaneously to the posted messages. This public is already a public of travellers, moving between different territories, between near and faraway proxemics. It is finally an "online" public, properly equipped with computers, knowledge and know-how permitting access to and appropriation of the space which an online media constitutes. Aljazeera.net positions itself as a communal and diasporic information site intended for territorial and non-territorial publics as well as internet users throughout the world. Its animated slogan blinks: "Why exhaust yourself searching for the specific information relative to your position? Aljazeera.net is the alternative."

Through its columns, polls, forums and links, Aljazeera.net not only draws to the intention of its recipients a map of the near and the faraway, but also configures a space with a center and a periphery. The setting in columns constitutes the references according to which the contents can be distributed. These references only exist insofar as the media institutes them. It seems obvious to consider the setting in columns like a simple rational ordering established following a professional convention. This categorization reflects in fact the organization of the space which the media refers to as well as social movement and its contradictions along with the new sensitivities of the receptors.[20] Aljazeera.net operates three orderings of the information it organizes: the order to the events, the territory and the center of interest.

The space of the event uses the top half of the site's opening page. Everything that relates to content in this space—from right to left as is the practice in Arabic—and is not integrated in the other established categories is event for the gatekeepers. To inform is a deliberate conduct. The promotion of any occurrence to the rank of event comes from the needs of those that make this promotion.[21] What is considered event is that which the media configures as such according to its nature, its editorial policies, its relationship with its financial backers, its sources, its competitors, its understanding of public expectations and the profits it tries to maximize.[22]

History has already confirmed that only its tracks give existence to the event, regardless of the ruptures and the eddies this event generates in the order of things, individuals and societies. Over a century ago, journalism fixed through repetition the occasional disorder of the rupture[23] and made out of it the exchange rate in the commercial information system, industrially creating an inflation of traces intended for consumption. This system is what transforms war information into exceptional journalistic matter and an inexhaustible source of profit for the media. This generalized communication wealth[24] does not prevent concurrent constructions of the same event and specific consumption of its representations and its traces according to the priorities and anguishes of individuals and societies.

Aljazeera.net systematically distributes this space between four information categories, the most important being the only one graphically illustrated and occupying the top right-hand corner of the opening page, visible from right to left as is the case in Arabic (only advertising information, named e-marketing pages by the website, is in English). In the same opening page space but to the left, Aljazeera.net organizes what makes the added value of the online information: the polls (or "vote"), the discussions and the archived information search engine. The search option occupies the top right of this space, next to the poll, attached to the main event and followed by the discussion forum. The site uses web technology and resources to communicate an event, securing immediately the right amplitude and the maximum performance to attract the largest number of receptors.

To inform does not have as its objective to describe the world but to configure by signs an acceptable world.[25] Aljazeera.net reorganizes for its recipients the space of the world, distributing its territories in the following space categories: "The Arabic Homeland," located just after the event space, "Asia Pacific," "Africa," "Europe and Israel," and "The Two Americas."

The cartography is clear: "The Arabic Homeland" occupies the center of the representation—not as a nation, nor as a region, but as a representation that ties to a community the set of individuals and Arab societies. Although extensively united by language, history and religion, Arab societies are more than ever crumbled and broken up into state-controlled entities, rarely in agreement with each other and sometimes bluntly hostile to each other. Through this arrangement, the media designates its audience, thus reorganizing in continuous space the disconnected geographical spaces. It erases and reorganizes the borders, defining those in which its public is present, but also those outside of which this public is untraceable.[26] This "Arabic Homeland" is put in event, as it is the main source of the events built by the site. The other space categories constitute the peripheries as "a centre doesn't exist alone, without periphery ... Such identities could never exist alone, without the negative and the contrary."[27]

Finally, the centers of interest categories conclude the opening page of Aljazeera.net. They reflect the receptor's sensitivity: "Economy and

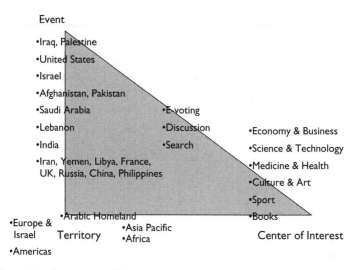

Figure 4.1   Cartography of Aljazeera.net

Business," "Science and Technology," "Medicine and Health," "Culture and Art," "Sport," and "Books." The refresh rate is high for the events and space categories, whereas the centers of interest categories have a longer temporality. This site cartography is schematically represented in Figure 4.1.

AGENDA SETTING

In societies that practice censorship and information control, the media is vested with the power to tell people what they must think. In societies where the exercise of information is driven by freedom of speech and market forces, the influence of the media is different. It rather consists of informing people about what they must think since media selects and organizes into a hierarchy events intended for the receptors to talk about. Setting the agenda is not done in an arbitrary fashion but varies according to the conjuncture. Public history, reception temporality and editorial policies are part of this conjuncture.

During the studied period,[28] the problematic of the moment was organized around the main event, the only one presented by pictures, that systematically made reference to the Third Gulf War or the Palestinian–Israeli conflict. These pictures, sometimes re-actualized in less than one hour, showed in close-up the dead, the injured, the old, women, children, destruction, fights, fighters, weapons and attacks—all in a big narrative of war. In contrast, the pictures illustrating the same information on the English-speaking and Arabic-speaking BBC news sites were among dozens of other pictures of the same format, and were smaller than those displayed on Aljazeera.net. Likewise, such pictures did not systematically occupy the space designating "the event" of the moment. These pictures had a longer temporality that could go beyond one day, and were systematically wide-angled. To show is the first level of the news content setting; to name is the next one: those that Aljazeera.net named "resistance fighters" or "martyrs," were named by other media "kamikaze groups," or "terrorists." Likewise, what the site described as an "invasion" was named a "liberation war" by the American and British media and "war against Iraq" by the other European media.

In online media, the agenda setting includes polls and forums: being interactive, it permits one to react. It also includes the internal links and gateways to information relevant to the main event as well as external links and gateways to other sites where the same event extends. In the case of Aljazeera.net, the only external links lead to advertising spaces. The site is thus closed on itself, which is more of a strategic decision than a technical limitation.

No media or real world can nowadays remain closed. The spaces of communication are open to the circulation of representations and people. They are articulated to fulfill the needs in the spaces of the people of our time who are no longer locked in the coercive space of the "here" and the "now."

The electronic and communal media is a specific modern time–space, and not a simple out of territory representation: it enables the management of tensions between the "here" and the "elsewhere," between the "now," the "past" and the "future"; it fulfills a linking function between the different identities and territories.

NOTES

1   E. Morin, *L'Esprit du temps* (Paris: Grasset, 1975).
2   G.H. Mead, *Mind, Self and Society* (Chicago: University of Chicago Press, 1934).
3   B. Anderson, *Imagined Communities* (London: Verso, 1991).
4   M. Mac Combs and D. Shaw, "The agenda setting function of mass media," *Public Opinion Quarterly*, No. 36 (1972).

5 According to Information & Technology Publishing <http://www. ITP.net>, these sites are: Albawaba.com, Aljazeera.net, Arabia.com, Maktoob.com and Ahram.org.com.

6 See Allied Media, <http://www.allied-media.com>.

7 See <http://www.aljazeera.net/e-marketing-eng/2004/2/2-9-1.htm>.

8 M. Mathien, *Le système médiatique: le journal et son environnement* (Paris: Hachette, 1989).

9 J. Habermas, *L'Espace public* (Paris: Payot, 1978).

10 R. Rieffel, *Sociologie des Médias* (Paris: Ellipses, 2001), p. 104.

11 Ibid.

12 D. Bougnoux, "L'indépassable chauvinisme de l'information," in M. Mathien (ed.), *L'Information dans les conflits armés* (Paris: L'Harmattan, 2001), pp. 131–6.

13 J. Baudrillard, *La guerre du golfe n'a pas eu lieu* (Paris: Galilée, 1991).

14 D. Wolton, *War game: l'information et la guerre* (Paris: Flammarion, 1991).

15 Ibid.

16 M.P. Grenier, "Aljazeera.net offers Arab news to wider audience through net: interview with Mahmoud Abdul Hedi," *Wall Street Journal Online*, October 23, 2001, <http://interactive.wsj.com/public/current/articles/ SB1003417218856711840.htm>.

17 M. Castel, *Le pouvoir de l'identité* (Paris: Fayard, 1999).

18 P. Flichy, *Les industries de l'imaginaire* (Grenoble: PUG, 1991).

19 Ibid.

20 Y. De La Haye, *Journalisme, mode d'emploi* (Grenoble: Ellug, 1985), p. 64.

21 Harvey Molotch and Marilyn Lester, "Informer: une conduite délibérée de l'usage stratégique des événements," *Réseaux*, No. 75 (1996), pp. 23–41.

22 Gloria Awad, *Du Sensationnel, Place de l'Événement dans le Journalisme de Masse* (Paris: L'Harmattan, 1995), pp. 22–5.

23 Gloria Awad, "Du papier à l'écran, l'espace au fil du temps," in A. Vitalis, J.F. Tétu, M. Palmer, and B. Castagna (eds), *Médias, temporalités et démocraties* (Paris: Apogée, 2000), pp. 45–59.

24 Abraham Moles, *Théorie structurale de la communication et société* (Paris: Masson, 1988), p. 185.

25 Bougnoux, "L'indépassable chauvinisme de l'information," p. 132.

26 D. Schnapper, *La relation à l'autre* (Paris: Gallimard, 1998), p. 158.

27 Edward Saïd, *Culture et impérialisme* (Paris: Fayard-Le Monde Diplomatique, 2000), p. 98.

28 We analyzed ten home pages of the site between February 6, 2002 and April 5, 2002, and ten between February 6, 2003 and April 5, 2003, and we compared the results with those of a similar analysis of the home pages of the site of the BBC News Middle East, in Arabic and in English.

II

Al Jazeera Programming

5

The Opposite Direction: A Program which Changed the Face of Arab Television

Faisal Al Kasim

One can hardly talk about the phenomenon of satellite television in the Arab world without focusing on live political programs, which many consider to be central to the satellite revolution. These are better known in Arab media jargon as views-exchange or dialogue-based programs. They are one of the most striking features of the new Arab media and arguably the most revolutionary, partly because exchanging opinions and venting feelings live on TV are novel practices. How has the public in the Arab world received talk shows? Why is it that Arab viewers lavish so much praise on them? Have they really led to more Arab fragmentation? Have they been a catalyst for unity, at least at the grassroots or public opinion level? What have they achieved politically and culturally? Are they a passing craze or are they here to stay for a long time? Do they merit the abuse heaped upon them by the official Arab media? This chapter attempts to answer these and other related questions by drawing on my weekly talk show, *The Opposite Direction* (*Al Ittijah Al Muaakis*), which is widely regarded as Al Jazeera's flagship program. The program, which is arguably the most popular and most controversial political Arab talk show, continues to generate exceptional emotional reaction throughout the Arab world.

In order to appreciate fully the importance and centrality of such talk show programs, it is necessary at the outset to compare them briefly with their terrestrial ancestors and explore the official reaction to them. Although many Arab regimes launched their television channels decades ago, they always kept live talk shows off the air, as talking in public—let alone in real time—is potentially unnerving in the Arab world. All televised material, including viewer request programs, were presented canned. When Arab states thought of modernizing their TV channels, they started allowing certain benign phone-in programs, including, for instance, interviews with singers.

But live shows remained for the most part taboo; criticizing official government policies was simply unthinkable.

With the advent of satellite television at the beginning of the 1990s, the *status quo* started to change. For the first time, Arab viewers could watch a group of politicians and journalists discussing a political issue live on the air. Initially, though, these types of shows were not totally free as the first Arab satellite channels to beam such programs belonged to politically and otherwise conservative regimes, to say the least. BBC Arabic television, which was a joint venture between the Saudis and the BBC, tried to be more adventurous in its political live programs. But its shows were not free-to-air to the masses; the signal was scrambled and made available only to subscribers. Even so, the project did not last for more than two years. The world's first modern Arabic news TV was brought to an end in 1996 as the investors fell out with the BBC over editorial policy.

Al Jazeera may not be the first or only channel to have aired live talk shows, but Al Jazeera's talk show programs are arguably the most captivating. For the first time, Arabs have been able to see live programs tackling sensitive political, religious, social and cultural issues. Being extremely controversial and exceptionally open to sensitive issues, *The Opposite Direction* has become the talk of the town all over the Arab world and amongst Arab communities abroad. Never before have Arab viewers seen the revered Muslim Sheikh Dr Youssef Al Qaradawi argue vehemently live on air with the staunch secularist thinker Sadik Jalal Al Azim over the conflict between Islam and secularism. Never before have they seen one of the most wanted Arab thinkers Nasser Hamid Abou Zaid face the well-known Muslim scholar Mohammad Amara. Never before have they seen the renown feminist Dr Nawal El Saadawi make mincemeat of the clergy, represented on the program by Sheikh Yussef Al Badri, over women's rights. Never before have they seen a debate on polygamy, which is permitted under strict conditions in Islam, between a veiled female Islamist and a liberal woman. This particular episode ended in an unusual way. As the program unfolded, many of the viewers phoning in to speak sounded angry over the debate and were calling upon the woman representing the view of the Islamists to withdraw from the discussion—and so she did as the discussion got heated. Episodes tackling highly sensitive religious topics such as this one have caused uproar in mosques and religious circles in many Arab counties. As if this were not enough, Arab newspapers and magazines, in turn, have launched fierce press campaigns against the program and Al Jazeera. The Arab press have published hundreds of articles and nasty caricatures attacking the program. Some television channels have also presented scores of programs hosting journalists and politicians to criticize Al Jazeera and vilify its programs. If anything, though, such attacks have helped publicize the program and make it more popular.

When Al Jazeera started tackling political issues, a greater controversy began to emerge and even governments started to take note of the debates. Overall, governments were uneasy about and even intolerant of programs such as *The Opposite Direction*. For the first time ever in the history of Arab television, TV programs led to diplomatic crises between Arab countries. Many countries temporarily closed down Al Jazeera offices; some countries lodged lawsuits against the channel; others launched aggressive and widespread press and political campaigns against it; still others went as far as withdrawing their ambassadors from Doha or summoning the Qatari ambassador in their countries to protest about the content of the programs.

It all started with the transmission of an episode of *The Opposite Direction* which touched on the dispute between Kuwait and Iraq.[1] Kuwait complained vehemently to top Qatari officials about a viewer who phoned in to speak unfavorably of the ruling family of Kuwait and to accuse the Kuwaitis of disrupting Arab unity. There was even a call for stern action against the presenter of the program, but nothing happened and no action was taken against me. Naturally, we began to make use of the amount of freedom given to us. Since then, the Kuwaiti press has taken delight in launching the most poignant attacks on the program and its presenter. Hundreds of articles have been written in the Kuwaiti papers against *The Opposite Direction*. Moreover, the Kuwaitis closed down the Al Jazeera office in Kuwait for some time after an episode of the program hosted a pro-Iraqi Egyptian journalist who accused the Kuwaitis of being the Jews of the Gulf and portrayed the ruling family in a very bad light.[2] Nevertheless, as one Kuwaiti acknowledged in an intervention on Al Jazeera, Kuwaitis remain glued every Tuesday night to their TV sets to watch *The Opposite Direction* which does not fail to keep them on their toes.

But Kuwait is not the only Arab country to have launched fierce press and political campaigns against the program. Jordan, in its turn, has been no less aggressive. When we presented an episode on the peace treaty between Jordan and Israel, the Jordanians could not swallow the accusations leveled at them by an Arab journalist in the program.[3] The guest of the program recounted the meetings between the late King Hussain and Zionist leaders years before the peace accords were signed, and argued that the Wadi Araba agreement had been extremely harmful and very unjust to Jordan. He even went as far as questioning the statehood of Jordan. This proved too much for the Jordanian authorities who immediately closed down our bureau in Amman and launched a widespread media campaign against the program for almost a month. Although our office in Jordan was reopened later, things got worse once again after we had presented an edition on Jordan's role in the American war against Iraq. This particular program turned out to be the straw that broke the camel's back. Jordan closed down the Al Jazeera office again, withdrew its ambassador from Doha and summoned the Qatari ambassador in Amman to protest very strongly over the content of the program. Al Jazeera was accused of being a dirty means of destruction and fragmentation that has nothing to do but to drive wedges between Arab countries. Still, this rhetoric did not stop many Jordanians from rushing to buy satellite dishes in droves.

Neighboring Saudi Arabia has also shown a great deal of unease over Al Jazeera programs, particularly *The Opposite Direction*, by allowing its press to write disparaging articles about Al Jazeera. The Saudi newspapers and magazines are always full of material attacking Al Jazeera. But things got worse at one point when we did a program on Saudi Arabia's sudden interest in the Palestinian cause, and had, for that matter, a Saudi official to defend the Kingdom's attitude against an Egyptian writer.[4] The latter argued that the Saudis got involved directly in the Palestinian issue only to improve their image with the Americans after the events of September 11. In other words, they were concerned with the plight of the Palestinians only to the extent that they could use it as a bargaining chip for their own gain. The Saudis reacted angrily to the program and pressed for an apology. Having failed to get one, they summoned their ambassador from Qatar a couple of weeks later and directed all Saudi journalists and politicians to boycott Al Jazeera.[5]

The Gulf information ministers went further in their notorious 2002 meeting in Oman. They dedicated their debate to talk shows on Al Jazeera and focused their attention on *The Opposite Direction*, which they regarded, along with its presenter, as highly dangerous. The ministers threatened the channel with commercial boycott if it did not stop its "campaign" against Gulf countries and even discouraged companies from advertising with the channel. Some countries have allegedly called company bosses and made them sign an undertaking to that effect. Not only commercials-wise but also news-wise, various countries have threatened to stop dealing with Al Jazeera.

The image Al Jazeera projects of itself is most unnerving. The channel publicizes itself as a rostrum for the other opinion or alternative viewpoint, which causes a great deal of anxiety amongst official circles in the Arab world. What has angered Arab regimes most is the fact that dialogical programs have given a platform for Arab opposition groups living abroad to express their opinions on various political matters. Previously, and because of censorship, dissidents living abroad were not very effective in speaking out on issues. It is true that some Arab dissidents have made use of the internet to reach a wide audience inside the Arab world, but Arab governments have been just as wily. Some of them have invested in very expensive technology to block opposition sites. Of course, they cannot jam Al Jazeera's transmission, nor can they stop the large number of viewers rushing to buy satellite dishes. Indeed, the channel has proved to be a godsend to Arab dissidents abroad. For the first time, they can communicate directly with their compatriots inside the homeland and propagate their ideas and opposing views freely and openly. Arab expatriates are particularly valuable for a channel like Al Jazeera. They are the ones who can appear on television, dare to speak their minds and return home safely. It is true that Al Jazeera has done them a great favor by giving them a platform to express their views, but they have been of paramount importance to us as well. A program like *The Opposite Direction* thrives on dissenting Arab voices. Not surprisingly, most of the episodes which have hosted expatriate Arab dissidents have raised a big row in the Arab world. Some of the speakers have become extremely popular amongst the masses for talking about issues that nobody dares probe within the Arab world.

In this sense, our programs have globalized alternative Arab political voices or "rebels" and made them known to a very large audience at home and abroad. They have also made Arab migrant communities in the West more involved in Arab politics. Arabs overseas are no longer passive viewers of what is happening back home. They have become active players in political Arab life thanks to satellite television. Their voices can now be heard loud and clear by both the ruling circles and their compatriots in the Arab world. That is why Arab expatriates follow our talk shows, particularly the *Crossfire*-types, avidly. Arab satellite channels, especially those with popular debate programs, have increased the involvement of Arab migrants in national issues back home. Such an interest has not gone unnoticed particularly by the host countries who fear the dis-integrationist potential of the newly-acquired media habits. It is hardly surprising that some European countries, such as France and Sweden, have expressed their worries over Arab satellite broadcast-ing coming from the Arab world. They are increasingly afraid that Arab communities in Europe could become ghettoized, thus pre-venting them from interacting with and integrating in their host societies.

If debate talk shows have been a pain in the neck for Arab rulers, the Arab masses inside the Arab world could not lavish more praise on them. This can be seen clearly in the polls conducted by various Arab newspapers, magazines and other media. For instance, *The Opposite Direction* has been voted as the best Arab TV program for six consecutive years.[6] Even magazines which are published in coun-tries whose regimes abhor the program cannot but point out that their readers have chosen the program as their favorite. Thankfully, most Arab magazines have also chosen me as the media man of the year more than once.[7] People have become addicted to such pro-grams to the extent that some of them arrange their time so as to be able to watch them.

I am always surprised when I travel to Arab countries to attend exhibitions and other galas. One tends to think that political talk shows appeal only to intellectuals and highly politicized people and that the young generally watch video clips, action movies, sports programs or the superficial shows that flood our screens. But that is no longer necessarily the case. Surprisingly enough, I have received the same reaction from young people as from older people when presenting a lecture or attending an event. For the first time ever in the Arab world, a television presenter can compete with pop or film stars and sometimes can outshine them. Particularly surprising is that teenagers have become greatly politicized and politically aware thanks in part to political talk shows. I am always astonished when I meet people in their teens and early twenties who are inquisitive about *The Opposite Direction*. They ask pointed questions about the program: "Why did you invite this or that guest on your show?", "Why did he say this and that?", "Why did you ask such and such a question?" "Don't you think that the other guest was right?" Some of them even remember my introductions and memorize certain sentences I have used.

Thrilling talk shows on Al Jazeera have brought about peace and quiet not only inside homes, but also in the streets of many Arab countries. The veteran British journalist David Hirst wrote that "cities can grow noticeably quieter when *The Opposite Direction* is about to go on air."[8] This has happened many times especially when the program has tackled a highly sensitive political issue concerning a certain Arab country. We have been told that when we did an edition on the so-called Shura Councils in the Gulf states, one could only see Asians on the streets of Riyadh in Saudi Arabia. Millions of Saudis stayed inside to watch a Bahraini dissident debating the alleged "democracy" of the ruling regimes of the Gulf states. Bahrainis, in their turn, set up huge tents to accommodate hundreds of people who wanted to watch an episode of *The Opposite Direction* dealing with the political reforms carried out by the Emir. Likewise, when the program touches on issues related to Syria, streets in Damascus and other Syrian cities grow quieter. Many people stay inside their homes as if they were watching a highly exciting football game involving their favorite team. The same thing could be said about a number of other Arab countries.

Of course, the program has received heavy criticism. There have even been attempts to torpedo the program. For example, the timing of a popular game show called *Who Wants to be a Millionaire?*, which is a somewhat successful replica of the famous English program hosted by Chris Tarrant, was meant to steal the thunder of *The Opposite Direction*. The case could be made that scheduling the airing of the program at the same time as *The Opposite Direction* was no coincidence. The motive could not be more obvious: to draw people away from Al Jazeera's program. Using the money factor to win viewers over, the show succeeded in pulling the rug from underneath *The Opposite Direction*, although not for long. A year or so on, the program began to lose viewers. It is true that it captured the hearts of about 40 per cent of the viewers when it was first introduced. But according to a Saudi poll, *Who Wants to be a Millionaire?* has since lost ground to live political talk shows.[9] There has even been talk of axing *Who Wants to be a Millionaire?* as it has outlived its popularity. *The Opposite Direction* competes strongly not just with *Who Wants to be a Millionaire?*, but also with other prominent and popular entertainment programs. When popular Arab magazines such as *Zahrat Al Khaleej* or *Al Osra Al Asriah* carried out opinion polls amongst their readers, they were surprised to discover that *The Opposite Direction* had scored top marks against raunchy and highly entertaining quiz shows which are supposed to have top viewership. *The Opposite Direction* scored 93 points where the popular Lebanese game show *Ya Lail Ya Ain*, which features half-naked women and "cool" guests, had earned 92 points.[10]

Unlike those Arab regimes which tend to demonize live political shows through their lackey press, some Arab academics have been alert enough to examine this new media phenomenon. Scores of M.A. and Ph.D. theses have been written on *The Opposite Direction* in various Arab countries and even in the United States. Western and Eastern journalists and researchers have been no less watchful of the new Arab media. I have been pleasantly surprised to receive a number of American, British, French, German, Swiss, Japanese, Korean, Indian, Dutch, Australian and other journalists who have been extremely interested in my program. Some of them have written extensively about it and what it means to the Arab world, while others have dedicated whole documentaries to examining the popularity of the show and its implications for the Arab world. Ironically, while the Arab press has been shredding Al Jazeera programs to pieces, some research centers in the West have studied them carefully and watched them with a great deal of interest. Thankfully, we are no longer local or national; we have become transnational, if not global.

However, there are those who argue that *Crossfire*-like programs have done great harm to Arab unity, and thus have become extremely disintegrationist and dangerous. Indeed, the official Arab media have always focused on the separatist nature of political talk shows. *The Opposite Direction* has been accused of sowing the seeds of discord, dissention and, for that matter, disunity amongst the Arab people and states. I have been portrayed in cartoons as a rabble-rouser, agitator, demagogue, troublemaker, muckraker and divisionist because I usually host two persons with opposing views in my program and let them argue fiercely live. Critics of this new type of program can only compare it to a cockfight. They argue that we are doing a diabolical job aimed at driving wedges between Arab states, between the governments and the people, between the regimes and the opposition, and more dangerously between the majorities and the ethnic minorities. In their view, we are doing nothing but encouraging discontent and social strife.

The most common criticism leveled at dialogue-based programs on satellite television is probably that they have done great harm to the national unity of certain Arab countries. In this respect, critics single out episodes of *The Opposite Direction* on the Berbers in the Maghreb. They have also taken us to task for doing editions of our talk shows on the Kurds and Copts in some Middle Eastern countries. In other words, the minorities issue has always been anathema to Arab governments. Whenever anybody gets close to it, he or she is instantly accused of playing with fire; but we know full well that the question of ethnic minorities in the Arab world has always been there. Arab researchers working on this issue have pointed out that civil wars in the Arab world have cost Arabs more than the Arab–Israeli conflict, which is supposed to be the main Arab concern.[11] Yet, no one is allowed to tackle such issues in the media. Isn't it better to discuss such topics openly instead of quarantining them as if they were an infectious disease?

Oddly enough, we have been accused of dismembering the Arab world, as if Arab states had always been unified. Nothing could be further from the truth than the accusation that live political talk shows have driven a wedge between Arab states. We all know that Arab states have always been at each other's throats clandestinely. It is true that live talk shows, particularly the *Crossfire* types, have led to trouble and caused tension between some Arab countries and it is true that programs like *The Opposite Direction* have caused diplomatic crises between the state of Qatar and other Arab countries, but this was not the intent of the programs and the causes of problems in the Arab world run far deeper. Arab regimes simply do not like the sound of voices other than their own. Arab rulers have a sort of gentleman's agreement amongst themselves not to touch upon each other's affairs in their media, except of course when they are in a state of war or when they have fallen out with each other over a serious problem. An ideal traditional Arab newspaper, magazine, radio or TV station is one which avoids anything that might be construed as offensive to any Arab country. Indeed, the Arab media have been so loyal to the Ottoman rule that the media should not comment on the politics of friendly countries. Being utilitarian, however, Arab regimes have always thought of the media as one of their possessions—one that should be harnessed to serve them first and foremost. That is why they were extremely shocked when Al Jazeera came about. Our channel, as mentioned earlier, has left no stone unturned. We have stormed the most fortified fortresses. Some Arab regimes have taken it personally. They have overreacted by recalling their ambassadors and protesting strongly to Qatar over the content of certain programs. Had a foreign television station presented similar programs, they would have never bothered to answer back. But simply because an Arab television station has done it, they have reacted. On our part, we have never sought to harm Arab relations or sow the seeds of disintegration amongst Arab countries as is often claimed. The changes that are taking place are inevitable as we live in today's global society. Gone is the time when journalists could be bought out and remote controlled. Arab countries have to learn to live with the new media.

The problem with Arab regimes is that they are not accustomed to hearing or listening to anybody opposing them. They have succeeded in muffling their people's voices for too long. Not any more, though. The open skies have given voice to the voiceless and the silent opposition groups can now shout and make themselves heard at home and abroad thanks to satellite television. Naturally, this makes Arab regimes uncomfortable. Instead of democratizing their societies, they tend to accuse the relatively new and independent Arab media of endangering the unity of the Arab world. However, what makes societies stronger and more unified is freedom rather than suppression. A close look at Western media practices suggests that the colorful variety of political and cultural opinions has not led to the disintegration of Western societies. It has rather made them more coherent and solid. Why is it that debate programs on Western TV—which have existed for a long time—have never been accused of harming the national unity of Western states? We have never heard a Western politician say that we should do away with live talk shows because they are causing us problems and affecting the ethnic texture or social composition of our homeland.

However, Arab regimes could be right in their belief that successful private Arab TV channels have widened the gap between the governments and the people. Indeed, debate programs on certain Arab satellite television channels have been eye-openers. The people have come to know more about what is happening in their societies. For the first time, they can hear the view of the opposition loud and clear. And the more people get to know the other opinions in their countries, the more they become at odds with their governments. Some are afraid that the new media might lead one day to alienation, or to a divorce between the regimes and their subjects. It is telling that some Arab governments have started to address their people through non-national TV channels; others have found themselves compelled to advertise on popular Arab channels to reach a wider audience. Indeed, satellite television has overtaken local terrestrial stations, which can be considered some kind of Arabization and arguably unification.

If anything, satellite talk shows have brought the Arab masses together and given them a pan-Arab identity. In other words, to a certain extent they have played a nationalist role by narrowing and sometimes bridging divides. In fact, one might argue that popular talk shows on Al Jazeera and other channels have succeeded where Gamal Abdel Nasser failed. Debate programs and live talks on satellite broadcasting are watched avidly by millions of Arabs and are contributing a great deal to the formation of pan-Arab public opinion over many issues. Arab viewers can now share each other's problems, issues and concerns. They have discovered that they suffer from a similar malaise. For example, people in the Middle East knew little about the Western Sahara dispute between Morocco and the Polisario before it had been debated on some popular *Crossfire*-style shows. Likewise, people in the Maghreb have learnt more about their brethren's causes in the Middle East and can now identify with them more. If anything, political dialogue-based programs have globalized Arab issues. Just as satellite talks have cemented relations between Arab expatriates and their homeland, they have also brought the Arab masses closer to each other.

In a way, the new phenomenon of talk shows is playing a role similar to that played by Voice of the Arabs (Radio Sawt Al Arab) in the 1960s. Although many accused that radio station of having misled the Arabs during the 1967 War by broadcasting false reports about Arab supremacy in the battlefield, no one can deny the fact that it produced the first pan-Arab broadcasters and journalists. Although the famous announcer, Ahmad Saeed is sometimes looked upon with scorn by some anti-Nasserite Arabs for having raised false hopes with the Arab listeners at the time, as a broadcaster, he captivated the minds and hearts of millions of Arabs all over the Arab region. Likewise, Mohammad Hasanein Haikal achieved a pan-Arab reputation thanks to Voice of the Arabs and the Egyptian press, which had at the time a noticeably nationalist flavor. No Arab radio or television station produced a similar transnational media figure until the emergence of satellite television at the beginning of the 1990s. Many of the Arab writers, journalists, intellectuals and thinkers who have appeared on our political and cultural debate programs have become household names in all Arab countries. The Palestinian journalist Abdel Barri Atwan, the editor-in-chief of the London-based newspaper *Al Quds Al Arabi*, has made a name for himself as a new nationalist pan-Arab speaker. Millions of Arabs identify with him as they relate to others who have achieved prominence across the divide. The same thing applies to the anchors of the talk shows themselves. Many of them have become household names for millions of viewers. We thankfully now have the pan-Arab presenter *par excellence* when in the past we used to have regional TV stars, whether they were Lebanese, Egyptian or Syrian.

Arabs have grown absolutely fed up watching the official TV channels which have nothing to present but news about whom his majesty, chairmanship or highness has received. I call it "the receive and see-off journalism." Our media have become specialized in reporting even the most trivial activities. Live political talks have damaged this decaying media and wetted the appetite of the Arab people for more talking. There is a great deal of yearning amongst the Arab masses for dialogue. People want to express their views; they want their voices to be heard; they are now united more than ever before. In fact, we can safely say that our programs have played a highly unifying and connecting role. They have brought Arab masses together in their quest for freedom of speech and search for more open societies both politically and socially.

NOTES

1   This episode on why Kuwait does not mend fences with Iraq was aired on March 25, 1997. For a detailed account on the Kuwaiti protest, see *Al Sharq Al Awsat*, April 3, 1997.

2   This episode was aired on February 5, 2002 and tackled the Kuwaiti press onslaught on the Secretary General of the Arab League, Amr Musa. It hosted Mr Sayyed Nassar, ex-editor of the Egyptian *Al Musawar Magazine*, and Nabeel Alfadel, a Kuwaiti columnist. As a result, a group of Kuwaiti solicitors lodged a lawsuit against Al Jazeera for defamation. For details on the furor, see the Kuwaiti press published the next day. The transcript of the program can be found on aljazeera.net.

3   The episode, which was aired on November 8, 1998, focused on the aftermath of the Wadi Araba Accords and hosted ex-foreign minister of Jordan Kamel Abu Jaber and veteran Syrian journalist Mohamad Khalifa. For the Jordanian reaction, see their press on the next day. All their papers without exception launched a press attack against the program.

4   This episode on Saudi Arabia and the Palestinian cause was screened on June 25, 2002 and had as guests Dr Fahd Alorabi Alharithi, a member of the Shura Council, and Egyptian journalist Mohamad Abdelhakam Diab. This particular episode drew heavy criticism from the Saudi press the next day.

5   See aljazeera.net, August 26, 2003.

6   "Faisal Al Kasim voted best media man for the sixth consecutive year," *Al Raya*, December 31, 2002, p. 14.

7   Ibid.

8   David Hirst, "Qatar calling: Al Jazeera, the Arab TV channel that dares to shock," *Le Monde Diplomatique*, August 8, 2001.

9   Unpublished survey carried out by the Saudi Ministry of the Interior.

10 See *Alosra Al Asriah Magazine*, December 22, 2000.

11 Ahmad Tohami, "The human cost of the Arab–Israeli conflict," The Cairo Centre for Human Rights Studies, pp. 50–1.

6

Media Brinkmanship in the Arab World: Al Jazeera's *The Opposite Direction* as a Fighting Arena

Muhammad I. Ayish

Since its inception in 1996, the Qatar-based Al Jazeera Satellite Channel has risen to prominence as the most professional and independent broadcaster in the Arab world. Drawing on the rich and diverse experiences of its staff, Al Jazeera seems to have managed to establish a foothold for itself in an Arab media scene long characterized by government censorship and restrictive policies. As much as Al Jazeera's daring attitude has won the admiration of millions of viewers around the Arab world, it has also generated countless diplomatic incidents involving its host and other Arab countries. The channel has been accused of sowing seeds of dissent and disintegration in Arab communities in the name of free speech and expression. Al Jazeera's opponents argue that the channel has drawn on sensational methods to build up its pan-Arab popularity, with no regard for the religious, social and cultural sensitivities of the issues involved. This, according to Al Jazeera critics, has turned the channel into a battlefield for fanatics representing marginalized religious and secular perspectives with little recognition in mainstream Arab world intellectual traditions.

This chapter draws on the notion of "brinkmanship" as a defining concept for understanding Al Jazeera's sensational approaches to political debates involving a wide range of personalities appearing on the channel's weekly show *The Opposite Direction*. The host of the show, Faisal Al Kasim, seems consistently bent on pushing guests to their limits in a dramatized fashion with the objective of achieving some form of impact on audiences at individual and institutional levels. By forcing guests to the "brink" of confrontation in front of live audiences, the host of the show seems to create an air of drama that often trickles down into concrete actions on the ground in the form of diplomatic incidents, office closures and mass protests, among other things. This aura of cliff-hanging sensationalism has not only heightened inter-Arab tensions, but has also meant a failure to deliver rational, sensible and balanced debates that represent existing intellectual and political trends in the Arab world.

THE AL JAZEERA NEWS AND PUBLIC AFFAIRS MODEL

The rise of private television in the Arab World since in the 1990s has been a highly significant media development in a region long dominated by government-monopolized broadcasting. Yet, what is more significant is the association of commercial television with the diffusion of Western-style media orientations and practices based on critical and pluralistic views of society. The emerging liberal media outlook, at least at face value, promotes the notion of a free market-place of ideas, providing for critical, free and balanced exchanges of information among politically diverse actors. Professional rather than political considerations seem to be driving news work practices at private stations operating in a highly competitive media market. For new broadcasters, what makes news is not a personality-centered event or issue, but a host of values and norms that derives from their perceptions of the public interest.[1] To this end, the launch of commercial television in the Arab world has not only broadened viewers' programming choices, but it has also provided them with better access to new formats hardly visible on government-controlled television.

Because most news staff either were trained in Western countries or worked in Western media organizations, their sense of news work draws on its perception as a highly selective process with important gatekeeping decisions. Private broadcasters have heavily invested in news work development by introducing state-of-the-art technologies and by establishing extensive regional and global networks of reporters and correspondents. The visual communication potential of television is often realized through rich infographics and video materials as well as sleek delivery formats. A newscast is made up of a series of news "intros" for reports and news items. Rarely does a news item appear without video. Conversational and friendly news delivery formats mark news presentations that sharply contrast with traditional rigid and formalistic delivery methods common in government-controlled television systems.

Al Jazeera Satellite Channel was launched in November 1996 "from the ashes of the BBC."[2] During its short existence, Al Jazeera has won a reputation for independent reporting that sharply contrasts with state-sponsored news carried by other media outlets in the Arab world. Al Jazeera has risen to prominence in the past few years with its daring handling of social and political issues traditionally dominated by monolithic and dull media reporting. As much as Al Jazeera proves appealing to millions of viewers, it has also incurred the wrath of numerous Arab governments for its critical coverage of sensitive social and political issues. The service draws on highly professional staff with extensive international experience as well as on state-of-the-art digital production technologies. In October 2001, Al Jazeera's live coverage of US raids on Afghanistan forced CNN and other television news services to feature its exclusive footage on their news shows. In the 2003 Anglo-American war on Iraq, Al Jazeera was viewed as a competent rival for global broadcasters like BBC World Television and CNN.

Al Jazeera is credited with the introduction of Western-style television journalism into the Arab world broadcasting scene through the airing of a series of live talk shows characterized by vigorous discussions and extensive viewer participation. Al Jazeera's public affairs programs include *The Opposite Direction, Without Borders, Open Dialogue, More Than One Opinion,* and *Beyond the Event.* These programs share one common feature: they seek to break away from dull television talk shows through hosting dissenting Arab world political figures and adopting an uncompromising approach to public issues. They seem to be held in high esteem by Arab world audiences generally because of their daring investigative spirit and their airing of unofficial points of view. By aligning itself more with grassroots and nonestablishment concerns, these programs seek to satisfy Arab viewers' quest to gain exposure to alternative media outlets that could furnish new perspectives on public issues in the region.

Al Jazeera's provocative political talk shows have generated serious tensions between its host country, Qatar, on the one hand, and other governments, on the other hand. There are numerous examples of Arab countries recalling their ambassadors from Doha to protest against what they view as Al Jazeera's incitements against their governments, leaders or value systems.[3] The channel has had some of its regional bureaus closed down following critical reporting of domestic issues or events. In October 2001, Al Jazeera came under US State Department criticism following the airing of a videotaped statement made by Osama bin Laden in which he called on Muslims around the world to carry out "Jihad" against America. US officials were concerned that bin Laden's videotaped statements included secret body language codes that might be used to relay certain messages. But, as Al Jazeera's Managing Director commented, the channel "gives the US viewpoint as much space as it gives the Afghani viewpoint," had three correspondents in the United States and was the only one authorized to broadcast continuously from Taliban-ruled territory in Afghanistan.[4] In March 2003, Al Jazeera was also criticized by the Bush administration for transmitting Iraqi TV video of US PoWs in Iraq.

The development of Al Jazeera has spawned numerous theories regarding its mission and agenda. Al Amin sees the meteoric rise of Al Jazeera as enigmatic to politicians and media critics.[5] One Western journalist noted that Al Jazeera came to exist in the aftermath of the termination of BBC Arabic Television following disagreements over the airing of statements made by a Saudi dissident.[6] It was also noted that Al Jazeera "is the lone Arabic broadcast outlet to put truth and objectivity above even its survival."[7] Hence, Al Jazeera has been conceived as a replica of the discontinued BBC Arabic Television Service, launched to furnish global publicity for the emerging Qatari leadership. According to one researcher, Al Jazeera is a true model for media pluralism in the Arab world.[8] Another view conceives of Al Jazeera as an Iraqi propaganda machine that served the interests of the former president Saddam Hussein through massive coverage of human miseries caused by the UN sanctions on Iraq which lasted over a decade.[9] Yet, other critics seem to go further by associating Al Jazeera with a variety of countries and groups such as Israel and Al Qaeda. Ajami sees extremist built-in tendencies among Al Jazeera staff who identify themselves as "anti-imperialists."[10]

THE OPPOSITE DIRECTION: A FIGHTING ARENA

Since its launch, Al Jazeera has generated stormy waves in long-time tranquil Arabian media seas. This satellite television broadcaster may have attracted many viewers from around the Arab world, but it has also generated spates of public criticism and diplomatic incidents in inter-Arab relations. Critics argue that in its quest for building up a broader audience base in the region, Al Jazeera resorts to *Crossfire*-style shows, drawing heavily on sensational media techniques. The most outstanding of these programs is probably *The Opposite Direction*, a weekly evening talk show. Hosted by Faisal Al Kasim, a British-educated presenter of Syrian origin, with a "talent for drawing out guests with opposing views and goading them to mix it up on air,"[11] the show includes audience participation through live phone calls from different parts of the world.

The Opposite Direction is arguably Al Jazeera's most controversial talk show—a program in which two guests vehemently argue opposite sides of an issue. The intensity of the debate, viewed by its host as analogous to the US TV program *Crossfire*,[12] has offended some guests and impelled others to storm out of the studio in the middle of the show. Faisal Al Kasim, described as "the hottest property on Arab television,"[13] told CBS's *60 Minutes* in May 2001 that "we Arabs have so much dirt buried under the carpet. So Al Jazeera is revealing that dirt, politically, culturally, socially and religiously."[14] The show's daring treatment of issues like polygamy, Islamic fundamentalism, political legitimacy, and corruption has made it the number one show on Arab satellite television channels among viewers in the region.[15]

On the other hand, the show has come under fire from some media critics as reflecting artificial rather than spontaneous work practices. Some writers see the Al Jazeera show as too staged to be true, with all telephone calls being prearranged.[16] Other writers suggest that Faisal Al Kasim has been keen on provoking guests to "heat up" their arguments in order to add more sensation to the show: "He would feel excited when guests start exchanging verbal insults and would seem delighted to see tension mounting to physical clashes."[17] According to Jawad, Faisal Al Kasim would also "interrupt guests in mid sentence to steer debates in a manner favorable to his political predisposition."[18] Kayyali charged that the Al Jazeera program presents issues and events mostly out of context and draws heavily on sensationalism and media hype.[19] A media seminar in the UAE noted that Al Kasim has often abandoned decency in dealing with his guests, thus transforming the show into a fighting game, broadcast live to worldwide audiences.[20]

Although the impact of *The Opposite Direction* on national and pan-Arab politics remains quite murky, the show seems to have served as a disruptive force in inter-Arab relations. There have been countless cases in which this talk show has led to diplomatic incidents with the government of Qatar which hosts Al Jazeera. While some governments have responded by recalling their ambassadors from Doha, others have closed down Al Jazeera's news offices or banned the entry of its staff. In October 2001, Al Jazeera came under fire from the US and British governments for hosting what were perceived as pro-Al Qaeda figures on the program, including the exiled Yemeni fundamentalist Abu Hamza Al Mesri, providing a media outlet for Osama bin Laden during the US war campaign in Afghanistan. These cases, of course, may not be interpreted as suggesting an absolutely negative "opposite direction" role in regional and global politics, but rather as proof of how sensitive and vulnerable Arab and Western governments have become to the talk show.

Although Al Jazeera's *The Opposite Direction* has been a subject of investigation by numerous academic studies,[21] the sensational features of the show do not seem to have received adequate scholarly scrutiny. The program has been especially noted for its daring handling of local and pan-Arab issues, and according to its host, for breaking significant social, political and cultural taboos.[22] In most academic investigations, the program has been approached more in terms of its editorial content than in terms of its technical format and non-verbal structure.[23] Interested in how different viewpoints are featured in the program, researchers have drawn up conclusions relating to issues of balance, objectivity, and fairness as components of professional Western-style broadcast journalism.[24]

This chapter draws on the concept of "brinkmanship"—originally denoting a political strategy drawing on military and rhetorical escalation to achieve specific goals—to describe how Faisal Al Kasim turns *The Opposite Direction* into a live breathtaking battle of words. In general terms, brinkmanship refers to the practice, especially in international politics, of seeking advantage by creating the impression that one is willing and able to push a highly dangerous situation to the limit rather than concede. Dixit and Nalebuff note that brinkmanship involves deliberately creating a risk that if other players fail to act as one would like them to, the outcome would be bad for everyone.[25] Introduced for the first time by Schelling, brinkmanship is defined as the "tactic of deliberately letting the situation get somewhat out of hand, just because its being out of hand may be intolerable to the other party and force his [or her] accommodation."[26] In the context of *The Opposite Direction*, media brinkmanship describes Al Kasim's use of tension-building techniques and media hype to attract viewers' attention. As manifested in *The Opposite Direction*, brinkmanship is a function of three factors—the three "Ps," so to speak: *the political factor*, as noted in the quest of Al Jazeera, as a government-sponsored broadcaster, for greater visibility in the evolving Arab media scene; *the professional factor*, as evident in Al Jazeera's adoption of the basic tenets of American-style journalism that provide for a free, detached and balanced flow of information; and *the personal factor*, which is associated with Faisal Al Kasim's conception of the Arab world as a rotten entity that needs to be reformed. The objective of this chapter is to demonstrate in quantitative and qualitative terms how the three Ps are combined by the moderator of *The Opposite Direction* to systematically push guests to the brink of confrontation as an audience-capturing strategy. A major casualty of this approach, as will become clear, is the viewer who ends up being faced with shouting bouts rather than intellectually stimulating exchanges.

METHODOLOGY

Ten episodes of *The Opposite Direction* (aired between November 26, 2002 and January 14, 2003) were recorded and their manuscripts downloaded from Aljazeera.net site for analyses of how the moderator of the show, Faisal Al Kasim, seems to "push his guests into the brink of confrontation" to win the broadest base of audiences in the Arab world. The article views media "brinkmanship" as a linear host-induced process of rising tensions leading to some sort of a sensational peak (plot) on which the show ends. Table 6.1 shows the topics and dates of broadcast for *The Opposite Direction* episodes covered by the analysis.

Table 6.1   Episodes *of The Opposite Direction* covered by the analysis

S	Program title	Broadcast date
1	America and Democracy in the Arab World	November 26, 2002
2	Saddam Hussein's Apology to the Kuwaiti People	December 10, 2002
3	The Kenya Attack and US–Israeli interests	December 3, 2002
4	Democracy and the Possession of Weapons of Mass Destruction	November 19, 2002
5	Afghanistan and the New Era	November 10, 2002
6	The Effects of the Intifada on the Palestinians	December 17, 2002
7	The Arabs' Views of the European Union	December 24, 2002
8	The Future of Israeli Labor Party	December 31, 2002
9	America Challenged by North Korea	January 7, 2003
10	The Arab Scientific Renaissance	January 14, 2003

Table 6.2 Behavioral themes in *The Opposite Direction* episodes

Music and logo	10
Introductory questions	10
Voice tone	5
Facial and non-verbal expressions	6
Verbal exchanges	7
Total & average score	38/7.5

This research draws on quantitative and qualitative analyses of the aforementioned ten episodes. In the quantitative analysis, each episode was divided along a timeline into six segments (12–15 minutes each) that would translate into six sequential scenes in a dramatic work. Each scene was analyzed in terms of several themes marking host behavior in the show, eventually generating a cumulative score for each scene. This means that the ten episodes of the show yielded 13.5 hours of television time, comprising 60 sequences that were subjected to analysis. In every scene, a score was assigned to each of the following host behavioral themes (the full score was 50) then the total was divided by five for an average score for each scene:

- Program music and logo: dramatic and fiery (always get a score of 10)
- Dramatic introductory questions (always get a score of 10)
- Voice tone of host, guests and audiences
- Facial and other non-verbal expressions of guests and host
- Inflammatory verbal exchanges

For example, Scene 1 (i.e., the first 12 minutes) of Episode 1 produced the scores for the five factors as shown in Table 6.2.

In addition to the quantitative analysis of the ten episodes of the show, the study offers a qualitative analysis which examines the moderator's use of such techniques as instigation, censorship, silence, rationality, anonymity and, to a lesser extent, polling.

QUANTITATIVE DATA

This study draws on a quantitative analysis of ten episodes of *The Opposite Direction* based on a graphical representation of the flow of tension within the programs. All ten episodes involve peaks of tension, whether in the form of shouting, aggressive verbal responses, undue interventions, abusive statements or offensive body language.

The flow of tension seems to experience notable rises as program time goes on (see Figure 6.1 and Table 6.3). The higher the score, the higher the level of tension. It should be noted that each episode starts out with a dramatic opening by the moderator in which he seeks to create a sense of appreciation on the part of viewers for what seems to be a fiery debate of a hot issue. The way issues are framed by Al Kasim draws on alarming voice tone, emotional guest reactions, distinct facial and other expressions, repeated interruptions, emotional viewer inputs, and aggressive verbal statements. The show can be said to be a forum for everything, except quiet dialogue.

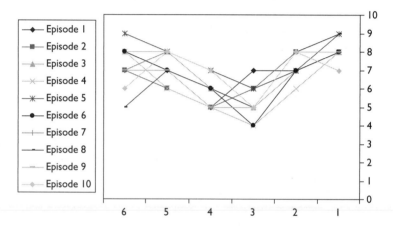

Figure 6.1   The flow of tension in ten episodes of *The Opposite Direction*

Table 6.3   Numerical representation of the flow of tension in *The Opposite Direction*

Episode number	Scene average score					
	Scene 1	Scene 2	Scene 3	Scene 4	Scene 5	Scene 6
Episode 1	8	7	7	5	7	7
Episode 2	8	8	6	5	6	7
Episode 3	8	7	5	6	8	8
Episode 4	8	6	4	5	6	8
Episode 5	9	7	6	7	8	9
Episode 6	8	7	4	6	7	8
Episode 7	8	8	5	7	8	7
Episode 8	9	8	5	6	7	5
Episode 9	8	8	5	5	7	7
Episode 10	7	8	5	7	8	6

The structure of the show in many ways resembles that of a work of drama with protagonists and antagonists acting out their roles on a theatrical stage. The major structural difference relates to the "highly sensational" introduction in which Al Kasim poses provocative questions to capture viewers' attention and to warm up guests for what looks like a live shouting game. In one episode about Iraq's relation with Kuwait, he opened the show as follows:

> Dear viewers, welcome ... What does the Kuwaiti regime want from Iraq? Why do Kuwaitis evade opening a new page with Iraq? Shouldn't Kuwait itself apologize to the Iraqi people? Didn't the Gulf regimes demand an apology from Iraq for years? Why wasn't the apology accepted and why has it been attacked with such an abominable force? Aren't the Kuwaiti reasons for rejecting the Iraqi apology too weak? Do the Kuwaitis dare to accept the Iraqi apology? Don't they need to receive the green light from America first? Was the Iraqi apology a real one or was Iraq forced to give it? Was the Iraqi message meant to drive a wedge between the Kuwaiti government and the people? How can Iraq apologize and incite people against the Kuwaiti government?

In a wrestling ring, an umpire seeks to observe the players' conformity to the rules of the game. In *The Opposite Direction*, Al Kasim seeks to make sure that both guests are always fully engaged in verbal fights with active audience participation. Once an episode opens up in the midst of heightened tensions as suggested by the introduction, continued exposure to the full program, as a shouting game, is better ensured. The dramatic momentum is carried on to the last minutes of the show when "combatants" are disengaged by the natural lapse of program time.

QUALITATIVE ANALYSIS

In his show *The Opposite Direction*, Faisal Al Kasim uses a number of host-centered strategies that maximize the realization of media brinkmanship: instigation, censorship, silence, rationality, anonymity and, more recently, polling.

Instigation
Against a cliff-hanging musical background, Faisal Al Kasim starts out his show with numerous questions that set the stage for what is intended to be a heated debate as indicated by the raging-fire logo of the program. The role of the host of the show suggests systematic

attempts on his part to keep goading guests into maintaining a state of heightened alarm and anticipation. Once a guest makes a fiery statement or exhibits a sensational non-verbal expression, it seems imperative in most cases that the other guest should respond in the same manner. Here we seem to see a vicious circle of sensational exchanges fueled by provocative input from the host. Such input is likely to be generated when verbal duels take on a more peaceful character or when both guests seem to come back to their rational senses. In some cases, guests were able to overcome their emotional urges and maintain a level of apathy to Al Kasim's instigations per-haps out of respect for audiences or out of excessive self-confidence in handling the situation in a less stormy fashion. This feature was noted in episodes about democracy and possession of weapons of mass destruction, Afghanistan and the new era, and the Arab scien-tific renaissance.

This issue of instigation brings into question the conventional role of a program host or moderator as a mediator between guests or as a facilitator of the flow of ideas between panelists, on the one hand, and audiences, on the other hand. In broadcast journalism, program hosts are entrusted with featuring authoritative sources with the highest intellectual standards in public affairs. The conver-sion of public affairs television shows in Western societies into sen-sational shouting rings for stormy exchanges has spawned a good amount of criticism.[27] Programs like CNN's *Crossfire* and BBC's *Hard Talk* have been seen as reflecting a good amount of "yellow journalism" and as lacking the minimum substance of intellectual complexity.[28] Researchers have found that TV talk shows thrive on fiery exchanges in which guests become "framed," and hence are prompted to "go out of their way" to get out of the corner they are pushed into. Program moderators have been taken to task for play-ing up hostile outward behavior to the exclusion of friendly rational dialogue.[29]

It is clear that Al Kasim's interventions in the show are tailored more towards keeping one of his guests always alarmed by the other guest. The host of the show does not hesitate to pose questions that seem bound to provoke more hostile statements. This seems to bear resemblance to wrestling fans who fill the ring with chanting and clapping noises to encourage their favorite wrestlers into a fast knock-down. In one episode about the Kenyan operation against an Israeli-owned hotel, an Egyptian guest with Arabist orientations criticized positions that argue against Palestinian suicide bombings as feeding into Israeli extremism. Al Kasim immediately jumped into support-ive conclusions that such positions are nonsense. By aligning him-self with either one of his guests, Al Kasim seems intent on keeping the heat on the antagonist to goad him or her into responding to those statements with equal vehemence. In the episode on the effects of the intifada on the Palestinian people themselves, Al Kasim asked Mohamed Nazzal of the Hamas movement about the other guest's claims that the militarization of the intifada has incurred huge losses for the Palestinians. In a third program on defiant North Korea positions, Al Kasim addressed a question to Mohamed Asaad Bayyoud Al Tamimi of Islamic Jihad on why Arab regimes who have socialized their people into hating America are not reaping the harvest of that socialization. The latter two ques-tions are not void of insinuations of downsizing anti-American sentiments in the Arab world.

The notion of the program host as an instigator fits well into the general perception of the show as a shouting arena, set up to capture attention through fiery verbal and non-verbal exchanges. This sen-sational media function seems in tune with growing perceptions of Arabs as "a noise phenomenon," suggesting strong emotional attachment to an oral culture (of words) rather than an action-based culture. The host of the show seems to believe that the instigating role he plays is a must for fueling the fight, and hence keeping the show hot. It is worth noting that Al Kasim initiates instigating inter-ventions only when he feels that both guests are getting along quite well. For him, this seems to work against the very essence of *The Opposite Direction* as a sensational *Crossfire*-style program. Should the program be stripped of these frequent "spats" and fiery exchanges, its brinkmanship objective would be defeated. The quantitative analysis suggests that spots of heightened tension keep rising through the course of the program, thus contributing to building up a sense of drama on the part of both guests.

Censorship

This technique of suppressing others' views has been evident in the host's frequent interruption of speakers making statements that inhibit his tension-building strategy. At different points of time, Al Kasim does not hesitate to interrupt guests in mid sentence or to block his or her statements in order to allow for more controversial ideas in a way that is conducive to keeping up the heat of the show. His eclectic approach to guest and audience input seems designed to

keep fanning heated exchanges in order to maximize dramatic tensions conducive to the realization of a brinkmanship strategy. In
most cases, Al Kasim's interventions are meant either to provide
momentum to controversial ideas or to suppress ideas that apparently
contribute to a peaceful atmosphere in the debate. This technique is
not confined to ideas generated by guests; it extends to statements
made by some of the viewers during live interventions or through
e-mailed and faxed feedback. The overriding principle governing
the gatekeeping of ideas in the show seems to derive from their relative enhancement of dramatic and sensational exchanges. When
both guests seem closer to sharing common positions on debated
issues, the host intervenes in such a way as to convert the discussion
into a fiery duel. Actually, as Al Kasim admits on several occasions,
the notion of an "opposite direction" show would be rendered
worthless should both guests act in a harmonious fashion. It seems
imperative that antagonists and protagonists act antithetically to
ensure program success.[30]

In a democratic society, the role of public affairs program hosts as
absolute gatekeepers has never been met with approval in the media
community. A show presenter is often viewed mostly as a facilitator
or a middle person between holders of different viewpoints, and is
not supposed to control the flow of information in favor of a certain
party or ideology. In a free media environment, a moderator draws
on his or her role as a neutral voice of truth and a reflector of public
opinion on the issues and events being debated. By steering debates
into certain directions, show hosts are in fact expressing their own
ideological positions to the exclusion of others.[31] Impartiality and
objectivity are precluded. However, given the nature of public affairs
shows as public forums for addressing issues of significance to society, a program moderator assumes a proactive rather than a reactive
role in managing live discussions. But this proactive role should in
no way be used as a tool for suppressing some views in favor of others.
Television show presenters are expected to approach both guests as
equal parties with equally legitimate viewpoints.[32]

Al Kasim's selective approach in dealing with the ideas presented
in the show has been evident in the amount of time appropri-
ated to different guests and in the eclectic use of audience feedback,
especially through faxes and e-mail messages. He seems to play up
feedback that is in tune with his specific political or ideological orientations while blocking out that which does not enhance the sensational nature of the show. In many cases, he tells us that he has

received more than 100 faxes, but he falls back on time limitations to highlight a feedback that fits into his brinkmanship strategy. He usually picks up on the most dramatic and sensational feedback from viewers and leaves out what seem to be ordinary responses. In some cases, it has been found that some guests get far less time than others not because of their deficient fluency, but because their responses either lack provocative features or are ideologically unpopular.

Episodes of *The Opposite Direction* are rife with examples of Al Kasim's gatekeeping functions. In an episode on the future of the Israeli Labor Party, Al Kasim diverted the discussion of the Palestinian views on the Labor Party to an explication of Mahmoud Abbas's claims of the Palestinian Authority's achievements and victories. One of the guests, Abdul Barri Atwan, editor of the London-based *Al Quds Al Arabi* newspaper, was criticized for speaking about the Palestinian issue from a distance, from his residence in London. In another episode about the Arab scientific renaissance, Al Kasim was pushing the view that Arab scientific and technological backwardness is due primarily to an international conspiracy spearheaded by the United States as evident in the campaign on Iraqi scientists. In a program about the Kenyan operation, Al Kasim tried to exclude Shafiq Al Ghabra, a Kuwaiti university professor with controversial political positions.

Silence

This wait-and-see strategy is evident in Al Kasim's extended silence as guests are engaged in verbal exchanges. The fiercer the debate, the more extended the host's silence. This pattern is evident in discussions of highly sensitive issues when tensions are running high in the program. The host of the show takes a more peaceful and detached posture, appearing to be a neutral observer of the fight. The duration of his silence seems in many cases to be proportionate to the intensity of the fight. In one of the episodes, one speaker talked for five consecutive minutes, uninterrupted by the host of the show. He was talking emotionally about the rotten and corrupt Arab world leadership, using language that was likely to be perceived as offensive by the other guest and by the audience. Underlying the host's silence is the belief that any intervention on his part would spoil the flow of drama. In one way or another, the guest was parroting Al Kasim's personal ideology of the Arab world as a gross case of political and cultural failure.

For some people, the host's silence might be indicative of his fairness to his guests; he is giving them adequate time to tell their views on the issue at hand. But as much as Al Kasim's interventions are meant to induce guests into engaging in fiery talk, his silence seeks to perpetuate shouting exchanges when they take place. There were numerous cases in which Al Kasim abstained from intervening when guests and viewers were using offensive language to refer to particular leaders or governments. For him, such abusive statements provide additional fuel for the show's end. The silence of the host of the show tends to be a dominant feature when speakers make hostile statements or utter fiery expressions as in the cases of Mohamed Asaad Tamimi and Abdul Barri Atwan. In *The Opposite Direction* episode featuring Jon Alterman and Abdul Hamid Qandil, more time was given to the latter while translated statements of the former were frequently disrupted by Al Kasim.

Rationality

This strategy is evident in the host's role as a rational observer of events and issues, a role that is intended to stave off any feelings of bias on his part regarding issues being debated. In some cases, and to stave off any potential suspicion of his biases and personal dispositions, Al Kasim acts as if he is the voice of reason in the debate. He assumes that both guests are running out of logic and going beyond reason, and it is his role to bring them back to the track of reason. He draws on facts, "widely held beliefs" and other evidence to make a statement that rationally seeks in the final analysis not to rationalize the discussion, but to inject more charge into the debate by misrepresenting guests as irrational actors. Al Kasim introduces himself as the impartial voice of reason with the intention of explicating ideas and arriving at the truth on the basis of objective clues.

Although the rational actor strategy has been used with both guests, the way arguments are presented seems to reinforce Al Kasim's determination to goad guests into making provocative statements more than into bringing up facts. For example, in an episode about America and democracy in the Arab world, Al Kasim posed the following question to Jon Alterman: "Jon Alterman in Washington, do you advise us to believe America this time around that it is serious about promoting democracy in the Arab world after decades of supporting fascist and dictatorial regimes in the region?" In an episode about the Kenyan operation, Al Kasim addressed Shafiq Al Ghabra of Kuwait:

A few days ago, Aljazeera.net published a public opinion poll in which over 90 per cent of those who participated said they were supportive of martyrial operations against Israel. In a democracy people state their position loud and clear and, in this case, the Arab people have made their position clear, so why not take that into account?

The rationality-shrouded questions seem also to place guests in critical positions, always on the defensive. Al Kasim knows the answer to both questions: American support for Arab dictatorial regimes is based on vested US interests, which are prioritized over human values. Arab people are not given a chance to translate their attitudes towards issues and events because they are suppressed by oppressive regimes. This strategy of assuming rationality to inquire about questions the answers for which are obvious serves two objectives: to increase pressure on guests to prod them into making irrational statements as a defensive strategy which leads in most cases to stormy exchanges and to assume an aura of impartiality and objectivity in the moderation of the debate.

Anonymity

In many cases, the host of the show can invoke unknown sources to substantiate his viewpoint or to raise an issue. As the audience has no means of verifying the authenticity of the source, the statement is taken for granted. This practice seems to contravene the basic norms of investigative journalism in democratic societies. Occasionally, reporters are not supposed to disclose their sources, but as a matter of principle, sources of information should be declared throughout the news story as a prerequisite for credibility. Source attribution is believed to be one of the cornerstones of objective and accurate journalism. The use of anonymous sources is likely to scale down levels of credibility on the part of news media and even to lead to serious legal troubles for journalists and media organizations.

The use of anonymous sources is used by Al Kasim as a strategy to substantiate his arguments or to counter those of guests and audiences. In a few instances, Al Kasim quoted "sources" on the use of depleted uranium in Iraq, on "Kuwaiti conspiracies" against the Iraqi people, on Palestinian Authority suppression of the intifada, and on imperialist powers "which plot to keep Arabs technologically and scientifically backward." This technique of source anonymity seems to amount to some form of editorialization. It goes against the very essence of journalistic accuracy as an ethical and professional value. In most cases, the use of anonymous sources with dramatic statements was intended to fuel debates as they were losing their intensity. Given the fast pace of the program, it was almost impossible to verify every piece of information cited by Al Kasim.

Polling

Recently, the introduction of online polling to evaluate audience views of both sides of the debate seems to have contributed to the process of rising tensions. The program host constantly reminds the "contestants" of their share of votes as if to prompt them to make more effort to improve their standing among viewers through more tense exchanges.

This strategy is not without effects. In an episode on the role of the Kurds in the new Iraq, aired on October 7, 2003, Al Kasim pitted Shirzad Adel Al Nereedy against Dr Salim Matar; the former defending the Kurds while the latter was questioning their Kurdish geopolitical agenda and doubting their allegiance to a national, unified Iraq. The subject of the polling was whether or not the Kurds are playing a positive role in the new Iraq. At the outset, Al Nereedy had a strong lead, and the host of the program took pains to emphasize that. Sure enough, this provoked Al Nereedy's opponent, so much so that, at one point, the polling itself became the subject of discussion. When the host of the program reminded Dr Matar that his Kurdish opponent was way ahead of him in the polls, Dr Matar lashed out at the practice itself claiming that the voting was channeled and that he was in no doubt that the Kurds who knew about the well-advertised episode of the program were calling other Kurds to urge them to vote. Interestingly enough, as the program unfolded, the tide changed and the numbers gradually shifted from 87 per cent versus 13 per cent at the outset, to 67 per cent versus 33 per cent half way through the program, to 51 per cent versus 49 per cent at the end of the program, with the total number of votes being 2,764. It was evident that Al Kasim was actively using the polling card. The contestants were reminded no less than seven times about the outcome of the online voting. The change in numbers prompted Dr Matar to be more confrontational while pushing his opponent to be more defensive. For the host of the program, polling ensured a threefold achievement: it heightened the tension between the two guests, it guaranteed "the show aspect" of the program, and exalted the kind of debate held as capable of swaying public opinion.

CONCLUSION

This study sought to investigate media brinkmanship as an audience-capturing strategy followed by Faisal Al Kasim's *The Opposite*

Direction. Brinkmanship describes the host's style of managing the program on the basis of maximizing its sensational value through engaging opposite figures in what looks like shouting games carried to live audiences. Three sets of factors have contributed to the realization of media brinkmanship: (1) political factors associated with the quest of Al Jazeera, as a Qatari television channel, for greater media visibility and hence greater political gains for its host country; (2) professional factors associated with Al Jazeera's adoption of American-style journalism that emphasizes "the opinion ... and the other opinion"; and (3) personal factors emanating from Faisal Al Kasim's personal view of the Arab world as a rotten entity that needs to be reformed by "forces of freedom and democratization." Quantitative and qualitative analysis suggests that *The Opposite Direction* thrives more on shouting exchanges than on intellectually-stimulating discussions. The role of Al Kasim in making this possible is very central. His strategy consists of pushing guests to the brink of confrontation as an attention-capturing goal.

While the advent of satellite television in the Arab world has been greeted with much fanfare as a long-awaited opportunity for broader political participation and democratization, the transfer of Western program formats into the emerging media scene seems to have been disappointing. In an Arab culture that cherishes consensus and collective attitudes, breaking down society along political, religious, ethnic and sectarian lines is often viewed as a very delicate issue. In the West, the notions of diversity and pluralism have been highly valued as the basis for democracy. Freedom of expression, as provided for by national constitutions, has been vital in the realization of a significant media role in public life. However, the experience of the past two decades suggests that, contrary to what many people would like to believe, the Arab world is disengaged from real Western-style democratic practices. The introduction of talk shows like *The Opposite Direction* is likely to hamper political development in its broadest sense. As one guest of the show told Al Kasim in an episode on Arabs' views of the European Union:

> This television show *The Opposite Direction* has contributed positively to the Arab nation in terms of quality debates and discussions. But I wish Dr Faisal you would come up with another program using the same format entitled "The Same Direction," suggesting that it is not adequate that we should have divergent views. We need to be closer to one another. You are focusing on one of the external factors behind Arab divisions.[33]

The sentiment was echoed by Schleifer who lamented the proliferation of Western-style talk shows in the Arab world:

> It is regretful not just for the vulgarity that is cheerfully migrating from the West to the Arab East ... but also because the whole justification for the public affairs talk show, with its aura of free speech, is presumably not to titillate or provide viewers with the intellectual equivalent of TV wrestling, but rather to inculcate an informed public opinion, as a requirement or hallmark of civil society and the democratic experience. And the drift of TV talk shows, while theoretically opening up new channels of public discourse on previously taboo subjects of social import, to quote the favorable literature, is receding away from opinion that is informed to opinion that is sensationalist.[34]

It is obvious that *The Opposite Direction* lends itself more to media brinkmanship than to rational media discussion. Brinkmanship, as a political and military strategy, provides the conceptual basis for explaining how the host of *The Opposite Direction* manages the show. The utilization of this concept helps shed light on the notion of media brinkmanship as a function of political, professional and personal factors that combine to maximize sensational aspects of the show as a media game that bears resemblance to political and military brinkmanship in the cases of North Korea's nuclear crisis and the Indo-Pakistani conflict. In the case of *The Opposite Direction*, the actors are not only the guests and viewers but also Faisal Al Kasim who drives them to the brink of confrontation to achieve some political, professional and personal goals. In international and regional conflicts, brinkmanship is driven by nations' desires for accruing political and military gains through pushing their positions to extreme limits. In international relations, brinkmanship may describe some form of "gunboat" diplomacy in which negotiations are equated with coercive measures on the ground designed to bear on relations between actors. In the case of *The Opposite Direction*, media brinkmanship is designed to maximize Al Jazeera's viewership in the Arab world through projecting the channel as daring, unconventional and not aligned with mainstream political establishments, rhetoric, and style.

The foregoing analysis of *The Opposite Direction* should in no way suggest that this program, which is unprecedented in Arab television, has been all but useful. The introduction of an "opposite direction" format for public affairs programs in the Arab world has actually revolutionized the long-time dull and monolithic talk shows that dominated television in the region. In many significant ways, the show has marked a breakaway from conventional television work practices by demonstrating the possibility of utilizing television as a forum for robust debates involving a wide range of viewpoints, and similar programs need to be encouraged on Arab television. However, such talk shows need to promote real dialogue rather than sensational shouting matches among participants. To achieve this, television needs to be more insulated from political alignments and professional broadcast conventions and to address seriously the public interests of the community.

NOTES

1 Muhammad Ayish, "Political communication on Arab world television: evolving patterns," *Political Communication*, Vol. 19, No. 2 (2000), pp. 137–54.
2 M. Moran, "In defense of Al Jazeera," MSNBC (2001), <http://www.msnbc.com/news/643471.asp?cp1=1>.
3 "Al Jazeera: a series of harassments," <http://www.aljazeera.net/news/arabic/2003/4/4.9.4.htm>.
4 D. Anderson-Ford, "Al Jazeera strikes back," ITP, <http://www.itp.net/features/100565682055132.htm>.
5 I. Al Amin, "Arab media from visual to audio: Al Jazeera as a model," *Al Hayat*, April 26, 2000, p. 10.
6 Moran, "In defense of Al Jazeera."
7 Ibid.
8 Suleiman Al Shammari, *The Opposite Direction: An Academic Study* (Doha: Dar Al Sharq, 1998).
9 Al Amin, "Arab media from visual to audio."
10 Fouad Ajami, "What the Muslim world is watching," *New York Times*, November 18, 2001.
11 Mohammed El-Nawawy and Adel Iskandar Farag, *Al Jazeera: How the Free Arab News Network Scooped the World and Changed the Middle East* (Boulder: Westview Press, 2002).
12 Faisal Al Kasim, "*Crossfire*: the Arab version," *Harvard International Journal of Press/Politics*, Vol. 4, No. 3 (1999), pp. 93–7.
13 Brian Whitaker, "Battle station: with its broadcast of Osama bin Laden's video and exclusive footage of the Afghan War, the tiny satellite TV channel Al Jazeera made a huge name for itself," *Guardian*, February 7, 2003, p. 2.
14 El-Nawawy and Farag, *Al Jazeera*.
15 R. Zednik, "Perspectives on war: inside Al Jazeera," *Columbia Journalism Review* (March 2002), p. 44.
16 H. Madan, "Live on the air," *Al Khaleej*, June 12, 2000, p. 40.
17 M. Khalifa, "A look at *The Opposite Direction*," *Al Sharq Al Awsat*, September 22, 2000, p. 19.

18   A. Jawad "On the direction that has become no longer opposite," *Al Sharq Al Awsat*, September 24, 2000, p. 18.
19   M. Kayyali, "Politics on Arab satellite television," *Al Bayan*, November 20, 1998, p. 5.
20   "Al Jazeera evaluation seminar ends with tough trial for *The Opposite Direction*," *Al Bayan*, May 10, 2000, p. 6.
21   Al Shammari, *The Opposite Direction*; El-Nawawy and Farag, *Al Jazeera*.
22   Whitaker, "Battle station," p. 3.
23   Al Shammari, *The Opposite Direction*.
24   Muhammad I. Ayish, "American-style journalism on Arab world television," *Transnational Broadcasting Journal*, No. 5 (2001), <http://www.tbsjournal.com/Archives/Spring01/Ayish.html>.
25   A. Dixit and B. Nalebuff, "Game theory," *The Concise Encyclopedia of Economics*, <http://www.econlib.org/library/Ecn/Gameth>.
26   T. Schelling. *The Strategy of Conflict* (Cambridge: Harvard University Press, 1960), p. 43.
27   A. Schleifer, "Looks are deceiving: Arab talk shows and TV journalism," *Transnational Broadcasting Studies*, No. 6 (Spring/Summer 2001), <http://www.tbsjournal.com/Archives/Spring01/Schleifer.html>.
28   G. Comstock and E. Scharrer, *Television: What's on, Who's Watching, and What it Means* (San Diego, CA: Academic Press, 1999).
29   J. Gamson, *Freaks Talk Back: Tabloid Talk Shows and Sexual Non-Conformity* (Chicago: University of Chicago Press, 1998).
30   Faisal Al Kasim, "*Crossfire*."
31   Gamson, *Freaks Talk Back*.
32   I. Fang, *Television News, Radio News* (St. Paul, MN: Rada Press, 1986).
33   *The Opposite Direction*, December 24, 2002.
34   A. Schleifer, "Looks are deceiving."

7

Women, Development and Al Jazeera: A Balance Sheet

Naomi Sakr

Development across the Arab world is being hindered by gender inequality. Such was the conclusion reached by the team of Arab thinkers who compiled the first Arab Human Development Report, published in 2002 under the joint auspices of the UN and the Arab League. Women's participation in the workforce and in political decision-making in Arab countries is lower in quantitative terms than anywhere else in the world, the report declared. It went on to warn: "Society as a whole suffers when a huge proportion of its productive potential is stifled, resulting in lower family incomes and standards of living."[1] Based on this assessment, it may reasonably be argued that marginalization and disempowerment on grounds of sex are issues of concern not only to Arab women but to the whole of Arab society. The report itself concluded that progress towards broader political and economic participation will depend on changing attitudes at all levels of society, "from top levels of government to local communities and individual households."[2]

How beneficial is it therefore for television stations serving Arab countries to address the specifics of women's inequality in programs that appear to be targeted exclusively at women? Television is a mass medium; its audiences include millions of people who may not have access to the printed press for reasons of illiteracy, limited distribution and high cost. The number of television programs of interest and relevance to ordinary people in Arab countries increased dramatically during the late 1990s, as competition for viewers and advertising revenue intensified among a proliferation of Arab satellite channels.[3] Growth in viewership and in the number of talk shows focusing on socio-political issues created an unprecedented opportunity for televised debates on women's status in the region. In some cases these debates took place in shows defined primarily by their format (face-to-face interview, two guests or panel of guests) or by their subject matter (religion, politics, law, current affairs, recent history, and so on). More often, they took place in shows clearly demarcated as intended for female audiences through titles like *Laki* (the feminine form of "for you"), *Kalam Nowaim* (*Talk of the Fair Sex*), and *Lil Nissa Faqat* (*For Women Only*).[4]

The exclusivity implied by titles like these proved contentious.[5] If women talk among themselves, asked Fairouz Nasr, Director of Development Programs for Syrian Television, "who will dialogue with men?"[6] It appeared to critics as though women were being homogenized and added into the schedules as an afterthought or sideshow. Such a trend seemed reminiscent of the Women in Development (WID) approach that international agencies had adopted in the 1970s out of concern that women were being excluded from development. The WID remedy was to treat women as a single category and help them out of their putative "private" spheres into the productive sectors of the existing economic system. In contrast, the later Gender and Development (GAD) approach took a holistic view of development that called for change in households and society at large. Questioning how and why particular gender roles and attributes are defined and assigned, GAD rejected the public–private dichotomy and examined women's situation inside the so-called private sphere as well as outside it.[7] Arguably, television programs that treat male–female power relations in the "private" realm as a matter for public dialogue among men and women could be considered compatible with a GAD approach.

Al Jazeera's programming includes the series *Lil Nissa Faqat*, in addition to periodic discussion of women's rights and responsibilities included in its other popular talk shows. This chapter draws on examples of both kinds of programming—those with single-sex and those with mixed-sex panels—to assess Al Jazeera's contribution, if any, towards rectifying women's empowerment deficit in the Arab world. The study starts by reviewing arguments for and against special women's programs. It then deploys the concept of the "counterpublic" (developed by scholars of the public sphere) as a tool with which to probe aspects of television debates about gender inequalities.

TELEVISION DEBATES AND COUNTERPUBLICS

In embarking on a discussion of television's capacity to empower women, it is useful to ask from the outset whether the medium is naturally equipped to redress women's lack of power in society or whether it is more likely to reflect it. As Gaye Tuchman said of American television in the 1970s, stereotyping and under-representation of women are often regarded as "distortion." Yet, she argued, these negative aspects may actually have "symbolically cap-ture[d]" women's real lack of power in American society.[8] In other words, the blame for unsatisfactory media treatment of women cannot be laid solely at the door of media institutions, since these are simply part of the wider fabric of power relations. Nevertheless, if the media form part of the apparatus through which gender roles are assigned, they can equally be deployed to renegotiate those assignments.

Women's employment in media institutions and media portrayal of women were identified as key global concerns in the Beijing Platform for Action at the Fourth World Conference on Women in China in 1995. Since then, efforts to end negative stereotyping and recruit more women to higher editorial ranks have had different degrees of success with different television stations, depending on the way those stations are financed and controlled. Public ser-vice broadcasters are susceptible to target-setting because of their public ownership and funding. In Germany, Spain, Italy and the Netherlands, for example, they are explicitly required to provide programming that contributes to gender equality.[9] Female senior executives at the British Broadcasting Corporation (BBC) increased from 3.6 per cent in 1985 to 30.8 per cent in 1999, after the BBC took deliberate steps to achieve a more equitable workforce balance of gender and ethnicity.[10] But such policies are not universal. Not only is independently regulated public service broadcasting absent in the Arab world, but pressure groups in the region remain unaware of its potential for giving a voice to all segments of the population.[11] Indeed, where regulations governing Arab broadcasting specifically prohibit material that criticizes religion and traditions or questions family ties and family values, the possibilities for even debating fac-tors contributing to women's disempowerment—let alone discussing how to overcome it—would seem to be severely limited.[12]

The challenge of framing gender-sensitive policies has thus been left to those Arab satellite broadcasters willing and able to avoid such stifling regulatory constraints. These have had to decide for themselves on the benefits and pitfalls of setting aside desig-nated program slots for women. Ghettoization, as the latter practice is sometimes pejoratively described, brings with it the "burden of representation," whereby "very few people with opportunities to make very few programs have to bear the responsibility for representing a diverse and complex social group."[13] Ghettoization is seen as creating more problems than it solves because it ignores the likelihood that members of an identified target group will in fact be irreconcilably split by basic political, economic and cultural differences.[14] Yet, there may also be occasions when ghettoization is a misleading term. Indeed, it is possible to regard television programs reserved for female guests and ostensibly aimed at a female audience as providing a much-needed space in which women may put their points across uninterrupted, on their own behalf. It could be said that television should provide such spaces, or else risk being accused of masking the fact that women often do have different priorities from men and different perspectives on issues of shared concern.[15]

Nancy Fraser's concept of subaltern counterpublics can help in assessing the pros and cons of discussing gender inequalities in women-only as opposed to mixed-sex forums. Fraser developed the concept in response to Jürgen Habermas's theory of the public sphere. Habermas applied the term "public sphere" to the "arena for discursive interaction"[16] that arose out of changing relations between capitalism and the state in Europe in the seventeenth and eighteenth centuries. Habermas's original account, of an egalitarian community of citizens openly, rationally and critically debating matters of public interest, has since been exposed as idealized, given the reality of exclusions based on gender and class. Yet the concept of a public sphere, where access is guaranteed to all citizens, retains normative value, since it can guide criticism of existing conditions and practices and provide a "social imaginary" to aspire to.[17] The concept becomes even richer as a theoretical tool if the discursive space to which it refers is envisaged not as an all-encompassing single sphere but a "multiplicity of dialectically related public spheres."[18] This is where the notion of the counterpublic comes in. Fraser points out that informal pressures may marginalize the contributions of members of subordinated groups, even when they are formally free to participate equally in a public sphere. Thus hierarchies may continue to function despite a pretence of participatory parity; indeed the very pretence of parity "works to the advantage of dominant groups in society and to the disadvantage of subordinates," because it leads to the strong claiming to speak in the name of the weak.[19] It is, as Fraser argues, the task of critical theory to "render visible the ways in which societal inequality infects formally inclusive existing public spheres and taints discursive interaction within them."[20] For subordinated groups, meanwhile, the task is to form subaltern counterpublics, or "parallel discursive arenas," where specific needs, objectives and strategies can be hammered out.

These insights suggest certain ways of examining whether or not programs on Al Jazeera are conducive to women's empowerment. Al Jazeera's wide geographical reach, large audience and active promotion of generally uncensored and critical discourse about subjects of general public interest make it eligible to be treated as contributing to the realization of a pan-Arab public sphere. The question for this chapter is whether *Lil Nissa Faqat*, by reserving a separate program space for women speakers, constitutes a form of ghettoization or whether it supports subaltern counterpublicity. For Fraser, the emancipatory potential of the counterpublic lies in the dialectic between its dual functions as a space both for withdrawal and regroupment of the subaltern group and also for agitational activities on behalf of that group, directed at wider publics.[21] That is to say, subaltern counterpublics are seen as having both an internal and an external orientation. They operate as a space in which participants can seek to argue out among themselves what counts as a matter of common concern to a wider public. Where such matters have hitherto been ruled off limits, the counterpublic then looks outward to contest that perception and "convince others that what in the past was not public in the sense of being a matter of common concern should now become so."[22] Fraser herself cites the issue of domestic violence, which was forced onto a public agenda through contestation in and by a feminist counterpublic.

Notions of "arguing out," "regroupment" and "contestation" help formulate questions about relevant Al Jazeera programs. It is indeed a hallmark of Al Jazeera programs that they favor contestation over consensus, because such contests are still relatively novel on Arab television and the station's management sees them as making for "interesting television."[23] Yet, there is a difference between arguing and "arguing out." Whether programs on Al Jazeera create a sense of direction or a sense of confusion regarding gender inequalities can only be answered through analysis of specific examples. Similarly, in light of the concept of "regroupment," it is worth reflecting on how these programs portray groups. Groups do not usually appear as such on television.[24] Where they are represented at all, it is generally by a single individual who will be pitted against another individual representing a different persuasion. Finally, there is the question of whether the issues identified for discussion are already widely accepted as matters of common concern to the general public or have previously remained beyond the bounds of public debate.

DISCUSSION OF WOMEN'S STATUS ON AL JAZEERA'S TOP TALK SHOWS[25]

Al Jazeera is the nearest approximation in Arab television to a public service broadcaster. Unlike the public sector monopoly broadcasters operating in most other Arab states, which are directly accountable to governments because they are supervised by ministers of information, Al Jazeera is organized in such a way as to serve and be accountable to a pan-Arab public. Its relationship with the government of Qatar, where it is based, has been likened to the relationship between the BBC and the British government,[26] in that the government has limited institutional means of day-to-day control over the station's editorial content. In addition, Al Jazeera's initial nucleus of staff was drawn from a BBC television news service in Arabic that had been closed down. These people, including the station's first two editors in chief, continued to make editorial judgments based on their understanding of BBC criteria several years after leaving the BBC.[27] Whereas Arab governments continue to fund monopoly broadcasters regardless of their profitability, Al Jazeera was established on the basis of a loan from the ruler of Qatar, with the aim of becoming self-financing through revenue from advertising, leasing of facilities and sales of exclusive film footage. This aim dictated an editorial policy geared to maximizing audiences. A Gallup poll in 2002 indicated success on this front, finding that viewers in countries such as Saudi Arabia, Kuwait, Jordan, Lebanon and Morocco were turning to Al Jazeera before other channels in order to catch up with the news.[28] On being set up in 1996, the station was initially given until the end of 2001 to become self-financing. In 2002, however, this deadline was extended, with the Qatari ruler also agreeing to inject more of his own money on an annual basis to keep the channel going.[29] On the one hand, politically motivated advertising boycotts had kept Al Jazeera's revenues artificially low.[30] On the other hand, the station had already expanded its output through development of a website and was planning further investment in a documentary channel and an English-language news channel.[31] These ventures could be seen as making a wider range of critical discourse on public affairs accessible to a wider public.

Although there is evidence to support Al Jazeera claims of editorial independence,[32] there are also noteworthy parallels between its allocation of editorial time to issues of women's empowerment and the efforts of Qatar's Emir to empower Qatari women. Qatar was the first Arab Gulf country in which women stood as candidates and voted in municipal polls, in 1999.[33] In municipal elections in 2003, the sole woman candidate won her seat after rivals stood aside.[34] The country's first female cabinet minister was appointed in May 2003, after voters had overwhelmingly approved a written constitution which guaranteed, among other things, women's right to vote and run for political office.[35] Irrespective of such developments, however, Al Jazeera had its own internal rationale during the period 1999–2003 to run items about women's status in the region and beyond, simply because these were sufficiently newsworthy and contentious to suit the station's characteristic *Crossfire* style. Controversy over women's involvement in elections in neighboring Gulf states, employment issues raised by reform programs and globalization, changes in legislation affecting women in various Arab countries, the spread of AIDS, the growth of women's organizations, the impact of conflict on Palestinian and Iraqi women—these and many other events and trends merited general coverage on the strength of their topicality alone. Al Jazeera consequently carried such coverage before *Lil Nissa Faqat* got under way at the start of 2002. After the toppling of the Taliban regime in Afghanistan in 2001, it explored the prospects for Afghan women in a program called *Oula Houroub Al Karn (First Wars of the Century)*.[36] In the same period the regular series *Al Sharia wal Hayat (Islamic Law and Life)* devoted an episode to polygamy, under the title "Polygamy: solution or problem?"[37] Earlier in 2001 the series *Bila Hudud (Without Borders)* had dealt with "The role of the Palestinian woman in the intifada."[38]

Al Sharia wal Hayat, a format copied by other Arab satellite channels, is a 90-minute program in which a prominent religious scholar, Youssef Al Qaradawi, advises on codes of conduct in Islam. His rulings have sometimes been at odds with those of Muslim scholars elsewhere. During elections in Bahrain in 2002, he formally approved women's participation as candidates, especially those past their child-bearing years. In this he was contradicted by a Saudi cleric.[39] During controversy over the appointment of Egypt's first female judge in 2003, Qaradawi approved the appointment of female judges, whereas Egypt's own most senior religious authority indicated that a female judge might be permitted to write opinions on the outcome of court cases, but not to judge the cases themselves. An episode of Qaradawi's series in February 2003 was entitled "The Islamic view of women participating in public life."[40] Since the early days of Al Jazeera, *Al Sharia wal Hayat* has been tackling questions about women's status in Islam. In 1997, an episode looked at "The Muslim woman in the West."[41] This was followed in 1998 by "The position of women in Islam," "*Misyar* marriage (a temporary marriage contract)," and "Why Islam organizes and regulates marriage."[42] Other related episodes included "Women's issues" in 1999 and "Women's liberation in the Arab world" in 2000.[43] This sample of programs does not list all relevant topics covered in the series, such as health, or all episodes during which women's status was mentioned. Even so, it gives a sense that *Al Sharia wal Hayat*, by discussing intimate personal matters like marriage and family life on television, accustomed viewers of Al Jazeera to public discussion of what goes on in the privacy of homes. A program in 2002, for example, covered "The family relationship and its effect on society," while another in 2003 tackled what it described as "Absent happiness in the life of Muslims."[44]

Al Sharia wal Hayat is interesting to the present study for three reasons. First, by providing a forum for religious opinions to be pronounced, it would appear to be designed to overcome confusion rather than create it. Second, by inspiring other Arab satellite channels to launch similar programs, it could be said to have played a part in expanding the public space available for rational discourse on matters that include gender roles and women's status. By adopting comparable formats, ART's religious affairs channel, Iqra, Abu Dhabi TV and the Egyptian Space Channel created unprecedented opportunities for women callers to discuss treatment they had received in matters of marriage and divorce. Third, through the phenomenon of intertextuality (whereby audiences inevitably and sometimes unconsciously "read" texts in relation to each other[45]), the content and tone of *Al Sharia wal Hayat* can certainly be assumed to have had repercussions in terms of audience expectations of other Al Jazeera talk shows, and vice versa. However, instead of examining specific episodes of *Al Sharia wal Hayat*, I propose now to turn the spotlight onto two talk shows in other series, in which women took part—one dealing with women's right to vote and stand for political office, the other with divorce. Aspects of these examples will be noted to allow comparison with the women-only talk show, *Lil Nissa Faqat*.

Akthar min Rai (*More Than One Opinion*), one of Al Jazeera's flagship discussion programs, is presented by Sami Haddad, a veteran of the BBC Arabic television service, who became one of the founding screen personalities of Al Jazeera. As its title implies, the point of Haddad's talk show is to highlight currents and counter-currents. An episode of the program, aired on May 28, 1999 and devoted to the political freedom of Gulf women, featured one woman and two men. The topical peg for this choice of subject was a decree by the Emir of Kuwait allowing Kuwaiti women to vote and stand as candidates in national legislative elections. The decree—being consistent with the Kuwaiti constitution, which guarantees equality between men and women—amended the country's electoral law which, by allowing male suffrage only, conflicted with the constitution. Later in 1999 (that is, after this particular episode of *Akthar min Rai* went on air), Kuwait's National Assembly overturned the emiri decree.

The guests on the show included Nouriya Sadani, long-standing campaigner for women's political rights in Kuwait and leader of two groups, the Arab Women's Development Society and Kuwaiti Women of the Twenty-First Century.[46] As a newspaper columnist and historian, Sadani has also written extensively on the subject. With her were Dr Abdel Razzaq Al Shayji, Assistant Dean of the Sharia College in Kuwait University, and Dr Abdel Hamid Al Ansari, former dean of the Sharia College at Qatar University. Sami Haddad introduced the episode by pointing out that both supporters and opponents of votes for women in Kuwait had quoted religious texts to support their arguments. He then launched the debate by asking Shayji whether men alone were responsible for public life in Kuwait, given the absence of the "other half" of society. Shayji, replying that democracy in the Gulf was still "immature," suggested that women did not regard elections as a "priority." Asked immediately by Haddad to explain, Shayji cited tradition and religion and disparaged what he called women's "little" groups in Kuwait, the purpose of which, he said, was "probably to strip women of their religion." Pressed by Haddad to cite a religious text forbidding women from choosing someone to represent them in public affairs, Shayji clarified his view to the effect that Islam allows women to vote but not to be parliamentary candidates. He indicated that it would be hard under current Kuwaiti law to allow women to vote but bar them from standing as candidates. To support his points Shayji quoted Quranic verses calling on women to "keep to their houses" and stating that men have the responsibility of providing for women.

At this, Haddad turned to Ansari for his interpretation of the first of these verses. With Ansari's reply, the "other opinion" alluded to in the series title (and in Al Jazeera's mission statement) became apparent, as he opened by disagreeing with Shayji on tradition. Restrained however by Haddad, who was still seeking a response to the point about women and their houses, Ansari declared that the consensus view of Muslim scholars was that the verse in question, being explicitly addressed to women in the family of the Prophet Mohammed, applied only to them. And yet, Ansari continued, they also left their houses when necessary. In response to questioning from Haddad, he insisted that women in the Prophet's family had been told in the Quran "You are not like other women," and that the instruction addressed to them did not apply to contemporary Muslim women.

Having established the opposing viewpoints of his two male guests, Haddad then briefly mentioned Sadani's background and asked her to comment on Shayji's opinion. Sadani's response was to point out that Shayji seemed to have no problem accepting orders from the female president of Kuwait University. Following on swiftly and addressing herself to Haddad, Sadani proceeded to dispute Haddad's introductory remarks about Kuwaiti Islamists objecting to women exercising political rights. Repeatedly blocking Haddad's attempts to interrupt, she noted that Islamist women in Kuwait were also campaigning for political rights. She applauded the head of state who, she indicated, was putting the interests of his society and country ahead of those of a few people resisting progress. Those opposing the decree, she said, should be thankful they lived in a democracy, protected by a constitution, and not in a police state. And yet, Sadani continued, despite more efforts by Haddad to cut her off, Shayji was effectively arguing against the equality enshrined in the very constitution that was protecting him.

It becomes apparent from these opening snatches that, although Sadani was in a minority of one female to three males, the more obvious outsider in this gathering was Shayji, as the sole self-professed opponent of women's political rights. The lone female guest started, as she meant to go on, by overriding interruptions for long enough to make her chosen points. The long program ended with Sadani and Shayji disagreeing over the contribution of women's organizations in Kuwait, thereby implicitly highlighting Sadani's position as spokesperson for active groups. Of the three guests, it was Sadani who literally had the last word, before Haddad turned to address his viewers and sign off.

Similarly hard-hitting debates take place on other Al Jazeera talk shows. In the series *Al Ittijah Al Muaakis* (*The Opposite Direction*), presented by Faisal Al Kasim, the format involves two guests confronting each other head to head. Al Kassim is proud that his program provides an arena for such exchanges. Off-screen, he has argued that live debates on Arab television help to liberalize attitudes to debate generally in Arab society, thereby changing a situation in which there is "no dialogue in families, no dialogue in schools" and where fathers, teachers and preachers are allowed to behave like dictators.[47] Al Kassim clearly appreciates participants who are practiced in defending their views. Referring to an episode of *Al Ittijah Al Muaakis* in which the outspoken Egyptian feminist Nawal El Saadawi took part, he once described her as having "made mincemeat" of an opponent. On another memorable occasion in 1999, his show hosted two female guests to debate the practice of polygamy. One, the Egyptian writer Safinaz Kazem, stormed out of the studio in mid-debate rather than be perceived to contradict the Quran.[48] Her sparring partner was Toujan Faisal, one of only two women ever to have been a member of the Jordanian parliament before it introduced a six-seat quota for women in 2003.[49]

On February 22, 2000, an edition of *Al Ittijah Al Muaakis* tackled the practice of *khula*, which had just been introduced in Egypt as an alternative to protracted litigation for women seeking divorce. Under *khula*, a woman is permitted to divorce her husband unilaterally and without delay on condition she returns her dowry and surrenders all financial rights, regardless of the length of her marriage and the reasons for her decision to end it. Although the Egyptian parliament approved the introduction of *khula*, it did not do so without a fight. Intense controversy, combined with wide public interest inside and outside Egypt, made the topic highly suitable for *Al Ittijah Al Muaakis*. The episode devoted to *khula* brought together two Egyptians: Farida Al Naqqash, female head of the Progressive Women's Union, and Ibrahim Al Kholy, a male professor from the University of Al Azhar in Cairo.

After a lengthy preamble setting out the issues, Al Kasim kicked off the debate by challenging Kholy to justify the "revolution" going on among men of religion just because women were "taking a few of their usurped rights." Rejecting the term "revolution," Kholy began with a defense of the system of religious scholars and a defense of women's rights in Islam, challenging "anyone" to name a religion that "gave" women more than Islam had given them. His opposition to *khula*, he said, was based on corruption in the judicial system, where lawyers were "messing around" and taking advantage of other people's problems. Kholy said changes in the courts would be preferable to *khula* as a means of ending the backlog of protracted divorce cases raised by women. He saw *khula* as opening the way to blackmail between couples. Naqqash, having briefly interrupted Kholy to correct the title of an official he had referred to, then proceeded (with encouragement from Al Kasim) to set out her opinion. She cited specific cases in which women had been denied the right to divorce. Apparently aware of viewers' concern that change was being imposed from abroad, Naqqash moved to pre-empt such a notion. She gave statistics for women's contribution to the economy, saying that these signaled a "new reality" and a need for "radical change" in the family. The "old relationship," according to Naqqash, was based "not on equality or justice but on oppression."

When male callers to the program suggested that Muslim women were better off than women in the West, Naqqash insisted that women wanted only justice and equality in accordance with models that existed in the region in an earlier era. "Arab houses are closed," she said, and "behind closed doors" there is suffering, isolation and enslavement. When Kholy argued that injured women already had the right to seek divorce, Naqqash pointed out that a woman suing for divorce through the courts could wait ten years for a settlement. In heated exchanges, the two guests stood their ground, battling to make themselves heard. Kholy maintained that men and women were suffering because secular laws were being used instead of Islamic law. Naqqash, goaded at one point by Al Kasim's interjection that women and the family were seen by some as the last bastion of Arab culture, responded that the last bastion would be formidable if built on love and compassion, not oppression and humiliation. Quoting the view expressed by some sheikhs that unveiled women bring dishonor and defeat on the whole nation, she seized the opportunity to stress that "secular" did not mean "atheist" or "against religion." The program ended with Kholy insisting that the point of reference should be the "Holy Book" and the traditions of the Prophet, and Al Kasim announcing "our time is up."

Here, as in the earlier example from *Akthar min Rai*, the female guest chosen to debate a controversial topic had long experience in parrying hostility and speaking plainly about actual examples of injustice visited upon a large group of people. Seizing on Kholy's statistic that corruption had caused a backlog of 1.5 million divorce cases, Naqqash said that nearly half of these cases had been raised by women whose husbands had injured them physically. For a woman to prove injury, Naqqash explained graphically, she had to display a blinded eye, broken leg or cut hand that a judge could see for himself. Invisible injuries were much harder to prove. With Al Kasim having suggested in his first question to Kholy that women's rights had been "usurped," the latter—being opposed to speedier divorce for women—was put on the defensive. In these episodes of *Akthar min Rai* and *Al Ittijah Al Muaakis*, women were numerically in a minority. Formally, this might be perceived as a lack of parity in participation. Informally, however, this disadvantage was mitigated by the factors outlined above. The programs demonstrated strong feelings and differing views with no attempt at resolution or summing up.

AL JAZEERA'S *LIL NISSA FAQAT*

Like Al Jazeera's other talk shows, the weekly *Lil Nissa Faqat* is a regular fixture in the station's schedules. How much of a fixture was demonstrated when it remained on air during the Israeli siege of Palestinian towns that started in March 2002 while some other programs were temporarily shelved at this time to make way for extended daily reports of the siege. In 2003, however, *Lil Nissa Faqat* lost its place for a few weeks to coverage of the invasion of Iraq, as Al Jazeera and other Arab satellite channels competed to be first with breaking news. As this scheduling policy confirms, timeliness is not a priority element of *Lil Nissa Faqat*. Since it started in 2002, its discussion topics have sometimes been prompted by events, as in the aftermath of the US-led invasion of Iraq, the elections in Yemen or the Earth Summit.[50] At other times, however, the program makers have chosen subjects of perennial interest to do with marriage and family relationships. On still other occasions, they have stepped back to take a fresh look at everyday phenomena such as popular sayings, social customs and women's magazines. Topics chosen for the series are equally likely to relate to what have traditionally been perceived as the public or private spheres, either separately or within the same program.

Topics debated on *Lil Nissa Faqat* have included: exchange of roles between men and women, violence against women, women's writing, businesswomen and Arab women's role in building the economy, women in the spotlight, the effect of September 11 on

Arab and Muslim women, women and fulfillment, women in popular sayings, the image of Arab women in video clips, the position of
women in war, the position of Arab women in professional unions,
the future of Arab women's movements, the understanding of gender, women and religious rulings, women and political change in
Iraq, the mother and her teenage daughter, women and diplomatic
work, and a husband's use of his wife's money.

Lil Nissa Faqat differs from either *Akthar min Rai* or *Al Ittijah Al
Muaakis* in having had a much shorter history, as well as a succession of four different presenters during its first two years. The first of
these, Khadija bin Ganna, who reportedly pushed for the program's
creation, was one of the original Al Jazeera team drawn from the
BBC Arabic Television Service. Muntaha Al Romhi, who succeeded
bin Ganna before leaving Al Jazeera in early 2003 for Al Arabiya,
shared a similar background. Al Romhi was followed by Laila
Chaieb, who in turn was followed by Lona Al Shebel. As prominent
women on Al Jazeera, they were clearly in a numerical minority,
along with the station's few female news reporters, including its
Ramallah correspondent Shereen Abu Aqla. The two episodes of *Lil
Nissa Faqat* described below were both screened in October 2002
while the program was being presented by Muntaha Al Romhi.
Although selected almost at random, as two episodes aired in quick
succession, it so happens that the ones chosen lend themselves to
comparison in terms of subject matter with the two shows (on Gulf
women's political participation and divorce law) discussed in the
previous section. One, broadcast on October 14, 2002, dealt with
the position of Gulf women in relation to leadership and management roles. The other, aired on October 28, 2002, was entitled
"Women's attitude to polygamy."

The *Lil Nissa Faqat* focus on Gulf women and leadership was
timed to coincide with a symposium taking place under the patron-
age of Qatar's first lady, Sheikha Moza, on women's advancement in
the six Gulf Co-operation Council countries. It featured three
panelists from Bahrain, Qatar and Oman. Dr Wajiha Sadiq Al
Baharna was introduced as head of the Bahrain Women's Society
and deputy head of the Society for Cultural and Social Innovation.
Dr Zakiya Ali Mallallah Abdel Aziz was described as head of the
Research Unit and Information Centre in the Qatari Public Health
Ministry's Pharmaceutical Administration. The third guest was
Mrs Aida Bint Salim Al Hajri, Director of Studies and Research in
Oman's Ministry of Social Development. Before presenting her

guests, however, Muntaha Al Romhi launched the program by explaining the issue to be discussed. The question, she said, was one of priorities. Should proficient and able women, faced with an enduring multitude of obstacles to entering jobs with executive authority, take a gradualist approach to reaching their strategic objectives, given the deeply-rooted social norms that currently bar them from such jobs? Or should deliberate steps be taken to enable them to break into such fields? How much distance separates qualified women from decision-making circles, asked Al Romhi, and what are the strategic landmarks on the way?

Having thus narrowed the debate to one around optimum methods of achieving a mutually agreed end, Al Romhi brought her guests into the discussion by appealing to Mallallah for information. Why, she wondered, was there such a big discrepancy between the number of Gulf women with higher degrees and the number occupying leadership positions in either the public or private sector? Mallallah replied by confirming that there was indeed a serious gap. She then proceeded directly to identify obstacles placed in front of women from their earliest upbringing as young girls. Arguing that traditions and customs put men in authority over women throughout their lives, she noted that, as girls grow up, they are subject to interference in what they wear, where they go, where they work and whether they can travel to gain experience and education. "These," she said, "are things we have all lived through, suffered from and still suffer from." Baharna, the next guest to speak, took Dr Zakiya's points further by noting that doubts expressed about women's leadership ability instilled doubts in women themselves and undermined their confidence. When Bint Salim's turn came to contribute, she began by highlighting rapid changes in women's circumstances in the Gulf during the second half of the twentieth century, including the rise of businesswomen. Soon, however, she was endorsing the previous speakers' arguments about upbringing, adding that female voters are more inclined to vote for male rather than female candidates. Girls, she said, are brought up to see their brothers and fathers as the ones who take decisions. On marriage, the decision-making role falls to the husband. The expectation that men will take decisions is consequently transferred to the workplace, Bint Salim said.

Other voices on the topic were introduced by means of a short report. Here women attending the Doha symposium were interviewed to say whether women should wait for gradual social change to elevate them to directorships or whether they should be calling for political intervention to accelerate that change. The report concluded that it was now up to women to push for equal opportunities while also boosting their skills and experience. It was followed by calls from viewers who, as often in *Lil Nissa Faqat* phone-ins, were predominantly men. The first proved to be out of step with the assumptions underlying the program, as he was strongly opposed to women becoming rulers, ministers or judges. He cited religious texts to argue that women should stay at home, not occupy positions of authority and not reveal any part of their anatomy. At this Baharna insisted, despite Al Romhi's cautioning against discussion of religious rulings, on stating that God had created men and women equally and given them equal responsibility for stewardship of the earth. When Al Romhi observed that Balkis was mentioned in the Quran as a wise female leader, Baharna concurred. The second caller declared that women had been claiming for the past 50 years that they were oppressed. When repeatedly urged by Al Romhi to be clear about whether or not he thought they were oppressed, he threatened to end the call. The program finally ended as an academic conference panel might, with a round-up of one-liners from each guest.

Several observations can be made about this episode of *Lil Nissa Faqat*. The first has to do with the way its assumptions and approach differed from those of the mixed-sex debates previously discussed. Instead of starting, as one of those debates did, by inviting a guest to argue against women's political participation, this program took as its starting point the view that qualified women should be aiming for decision-making jobs and that the subject of debate was not whether to aim for them but how. Second, an obvious and explicit level of agreement among all participants and the presenter allowed them to build on each other's contributions. In observing at one point that "these are things we have all lived through," Mallallah even took the initiative of speaking on the others' behalf and was not contradicted. Whereas Sami Haddad in his program on female suffrage blocked early attempts to discuss tradition, the guests in this show were quickly able to articulate their own shared experiences of traditions prevalent in the raising of girl children in the Gulf. In this way, a debate that was apparently focused on public affairs soon drew in evidence and explanations from the supposedly private territory of families and homes. Third, the program did not end with a slanging match in full swing. Instead it was rounded off with the producer establishing a sense of direction through final proposals for action from her panelists. As will be seen, these conventions were not so much in evidence in the program two weeks later on women's attitudes to polygamy, which featured guests with opposing views on a contentious subject.

Muntaha Al Romhi introduced the debate on polygamy by noting that an old topic had been given a new twist by the emergence of female voices calling for men to be allowed to take more than one wife. Some women, she explained, had come to see the abolition of polygyny as protecting men and hurting women, because it sanctioned men abandoning their first wives. By conveying the view that polygyny could "guarantee women the achievement of motherhood," Al Romhi seemed to allude implicitly to existing rules giving divorced men custody over their children above a certain age. Having briefly introduced the "new thinking" in this manner, Al Romhi pointed out that the program was to discover the reasons for it. She then presented her three guests: Hiyam Darbak, Egyptian media writer and head of the Society Calling for Polygamy; Afaf Al Sayyid, "active" writer from Egypt; and, via satellite from Rabat, the writer and thinker Khadija Moufied, head of the Society for Women's Custody (of children). Addressing both guests and viewers, Al Romhi stressed that the aim of the program was not to deal with the Islamic law (Sharia) aspects of the issue but to "open the door wide to discuss the logic of women's voices calling for or against polygyny."

Turning first to Darbak, Al Romhi reiterated that there was nothing new in women rejecting polygyny; what's new, she said, was women's tendency to support it. Mentioning again that Darbak headed a society calling for polygamy, she asked for her interpretation of this "radical change" in women's attitudes. Darbak started off with an anecdote, recounting how a close friend of hers had discovered that her husband had married a second wife three years earlier. Her friend's husband had treated her nicely during that time, but as soon as she discovered the second marriage she felt she had to divorce him. Darbak told viewers the advice she had given her friend. This was to remember that the husband had not committed adultery or gone against his religion and that divorce would complicate the problem. In fact, divorce would hurt the three children of the first marriage, persecute the second wife and destroy the first household. Concluding her narrative, Darbak said her friend had taken the advice and found that her husband felt indebted to her for not destroying the first marriage or depriving him of the children.

Sayyid had a different interpretation from Darbak's. Arguing that promoting polygyny would discourage men from seeking fulfilment from their first marriage, Sayyid said it would lead men to keep searching for satisfaction through a second, third, or fourth wife. Darbak's society was only a number of individuals, she noted, not a significant phenomenon in relation to the population as a whole. The third guest, Moufied, offered yet another view in defining polygyny as a right for women as well as men. Asked what she meant by that, Moufied gave her view that Islam allowed men to have more than one wife in order to solve problems. It had not legislated for polygyny, she said, but had regulated it and put it in a legal framework. Yet men had monopolized the interpretation of Islamic law and turned it to their own benefit. Women's voices on the subject had been absent, she continued. Women needed to know about Islamic law and had to avoid regarding certain matters as taboo. Since wives could not restrain their husbands, Moufied argued, they should, if necessary, uphold their right to remain as the first wife. This was a right, not a deprivation, she explained.

The outside report compiled for this program consisted mainly of vox pops—soundbites from individuals intercepted on the street in Arab countries and asked for their views on the principle of polygyny. This straw poll brought in the opinions of eight men and two women in the United Arab Emirates, six women and two girls in Lebanon and three men and three women in Egypt. None of the female interviewees corroborated the stance taken by Darbak or Moufied. Instead they expressed either flat rejection or grudging and conditional acceptance based on the need to observe Islam. A female caller to the program, who described herself as young, religious and a defender of Islamic law, voiced concern that Darbak's approach risked weakening a wife's position vis-à-vis her husband, as he could use an additional marriage to "defeat her because she has a strong personality." The program ended with Sayyid putting Darbak on the spot. Asked by Al Romhi to state whether she would accept that her husband marries another wife, Darbak said that, if he was ready to follow his desires come what may, it was up to her to ensure he took the route permitted under Islamic law. With Sayyid pressing Darbak to be clearer about her own motivation, Al Romhi intervened to apologize that time was up and remark that the dialogue would have to continue off the air.

It is hard to imagine the range of views expressed in this program having had an equal chance of being aired in a talk show involving both women and men. Discussions of polygyny in a mixed-sex panel risk being perceived as a dichotomous contest of male versus female. The two women speaking up for polygyny in the Al Jazeera debate were doing so in what they claimed to be the interests of women. By providing space for them to speak their minds, the program demonstrated that the two did not share the same rationale and that there could be nuances of interpretation. This was also possible because the debate was not conceived as a clash of opposing viewpoints but as an attempt to examine the thinking of those female defenders of polygyny who claim to be pro-women. The program differed in format and tone from the earlier one on Gulf women and leadership jobs. Yet, in the same way that the previous episode highlighted inequalities in child-rearing, this one enabled public discussion of inequalities in marital commitment.

CONCLUSION

Based on a brief assessment of the way gender inequalities are confronted in Al Jazeera's programs and a more detailed assessment of four specific programs, it can be argued that Al Jazeera has expanded the space for critical and contestatory discursive interaction over issues related to women's empowerment. This assessment is based on qualitative, not quantitative criteria. The conclusion is not that *Lil Nissa Faqat* contributed to a net expansion of discursive space through the mere insertion of a weekly slot for all-women debates. Instead, it made this contribution through the nature and management of those debates. For one thing, they complemented discussions already taking place among all-male or mixed-sex panels on Al Jazeera's other talk shows. For another, they allowed female representatives of groups and opinions in wider society to handle gender issues holistically, switching freely back and forth between the so-called public and private spheres, without their contributions being subject to reinterpretation, misrepresentation or even validation by male speakers or presenters.

Far from ghettoizing discussion of gender inequality, *Lil Nissa Faqat* added an extra dimension for discussion. In this additional space, women gained the opportunity to adopt debating styles that differed from the head-to-head clashes of other Al Jazeera talk shows. The format of the two programs discussed here, consisting of a three-woman panel, a female presenter and short documentary clips containing interviews and vox pops, not only increased the number of voices and opinions represented but created new opportunities for participants to gain media exposure and experience. Moreover, it was clear that, although supposedly a "women's program," *Lil Nissa Faqat* had no brief to homogenize women. Quite the contrary, the debating agendas set out at the start of both episodes highlighted the aim of representing a plurality of women's views about priorities and objectives in pursuit of their own interests and those of society at large. By taking calls from male viewers, the series demonstrated how a space that has been reserved for agendas decided and pursued by women can also be outward looking. In these circumstances, callers who opposed gender equality found themselves momentarily alone as they sought to defend their views on air.

The concept of the counterpublic proved highly revealing in assessing Al Jazeera's contribution to development. When gender inequality impedes development, one way to confront it is through public discourse. But, no matter how well intentioned, public debates about inequality will remain lopsided if groups on the receiving end of unequal treatment can only ever discuss their treatment with those who are complicit in handing it out. The group seeking redress needs its own separate spaces in which to articulate shared concerns, free from manipulation or domination. In *Lil Nissa Faqat*, Al Jazeera provided something approximating to such a space.

NOTES

1   UNDP, *Arab Human Development Report 2002* (Oxford: Oxford University Press), p. 3.
2   Ibid., p. 11.
3   Naomi Sakr, *Satellite Realms: Transnational Television, Globalization and the Middle East* (London: I.B. Tauris, 2001); Naomi Sakr "Maverick or model?: Al Jazeera's impact on Arab satellite television," in Jean Chalaby (ed.), *Transnational Television Worldwide* (London: I.B. Tauris, 2005), pp. 66–95.
4   These titles were adopted by Abu Dhabi TV, Middle East Broadcasting Centre (MBC) and Al Jazeera Satellite Channel, respectively.
5   Objections were voiced to this author by a number of female media professionals working in the Arab media.
6   Quoted in Noureddin Aathar, "Women's screens: return to the pre-Islamic age," *Al Hayat*, September 6, 2003.
7   Nalini Visvanathan, "Introduction to Part 1," in Nalini Visvanathan, Lynn Duggan, Laurie Nisonoff and Nan Wiegersma (eds), *The Women, Gender and Development Reader* (London: Zed Books, 1997), pp. 18–19.
8   Gaye Tuchman, "Women's depiction by the mass media," *Signs*, Vol. 3 (1979), condensed and republished in Helen Baehr and Ann Gray (eds), *Turning It On: A Reader in Women and Media* (London: Arnold, 1996), p. 12.

9   Tomas Coppens, "The goal of public broadcasting: a comparative study of the missions, tasks and roles of public broadcasters in 13 European countries." Paper presented to the Third Annual Conference of the Media Communication and Cultural Studies Association, London, January 2002.

10 Caroline Millington, "Getting in and getting on: women and radio management at the BBC," in Caroline Mitchell (ed.), *Women and Radio: Airing Differences* (London: Routledge, 2000), pp. 211–12.

11 Dima Dabbous-Sensenig, "The Arab world and the challenge of introducing gender-sensitive communication policies." Paper presented to the Expert Group Meeting of the UN Division for the Advancement of Women on Participation and Access of Women to the Media, Beirut, November 12–15, 2002.

12 Naomi Sakr, "Seen and starting to be heard: women and the Arab media in a decade of change," *Social Research*, Vol. 69, No. 3 (Fall 2002), p. 841.

13 Jane Arthurs, "Women and television," in Stuart Hood (ed.), *Behind the Screens: The Structure of British Television* (London: Lawrence and Wishart, 1994), pp. 83–4.

14 Ibid.

15 Ros Coward, "Women's programs: why not?," in Helen Baehr and Gillian Dyer (eds), *Boxed In: Women and Television* (London: Pandora Press, 1987), p. 105.

16 This terminology relating to the public sphere is drawn from Nancy Fraser's formulation in her "Rethinking the public sphere: a contribution to the critique of actually existing democracy," in Craig Calhoun (ed.), *Habermas and the Public Sphere* (Cambridge: MIT Press, 1992), pp. 110–11.

17 Lisa McGlaughlin, "From excess to access: feminist political agency in the public sphere," *Javnost/The Public*, Vol. 2, No. 4 (1995), p. 37.

18 Robert Asen and Daniel C. Brouwer, "Introduction: reconfigurations of the public sphere," in Robert Asen and Daniel C. Brouwer (eds), *Counterpublics and the State* (Albany: State University of New York Press, 2001), p. 6.

19 Fraser, "Rethinking the public sphere," pp. 120, 123.

20 Ibid., p. 121.

21 Ibid., p. 124.

22 Ibid., p. 129.

23 According to Mohammed Jassim Al Ali, speaking as Al Jazeera's General Manager. See Chris Forrester, "Broadcast censorship: it's a question of culture," *Middle East Broadcast & Satellite*, Vol. 6, No. 7 (October 1999), p. 15.

24 Leonor Camauër, "Women's movements, public spheres and the media: a research strategy for studying women's movements' publicist practices," in Annabelle Sreberny and Liesbet van Zoonen (eds), *Gender, Politics and Communication* (Cresskill: Hampton Press, 2000), p. 175.

25 Discussion of specific programs in this and the following section is based on verbatim transcripts posted on Al Jazeera's website. The author thanks her husband, Ahmad Sakr, for help with Arabic–English translation.

26 Brian Whitaker, "Battle station," *Guardian*, February 7, 2003.

27   "From day one most of our editorial staff were from this BBC envir-
     onment," Ibrahim Helal told an interviewer in 2001. "Even after five
     years if we're in doubt in a certain situation, we convene and ask our-
     selves, if we were in London now what would we do." See Sarah Sullivan,
     "The courting of Al Jazeera," *Transnational Broadcasting Studies*,
     No. 7 (Fall/Winter 2001), <http://tbsjournal.com/Archives/Fall01/
     Jazeera_sjs.html>.

28   "Viewers say Al Jazeera objective and daring," *Gulf News*, November 21,
     2002.

29   Albawaba.com, "Al Jazeera struggles from beneath financial pressures,"
     Global Vision News Network (gvnews.net), November 1, 2002.

30   According to internal estimates compiled by the Pan-Arab Research
     Centre (PARC), Al Jazeera achieved advertising income of very roughly
     US$48 million in the first nine months of 2002, compared with levels of
     US$174 million for MBC, US$133 million for LBC-Sat, US$115 million
     for Future International and US$ 74 million for Abu Dhabi TV.

31   Abdullah Schleifer, "Interview with Mohammed Jasim Al Ali, Managing
     Director, Al Jazeera," *Transnational Broadcasting Studies*, No. 10 (Spring/
     Summer 2003), <http://www.tbsjournal.com/Archives/Spring03/
     jasim.html>.

32   Sakr, "Maverick or model?"

33   Universal adult suffrage came later to Oman and Bahrain. National
     Assembly elections in Kuwait in 2003, as previously, were by male suf-
     frage only. By late 2003, legislative elections had yet to be introduced in
     the UAE. October 2003 saw the Saudi government promising elections
     but without stating that women would have the vote.

34   "Qatar appoints first woman cabinet minister," *Middle East Times*, May 9,
     2003.

35   Ibid.

36   First screened on November 24, 2001.

37   First screened on December 30, 2001.

38   First screened on May 30, 2001.

39   Anthony Shadid, "Maverick cleric is a hit on Arab TV," *Washington Post*,
     February 14, 2003.

40   First screened on February 9, 2003.

41   First screened on October 5, 1997.

42   First screened on March 15, May 3, and October 4, 1998.

43   First screened on September 5, 1999 and March 5, 2000.

44   First screened on August 11, 2002 and August 17, 2003.

45   John Fiske, *Television Culture* (London: Routledge, 1987), p. 108.

46   See Haya Al Mughni and Mary Ann Tétreault, "Engagement in the pub-
     lic sphere: women and the press in Kuwait," in Naomi Sakr (ed.), *Women
     and Media in the Middle East* (London: I.B. Tauris, 2004), pp. 132 and 134.

47   Comments on "The centrality of live talks in Arab satellite broadcast-
     ing," made at the conference on Arab Satellite Broadcasting in the Age of
     Globalization, University of Cambridge, November 2002.

48   Mohammed El-Nawawy and Adel Iskandar Farag, *Al Jazeera: How the Free
     Arab News Network Scooped the World and Changed the Middle East*
     (Boulder: Westview Press, 2002), p. 98.

49 Rana Husseini, "53 women express interest in running for Lower House," *Jordan Times*, March 4, 2003.

50 "Women and political change in Iraq" was first screened on May 12, 2003. "Women's defeat in the Yemeni elections" was first screened on May 26, 2003. "Arab women and the Earth Summit in Johannesburg" was first screened on September 2, 2002.

III

Al Jazeera and Regional Crises

8

Al Jazeera and the War in Afghanistan: A Delivery System or a Mouthpiece?

Ehab Y. Bessaiso

Few would probably disagree with the contention that the real battle in the war in Afghanistan took place on the airwaves. In this widely televised battle, Al Jazeera was a player to contend with. Its exclusive coverage of the war, at least in its early stages, not only catapulted it to international prominence but also sparked a blaze of controversy. While Al Jazeera claims that by broadcasting bin Laden's tapes and by showing images of civilian casualties, it gave its audience the chance to hear the other side of the story, the US—which was not able to control the flow of information from the battlefield—maintains that bin Laden's communication with Al Jazeera deliberately fanned the flames of Muslim outrage and Arab hatred for the US. Focusing on the controversial coverage of the war on Afghanistan, this chapter examines whether Al Jazeera acted as a delivery system or as mouthpiece for bin Laden and his Al Qaeda network.

While American and British troops were bombing Afghanistan, Osama bin Laden was allowed to rebut the Western viewpoint through Al Jazeera. The channel formed what could be described as a "delivery system" to "bomb" the Arab and Muslim world with bin Laden's ideas, explanations and views. During the war on Afghanistan, Al Jazeera transmitted the first video message from Al Qaeda and bin Laden. Several video messages followed on different occasions. The released tapes indicated that bin Laden was well prepared for the American and British attacks. The carefully staged videotapes suggest that, while totally outgunned by his opponents, bin Laden was fully aware of the importance of the propaganda battle that would accompany the military conflict—so much so that some observers think that the real battle took place on the airwaves of Al Jazeera. The ensuing events changed the Western perception of Al Jazeera from a "phenomenon of democracy" to a "mouthpiece of bin Laden"— although Al Jazeera perceives itself as nothing more than a delivery system in a competitive media environment.

Following the first aired message, Al Jazeera was criticized for providing bin Laden with the opportunity to state that the war in Afghanistan was "a religious war" and to call on Muslims throughout the world to join this "holy war." Renaming the war, applying one of the common propaganda tactics,[1] pushed Western leaders to strongly deny any link between Islam as a religion and the so-called War on Terrorism. Meanwhile, bin Laden was exploiting the anger of the Arab and Muslim societies caused by the US foreign policy in the Middle East, its military presence in Saudi Arabia and other Gulf states, and its unconditional support for Israel in its occupation of the Palestinian Territories. He presented himself to the Muslims and Arabs as a "hero" whose ultimate goal was to purge the Holy Land and to liberate Palestine. In the first video released by Al Jazeera, bin Laden declared his intention to tap into the vein of Arab discontent. It became obvious that, without Al Jazeera, bin Laden could not spread his message and proclaim himself as a "liberator." Bin Laden tried to promote opposition in the Arab streets against the US war in Afghanistan. This message emphasized that the war was against Islam and Muslims and not on terrorism, as the Americans claimed. Bin Laden's communication with the media skewed the coverage of the September 11 attacks. He wanted to justify his acts as retaliation against US policy in the region and America's support of Israel. At the same time, he wanted to raise questions in the West in general and the US in particular about the reason behind his acts.

In *Terrorism and the Media*, Brigitte L. Nacos argues that it is through the media that international terrorists gain access to the public at large and to the decision-makers of their target society. In her view, "violent incidents can advance the terrorists' goal only if these kinds of incidents are widely reported. For this reason the press is frequently accused of providing terrorists their lifeblood or oxygen in the form of publicity."[2] Bin Laden wanted access to international public opinion and chose Al Jazeera to deliver his messages. These were consumed as prime time news on TV and front-page articles in newspapers throughout the world. The West's view of Al Jazeera's handling of the news during the war on Afghanistan was highly critical. American and British officials and media outlets accused the Qatari channel of inciting hatred and acting as bin Laden's loudspeaker for his propaganda. Accordingly, the channel was vilified and described as highly irresponsible.

For its part, Al Jazeera claimed that by broadcasting bin Laden's messages it gave its audience the chance to hear the other side of the story and to know more about the most "wanted man" in the world. Ibrahim Helal, Al Jazeera's chief news editor, asserted that the bin Laden videotapes were initially available to many other networks, but the central question was the ability of these networks to take a decision to air the tapes or not.[3] Helal justified the decision to air them:

> The supporters of bin Laden tried to deliver his messages in any possible way to the world. They have contacted some other Arab and non-Arab networks before seeking Al Jazeera, but those networks refused to communicate with them because "they are terrorists." For us they are terrorists and we are journalists looking for news.[4]

Helal justified transmitting bin Laden's videotapes on grounds that they presented the other side of the issue and, in the case of bin Laden, the other side of the story is important because the whole world is looking for him: "Broadcasting these videotapes indicated the red lines in the Western media and proved that objectivity and neutrality do not exist even in what they call 'the Land of Freedom'."[5] The common view at Al Jazeera was that bin Laden chose their channel partly because they were in Kabul, and thus it was easy to reach them, and partly because it broadcast in Arabic, bin Laden's own language.

However, these explanations did not affect the American position towards the channel. When Al Jazeera broadcast bin Laden's videotapes, it prompted a current of anger and criticism. On the first day of the bombing campaign in Afghanistan, Secretary of State Colin Powell denounced the network for airing "vitriolic, irresponsible statements"; he criticized it for broadcasting bin Laden's threat of a "terrorist war," which was picked up by every American network and played to the horror and shock of many.[6] National Security Advisor Condoleezza Rice requested networks not to air Al Jazeera's bin Laden footage because it might be transmitting coded messages, although "many realized that terrorists could easily get bin Laden's alleged messages through web or satellite broadcasts."[7] Later on, this rationale clearly became an American strategy to control the flow of information and to isolate bin Laden and the Taliban in order to win over public opinion in the campaign against "terrorism." It is hardly surprising that American news outlets echoed the official position, describing Al Jazeera as a channel that "often slants its news with a vicious anti-Israeli and anti-American bias" and airs "deeply irresponsible reporting [that] reinforces the region's anti-American view."[8] The American administration's requests to isolate bin Laden and to face Al Jazeera probably opened the door for some writers to launch a campaign against Al Jazeera and to call for its closure. In a withering critique, Zev Chafets described Al Jazeera as an Arab propaganda machine in the guise of real journalism:

> Al Jazeera is far from legitimate. It is an Arab propaganda outfit controlled by the medieval government of Qatar that masquerades as a real media company. For years, it has inflamed the Arab world against the United States and its allies. Its occasional interviews with Western statesmen ... are designed to provide it with a fig leaf of objectivity ... Dealing with Al Jazeera is a job for the military. Shutting it down should be an immediate priority because, left alone, it has the power to poison the air more efficiently and lethally than anthrax ever could.[9]

During the 1991 Gulf War, the Americans were able to control the flow of information from the battlefield. According to Hudson and Stanier, the American administration viewed four aspects of media reporting which could prove critical to their cause: the need to maintain the security of their plans; the need to convince the world of the justice of their cause; the need to avoid reporting anything that might damage the coalition with their allies; and finally the need to avoid reporting or showing anything that might affect the support of their own people at home.[10] The monopoly of live coverage, which CNN secured during that war, helped the American administration maintain these aspects. However, during the war in Afghanistan, the situation was different. The need to maintain these four aspects of media reporting still existed, only the monopoly of live coverage from Afghanistan lay this time in the hands of a 24-hour Arab news channel. The Western media found themselves relying on a relatively new and obscure network for the only live footage available from Afghanistan. The major American concern was that the exclusive coverage by Al Jazeera of the consequences of the war and the transmition of bin Laden's statements would have the undesired effect of galvanizing Arab support for his cause by identifying his actions with the suffering of the Palestinians and the plight of the Iraqis. The US government criticized Al Jazeera's coverage, expressed great displeasure with its extensive coverage of anti-American sentiments following the September 11 attacks and objected to the station's repeated airing of its exclusive 1998 interview with Osama bin Laden.[11] White House spokesman Ari Fleischer justified the American position against Al Jazeera on grounds that "at best, Osama bin Laden's message is propaganda, calling on people to kill Americans. At worst, he could be issuing orders to his followers to initiate such attacks."[12]

For Warren Richey, three of the most defining images of America's War on Terrorism did not come from CNN, the BBC or any other Western network, but from Al Jazeera. These images depicted Osama bin Laden flanked by his chief aids in an Afghan mountain hideout, a bin Laden spokesman delivering a chilling threat that "the storm of airplanes will not be calmed," and young Afghan children bruised and bandaged in Kabul hospital beds after US military bombing raids in Afghanistan.[13] According to the *Guardian*, the White House was concerned about the impact of reports on civilian causalities from the US bombing. This pushed the US press outlets to reduce the amount of detailed coverage in their reports for the sake of national security, especially when the reports involved the activities of special forces. The five major US networks agreed to censor themselves at the request of "an administration increasingly anxious that it is losing the propaganda war."[14] For instance, CNN openly said that it would not air any of bin Laden's addresses live and promised "to consider guidance from appropriate authorities" in deciding "what to broadcast."[15] To further isolate bin Laden, the US administration asked Qatar to rein in Al Jazeera. The Emir of Qatar confirmed after a meeting with Colin Powell in Washington that he had been asked to exert influence on the Qatari channel.[16] The US embassy in Doha even filed a formal diplomatic complaint about Al Jazeera with the Qatari government. As if this were not enough, Al Jazeera's bureau in Kabul was bombed on November 12, 2001, allegedly by mistake.

The fear of undermining the justice of their cause and losing the precarious coalition with their allies apparently brought several prominent American and British politicians, diplomats and spokesmen to appear on Al Jazeera after the first strike on Afghanistan. According to the *Washington Post*, these interviews with Al Jazeera were a sign of the leaders' intensifying interest in a "public diplomacy" which seeks to sell the American policies to the public, especially in the Middle East where the US position has been unpopular for years: "Nearly five weeks into the war on terrorism, numerous government officials and outside experts say the United States badly needs improved capabilities on the propaganda front, especially as it seeks the support of countries whose publics react negatively."[17]

Naturally, the United States was not alone in what has been identified as a "propaganda war." Feeling that the West was starting to lose the propaganda war in the Arab world, No. 10 Downing Street also joined the battle by taking serious measures. The *Daily Telegraph* asserted that Al Jazeera could be banned from broadcasting in Britain if its transmission of Osama bin Laden's video statement was perceived as inciting racial and religious hatred: "The Independent Television Commission would be monitoring Al Jazeera's output in order to examine the content of bin Laden's video in which he urged Muslims to wage religious war on the 'infidel'."[18] The British government had serious concerns about the influence of Al Jazeera, especially since the channel had been available free in the UK since August 2001 in 6 million British homes subscribing to Sky Digital, providing a potential audience of 10 million people in the country.[19] This could be one of the factors that led the Prime Minister, Tony Blair, to give an interview to Al Jazeera, in an attempt to convey to Muslims in the UK and elsewhere the message that the war was not against Islam. According to the *Independent*, the interview was part of Britain's policy of "winning hearts and minds"[20] and intended to correct the perception about the coalition in the Arab world. At the same time, Whitehall was doing its utmost, in private briefings, to discredit Al Jazeera and to present it as "naturally biased towards the Taliban/Osama bin Laden cause" and was playing a major role in losing the propaganda war in that part of the world.[21]

Meanwhile, the British tabloids launched their own war on Al Jazeera. On the day following the interview with the Prime Minister, the *Sun* newspaper (which is owned by Rupert Murdoch, the Australian-born media magnate who also owns Fox News and News International), described the channel as the "bin Laden TV station." Trevor Kavanagh, the political editor at the *Sun*, started his article with the heading "PM goes on bin Laden TV station."[22] Charles Riess, the political editor at the London *Evening Standard*, also adopted the same slogan: "bin Laden station puts PM on spot over raids."[23] The *Mirror* described Al Jazeera as "the Arab TV station used by Osama bin Laden."[24] The war launched by the tabloids seemed to be going along with the British government policy of facing up to Al Jazeera. Downing Street fired a warning shot on October 15 across the bows of Britain's television broadcasters over their role in the "increasingly jittery propaganda war between the US-led coalition and Osama bin Laden and the Al Qaeda network."[25] The *Guardian* revealed the concern of Alastair Campbell, Tony Blair's communications chief, that the broadcasters would undermine the long-term anti-terrorist strategy that Washington and London had set out. At a meeting on October 16 with key staff from British broadcasters, Campbell warned his audience to be careful in their use of material taken from Al Jazeera. In Campbell's words, "the media have responsibilities beyond simply saying, one side says this, and the other side says that. That way lies a sense of moral equivalence. I do not think the media should suspend its own moral judgment."[26] This warning was unlikely to change the broadcasters' commitment to obtaining information and pictures from Al Jazeera. It is assumed that No. 10 tried to avoid charges of censorship, which had surfaced as a result of similar policies in the US. However, the warning was enough to make broadcasters think twice about sensitive editorial decisions and, possibly, to consult the government rather than face accusations of "unpatriotic conduct, such as governments of both main parties have levelled during every recent military action."[27]

The *Guardian* revealed that senior executives from the BBC, ITN and Sky, Richard Sambrook, Richard Tait and Nick Pollard respectively, had discussed in the meeting with Campbell the protest of No. 10 about the familiar problem during war times or conflicts. The concern, prefigured in a Downing Street press briefing on October 15, 2001, was that the Taliban's invitation to foreign reporters to visit bombed villages inside Afghanistan after the air raids "should be treated extremely sceptically" because "access would be manipulated for propaganda purposes." According to Michael White of the *Guardian*, the broadcasters did agree at the end of the meeting to follow the practice in Northern Ireland before the ceasefire.

Despite the efforts made by the British government and the US administration, the information war during this crisis proved to be tougher than destroying airfields in Afghanistan. As many observers pointed out, the propaganda war was not an easy one to win. For instance, Fouad Ajami expressed his doubt that the United States would be able to convince the Arab population of the Middle East that the War on Terrorism is just. William A. Rugh attributed the decline of American credibility in the Arab world to the American policy in the Arab–Israeli peace process over the past few years and to the effect of ten years of sanctions on Iraqi civilians. Baker concurred:

> The challenge facing them resulted partially from neglecting Arab public opinion. For a long time after the Gulf War, the US assumed that its allies—most of which are authoritarian regimes—could impose their views on their people. The error of this approach has become apparent in recent years. The plight of Iraqis living under United Nations sanctions moved public opinion and forced rulers to distance themselves from US policy towards Iraq.[28]

More than anything else, the Palestinian intifada preceding the American War on Terrorism had shaped Arab public opinion in relation to Washington. The position of the US government on this issue promoted anger towards US policy in the Middle East. Negative perceptions of the US—and bin Laden's attempt to use the Palestinian issue to justify his actions—counted against the US in its efforts to explain its bombing of Taliban targets: "For Arabs, the image of this war—that of a rich, strong superpower hitting a small country—does not lend itself to sympathy and creates a gap that cannot be bridged by propaganda."[29] Images of Afghan victims were extensively captured and transmitted by Al Jazeera. Many of the reports by Tayseer Allouni, Al Jazeera's correspondent in Kabul, included stories on civilians subjected to indiscriminate shelling on their villages and homes causing death and injury. Such stories were widely copied by other Arab broadcasters and newspapers. This may have led Michel Jansen of the *Irish Times* to describe Al Jazeera as "the Arab TV which wins the war exclusive,"[30] and James Drummond of the *Financial Times* to point out that "just as the Gulf war made CNN, so today's conflict will be the making of the Al Jazeera service."[31] On October 9, 2001, the *Guardian* had a picture of Kabul being hit by missiles with the logo of Al Jazeera on its front page with a caption saying "Who needs CNN?"

Beyond all the accusations and criticisms facing Al Jazeera, the channel has proven its ability to handle the news during the War on Terrorism, feeding the world's media channels its exclusive footage from Afghanistan, in a role similar to that of CNN during the Gulf War. But this time around, as Brian Whitaker put it, "CNN found itself in the wrong place and Al Jazeera has become our window to the war, providing exclusive footage from Taliban-held areas of Afghanistan."[32] Al Jazeera's exclusivity negated the American and

British efforts to control the flow of information and to restrain the footage transmitted from Afghanistan by Al Jazeera. Tony Blair reached a point where he warned frankly, on October 11, 2001, that the West was in danger of losing the propaganda war against Osama bin Laden and the Al Qaeda network.[33]

Not surprisingly, on November 12, 2001, Al Jazeera's bureau in Afghanistan was hit by an American missile resulting in total destruction of the building. The same missile that destroyed the Al Jazeera office also damaged the AP and BBC bases in Kabul.[34] The Pentagon denied that it had deliberately targeted Al Jazeera, but said it could not explain why the office was hit.[35] Speaking by telephone to the News World Conference in Barcelona, Ibrahim Helal said that he believed that the Al Jazeera office in Kabul had been on the Pentagon's list of targets since the beginning of the conflict but the US did not want to bomb it while the broadcaster was the only one based in Kabul.[36] Mohammed Jassim Al Ali, Al Jazeera's former managing director, stated that the office was hit about two hours before the Northern Alliance took over Kabul, adding that "if the office was not hit we could have covered the entering of the Northern Alliance and the massacres committed in Kabul."[37]

Al Jazeera's correspondent Tayseer Allouni, who fled Kabul an hour before the attack on the office when the city became chaotic with the arrival of the Northern Alliance, doubted any mistake in the American calculations and believed the office was hit deliberately:

> We were transmitting our reports via satellite, therefore locating our office very precisely would be an easy job for military technology and especially for the American ones, which are very developed and could sense our signals to the satellite easily.[38]

Journalists and officials at Al Jazeera headquarters in Qatar believe the attack was a punishment because Al Jazeera covered the war in Afghanistan in a way which did not please the American administration in its efforts to build a coalition. According to Matt Wells of the *Guardian*: "When correspondent William Reeve dived under his desk in Kabul to avoid shrapnel from the US missile that had landed next door [Al Jazeera's office], some think it marked a turning point in war reporting."[39] Matt argued that this event would open up a worrying development for news organizations covering wars and conflicts because they could be targeted simply for reporting a side of the story that one party wanted suppressed. BBC World presenter

Nick Gowing raised this issue at the News World Conference in Barcelona in November 2001. Gowing's argument was that Al Jazeera's only crime was that it had been "bearing witness" to events that the US would rather not see:

> Indeed there is no clear evidence that Al Jazeera supported the Taliban— simply that it enjoyed greater access than other stations. Certainly, Al Jazeera reflects a certain cultural tradition, but only in the same way that CNN approaches stories from a Western perspective.[40]

Still, questions persist: Why did Al Jazeera transmit bin Laden's tapes? Why did bin Laden choose Al Jazeera? Did Al Jazeera provide unfiltered news? Did it broadcast more accurate and in-depth war coverage in Afghanistan than the American networks? Or was it biased towards bin Laden and the Taliban?

"The so-called War on Terrorism" is a phrase that was adopted by Al Jazeera's policy-makers during the war in Afghanistan. Osama bin Laden was mentioned without being named as a "terrorist." He was given airtime and his messages were transmitted without editing. The coverage of war casualties was no less bold. "Why are you bombing civilians?" was a common question facing American officials whenever Al Jazeera hosted them. Images of innocent casualties and destruction were repeated over and over again. What was obvious was that Al Jazeera questioned the legitimacy of the American war in Afghanistan. What was new was that Al Jazeera was not a "Western channel"; it was a channel with a different cultural background from Western media organizations. As one of Al Jazeera's prominent anchors, Mohamed Krichene, put it, "Al Jazeera ruined the international media symphony ... We were like a fly which fell in a dish of cream or honey prepared by the US and Britain."[41]

Ibrahim Helal believes that the Americans were not able to accept a channel that does not follow their political line. In his view, no one should expect Al Jazeera to operate as other networks in the West because of the difference in perspective: "Our understanding differs from that of the US. The Americans have the right to think how to protect their national security, and we have the right to say what exactly is happening."[42] Likewise, Hassan Ibrahim, a senior program producer at Al Jazeera, emphasizes the cultural differences between the journalists of Al Jazeera and Western journalists. He attributes the difference in coverage in part to a difference in cultural perspective:

> We cannot cover the news the way the BBC or CNN do. We in the "Third World" have our own cultural perspective in looking into issues. Whenever I ask myself the question, "what did we want to say?" I always find that we wanted to prove to the world that the truth is not always in the hands of the CNN or the spokesman of the White House or the Pentagon; we in the "Third World" have the right to look at the issues from our own cultural perspective.[43]

Ibrahim considers the Western media's lack of deep understanding of the specificity of the Muslim and Arab World to be one of their weakest points. He believes that this was an advantage which enabled Al Jazeera to claim a prominent position on the world media map: "I do not think that bin Laden and the Taliban have used us to transmit their propaganda. In fact we have used them to gain our international reputation."[44]

It should be emphasized that Al Jazeera was already in Afghanistan before September 11. Al Jazeera's attempts to establish a bureau in Kabul extended back to 1997. There were negotiations between the channel's administration and the Taliban regime to allow the opening of a bureau in Afghanistan. The Taliban had previously declined this request because they forbade filming for what they would presumably describe as "religious reasons." However, in 1999, Al Jazeera succeeded in obtaining the permission to open a bureau. In fact, the Taliban gave permission for two channels and a news agency to operate in Afghanistan: Al Jazeera, CNN, and Reuters. Al Jazeera took up the offer but CNN declined. For Mohammed Jassim Al Ali, CNN's refusal emanated out of a lack of interest in a region that had become fairly stable after the Russian withdrawal:

> The Western media became less interested in Afghanistan after the Russian withdrawal. The tribal fights that followed were not an important news items for them. But for Al Jazeera, the situation was different. Firstly, Afghanistan is an Islamic state. Secondly, many Arabs were still living there— Arabs who volunteered to fight next to the Afghans during the Russian invasion in the seventies and then continued to live in Afghanistan after the withdrawal of the Russians.[45]

Tayseer Allouni, who was the head of the Al Jazeera bureau in Afghanistan and the reporter often accused of transmitting bin

Laden's propaganda, cited other reasons behind Al Jazeera's determination to open a bureau in Kabul:

> Afghanistan is the country where bin Laden and many Islamic and fundamentalist groups are located; groups that are in continuous confrontations with their governments. Al Jazeera's ambition was to get exclusive stories about them, also to get exclusive coverage about the Taliban and their relations with their neighboring countries and the other groups in Afghanistan. I can say Al Jazeera had a strategic vision in opening this bureau at that time.[46]

However, proceeding with the job was hazardous at times. According to Allouni, Al Jazeera crew were warned on several occasions by the Taliban to leave the county because they had broken the law through filming. Adding to the complexity of the situation was the fact that Islamic groups considered any journalist a "spy." Not surprisingly, perhaps, Al Jazeera's crew, as Allouni points out, were treated as "suspects" all the time. Despite all these restrictions, Al Jazeera managed to scoop the world with its coverage of the bombing of the Buddha statues in Bamiyan and the wedding of bin Laden's son, which was attended by members of the Taliban and other Islamic groups in Afghanistan.

The period of a month or so between September 11 and the air strikes on Afghanistan was frightening for Afghans as well as for foreigners. The Taliban ordered foreigners, including reporters, to evacuate the country. However, Tayseer Allouni convinced Taliban officials that he had been a resident in Afghanistan for more than two years, which distinguished him from the other foreign reporters who came only to cover the trial of "Shelter Now" employees who were accused by the Taliban of "preaching for Christianity." As Allouni indicates, the Taliban came to approve his presence as they realized the need for a television network to communicate with the outside world and to send out the images of the Afghan civilians who were victims of the indiscriminate American shelling.

When the strikes on Afghanistan started, Tayseer Allouni appeared on the screen with the other version of the story—"the version of the victims" as he put it. His reports were heavily criticized in the Western media for being biased. However, extending over the period of five weeks or so, Allouni's coverage started to draw much sympathy for the victims and to sink in as factual. In some reports, Allouni contradicted the information released by the White House or the Pentagon. For example, on October 6, 2001, Allouni reported the destruction of two US fighter planes by Taliban forces (one was a reconnaissance aircraft and the other was an Apache helicopter). He went to the site where the planes were shot down in Gezno, filmed the ruins of the planes and filed the footage in his report. In the meantime, the Pentagon admitted the downing of one plane but not two. However, Allouni's report was hard to ignore as it was backed up with visual evidence. The disparity between Al Jazeera's version of the story and the US official version may provide an explanation for why Al Jazeera was demonized and why the American networks were urged to exercise self-censorship.

It is worth adding that Allouni also communicated the Taliban's political responses through extensive interviews with its leaders. He reported the movement's military preparations to resist any invasion of Afghanistan. In his reports, Allouni used many phrases from the holy book and comparative Islamic stories which reflected his cultural and religious background. Allouni's Islamic commitment and his profile further enhanced his journalistic mission. He wore a beard and at times put on the Afghans' traditional outfit. He admitted that this helped him in approaching both ordinary and official people in Afghanistan:

> religion plays a vital role in shaping the Afghans' understanding of people and societies. Thus, if they are approached by a person who does not follow the same religious traditions as them, does not try to speak their language and wear their costume, they would treat him with suspicion.[47]

Besides Allouni, Al Jazeera sent two reporters to Khandahar soon after September 11, and their reports also revealed the sufferings of the Afghan people. Yousif Al Sholi, a Qatar-based news producer, was assigned to cover the consequences of the war from Khandahar. During his stay, he transmitted daily stories of death, casualties, fear and sorrow, revealing some of the Afghans' pain and suffering. It was difficult to capture these images at the beginning of the attacks not only because of the inconvenience in getting to all the places which were attacked, but also because of the Taliban's rules and restrictions not to allow filming of human beings:

> Capturing images in the streets of the city was difficult, although we had permission to shoot images. The Taliban justified this permission by shooting the destroyed houses and the results of the air raids. In other words, we were only allowed to shoot "things that did not have souls"; that is, we were

not allowed in the early days to take images of humans beings whether they were dead or alive. Various incidents occurred where the Taliban police used to take us for interrogation when they discovered us filming. The matter was fully dependent on their personal whim.[48]

Al Sholi negotiated continually with the authorities to allow him to shoot. These difficulties suggest that Al Jazeera's job in Afghanistan was not easy to conduct and that the authorities were not making it easier for them. The reporters were faced with the restrictions of the Taliban and the suspicion of the Islamic groups, including bin Laden's. These constraints and difficulties do not suggest that Al Jazeera was a propaganda tool of the Taliban and bin Laden. For Muhammad Al Bourini, a news producer assigned to cover the situation in Khandahar after Al Sholi departed, Al Jazeera crew were not welcomed in Afghanistan by the Taliban:

I was always scared of the Taliban's reaction towards us because their understanding of the nature of our work as a TV crew varied from one person to another. They have told us once that we were in Afghanistan upon our own request and that we could stay if we were able to protect ourselves. We were not welcome as was propounded on the Western media.[49]

Despite these difficulties, Al Jazeera kept covering the war and benefited from it. The channel was guaranteed a prominent place on the world media map and earned huge sums of money from selling images from Afghanistan to various networks for as much as $20,000 a minute, although some of the images were provided for free to news agencies. Interestingly enough, most Western networks were ready to pay money for bin Laden's images and speeches, but not for the images of civilian casualties.[50]

Even CNN did not fail to court Al Jazeera, although the partnership did not last long. Days after the September 11 attacks, Al Jazeera and CNN negotiated a deal to exchange footage and resources. Originally, CNN would receive six hours of exclusive rights to Al Jazeera footage and remote access to news-breaking locations like Kabul through an Al Jazeera correspondent. In return, Al Jazeera would receive access to Northern Afghanistan through a CNN correspondent, professional assistance with crews and equipment in other areas of Afghanistan and access to CNN's syndicated news feed. In addition, CNN shipped a satellite uplink facility for both networks to use.[51]

This partnership soon ended in a crisis. On October 20, 2001, Tayseer Allouni conducted an interview with bin Laden which Al Jazeera chose not to broadcast. According to Allouni, one of the Al Qaeda associates told him that bin Laden agreed to give an interview for two networks, one Arabic and one foreign. Accordingly, the questions were prepared and CNN had been informed in accordance with the agreement held between the two networks during the Afghan events. A few days later, the list of questions from CNN and Al Jazeera was submitted to an Al Qaeda associate. Ten days later, Allouni received a message informing him that an important event was about to happen and that he could cover it. Consequently, he was transported blindfolded by a group of armed men to the presumed location of the event. He then received a list of prepared questions he could ask bin Laden, which included only some of the questions submitted by Al Jazeera and CNN. During the 90-minute interview, bin Laden ignored a lot of the questions from both Al Jazeera and CNN.[52] He refused to answer such questions as "what is your future target?" because the assumption behind such a question is that bin Laden and Al Qaeda carried out the September 11 attacks. Al Jazeera did not air the interview, claiming it was not newsworthy. Following this, the channel was accused of hiding material regarding bin Laden. Surprisingly, and much to the dismay of Al Jazeera, CNN broadcast the tape on January 31, 2002 in what has been perceived as a humiliating act. CNN disputed the view that the interview was not newsworthy, noting that it included new statements about anthrax attacks which had taken place a few months earlier, the restrictive effect of new security precautions in the United States and the Bush administration's handling of the news.[53] A CNN spokesman said the network was well within its rights in broadcasting the excerpts of this bin Laden interview: "Our affiliate agreement with Al Jazeera gives us the express right to air any footage by Al Jazeera."[54]

However, Al Jazeera expressed its surprise about CNN's attitude. In its view, CNN obtained a copy of this interview by unknown means and aired it without the consent of Al Jazeera and without explanation regarding the conditions in which this interview had been conducted. Al Jazeera officials announced that the channel received the interview via satellite from their bureau in Kabul on October 21, 2001, then decided not to air it on the basis that the conditions under which the interview had been conducted "did not present the minimum of objectivity and professionalism." Al Jazeera also chose not to acknowledge the existence of this interview for the sake of the safety of its correspondent in Kabul. The dispute between Al Jazeera and CNN made the headlines of Arabic newspapers on February 2, 2002. The London-based *Al Hayat* newspaper stated on its front page that "Al Jazeera will sue CNN for broadcasting of bin Laden with Al Jazeera's correspondent in Kabul." *Al Quds Al Arabi*, another London-based newspaper, reported that

> CNN humiliated Al Jazeera by broadcasting an interview for bin Laden. The tape was not broadcast on Al Jazeera due to the American and Gulf states' pressures. Al Jazeera will terminate its agreement with CNN and open an investigation on how CNN acquired the tape.[55]

Beyond the details, the short-lived partnership between Al Jazeera and CNN is telling in other ways. It is a reminder of an ongoing mistrust, if not a chasm, between the media discourse in the West and the media discourse in the Arab world. There is a tendency among Western media and officials to see Al Jazeera as being biased toward the Taliban and Al Qaeda and to view it as a means of transmitting Taliban and Al Qaeda propaganda, while Al Jazeera denies being used as a propaganda machine, claiming that it succeeded where Western media failed. For Al Jazeera, the coverage of the war was not aimed against the US or the West; the channel was simply giving an appropriate Arab perspective, although remaining balanced was not an easy task at times. Just as Al Jazeera was the channel which "broke the taboo in the Arab media," it has also become the channel which broke the "American taboo" in reporting this conflict by providing the world with extensive coverage of "the terrorist and the victim." Without Al Jazeera, bin Laden and his network would have stayed a mystery and hardly anyone would have known about them; nor would the world have known about Afghan civilian victims killed by indiscriminate shelling. Al Jazeera has provided the world with another version of the conflict, one which would have been difficult to know through the lenses of Western media. When Al Jazeera set its agenda to cover this conflict, it influenced the world media coverage, which relied on the channel's footage to report the conflict. In the process, it helped American and British governments lose their "propaganda war" in the Arab and Muslim world.

NOTES

1 R. Jackall, *Propaganda* (London: Macmillan, 1995), p. 217.
2 B. Nacos, *Terrorism and the Media* (New York: Columbia University Press, 1994), p. 10.
3 I. Helal, Interview with author, April 10, 2001.
4 Ibid.
5 Ibid.
6 T. Straus, "The CNN of the Arab world," *Alter Net*, October 26, 2001, <www.alternet.org/print.html?StoryID=11811>.
7 Ibid.
8 H. Ibish and A. Abunimah, "The CNN of the Arab World deserves our respect," *Los Angeles Times*, October 22, 2001. See also Straus, "The CNN of the Arab world."
9 Z. Chafets, "Al-Jazeera unmasked: an Arab propaganda machine in the guise of real journalism," *New York Daily News*, October 14, 2001, <www.nydailynews.com/2001-10-14/News_and_Views/opinion/a-128499.asp>.
10 M. Hudson and J. Stanier, *War and the Media: A Random Searchlight* (Stroud: Sutton, 1999), p. 222.
11 N. Abu-Fadil, "Al Jazeera surpasses CNN in live Afghan war coverage," *Poynter*, October 8, 2001, <http://63.208.24.134/terrorism/magda1.htm>.
12 A. Fleischer, cited in R. Fisk, "Al Jazeera: a bold and original TV station that America wants to censor," *Independent*, October 11, 2001.
13 W. Richey, "Arab TV network plays key disputed role in Afghan war," *Christian Science Monitor*, October 15, 2001.
14 J. Borger, "US television to censor videos from bin Laden," *Guardian*, October 12, 2001.
15 Ibid.
16 "US urges curb on Arab TV channel," BBC News Online, October 4, 2001, <www.news.bbc.co.uk/hi/english/world/americas/newsid_1578000/1578619.stm>.
17 R. Kaiser, "US message lost overseas," *Washington Post*, October 15, 2000.
18 S. O'Neill, "Al Jazeera TV faces ban for inciting hatred," *Daily Telegraph*, November 6, 2001.
19 Ibid.
20 M. Woolf, "Prime minister grilled, Paxman style, by Arab TV," *Independent*, October 10, 2001, p. 7.
21 C. Blackhurst, "Propaganda war," *Independent*, October 14, 2001.
22 T. Kavanagh, "PM goes on bin Laden TV station," *Sun*, October 9, 2001, pp. 4–5.
23 C. Riess, "Bin Laden's station puts PM on spot over raids," *Evening Standard*, October 9, 2001, p. 3.
24 *Mirror*, October 10, 2001.
25 M. White, "Downing Street gives propaganda warning," *Guardian*, October 16, 2001.
26 A. Campbell, cited in *Guardian*, November 9, 2001.
27 White, "Downing Street gives propaganda warning."

28 G. Baker and R. Khalaf, "A different script," *Financial Times*, October 12, 2001.
29 Said, cited in Baker and Khalaf, "A different script."
30 M. Jansen, "Arab TV wins war exclusive," *Irish Times*, October 9, 2001, p. 8.
31 J. Drummond, "Qatari broadcaster emerges as key channel of communication," *Financial Times*, October 9, 2001, p. 4.
32 B. Whitaker, "Battle station," *Guardian*, October 9, 2001,
33 "West is losing propaganda war, ways Blair," *Metro London*, October 12, 2001, p. 2.
34 *Guardian*, November 13, 2001.
35 M. Wells, "How smart was this bomb?," *Guardian*, November 19, 2001.
36 Ibid.
37 M.J. Al Ali, Interview with author, April 10, 2002.
38 T. Allouni, Interview with author, April 11, 2002.
39 Wells, "How smart was this bomb?"
40 Gowing, cited in Wells, "How smart was this bomb?"
41 M. Krichene, Interview with author, April 12, 2002.
42 Helal, Interview with author.
43 H. Ibrahim, Interview with author, April 7, 2002.
44 Ibid.
45 Al Ali, Interview with author.
46 Allouni, Interview with author.
47 Ibid.
48 Y. Al Sholi, Interview with author, April 11, 2002.
49 M. Al Bourini, Interview with author, April 6, 2002.
50 Krichene, Interview with author.
51 M. El-Nawawy and A.I. Farag, *Al Jazeera: How the Free Arab News Network Scooped the World and Changed the Middle East* (Boulder: Westview Press, 2002), p. 164.
52 Allouni, Interview with author.
53 J. Rutenberg, "A nation challenged: video tape," *New York Times*, February 1, 2002.
54 S. Beatty, "CNN ends ties with Arab TV network," *Wall Street Journal*, February 4, 2002, p. 12.
55 "CNN humiliates Al Jazeera by broadcasting an interview of bin Laden," *Al Quds Al Arabi*, February 2, 2002.

9

Witnessing the Intifada: Al Jazeera's Coverage of the Palestinian–Israeli Conflict

Mohamed Zayani

Al Jazeera distinguished itself by its attempt to reach out to a large Arab audience, discussing issues that are both timely and pressing in the Arab and Muslim world in general and the conflict-ridden Middle East in particular. Covering certain events, crises or wars in the region has created milestones in the history of Al Jazeera—although seen from a different perspective, such a focus is a short-coming as it dwarfs other issues. The inception of Al Jazeera as a global broadcaster came with the coverage of the Anglo-American bombing of Baghdad in Operation Desert Fox in December 1998. Having an office in Baghdad enabled Al Jazeera to stand alongside and to compete with international media organizations like CNN and the BBC. The various documentaries, reports, and programs which Al Jazeera aired on the plight of the Iraqi people under the sanctions for over a decade have further enhanced its in-depth treatment of the question of Iraq. It was not, however, until the war in Afghanistan that Al Jazeera became the center of the world's attention. The so-called War on Terrorism has given Al Jazeera an international prominence. The network's coverage of the invasion of Iraq in 2003 further enhanced the image of the channel as an international broadcaster to contend with, which it claimed in 2001 during the war in Afghanistan.

No less important is Al Jazeera's reporting on the Palestinian–Israeli conflict. While Desert Fox was the first world event to give Al Jazeera regional importance, the coverage of the second intifada has given Al Jazeera a truly pan-Arab dimension. The question of Palestine is part of the socio-political consciousness of the Arab nation as a whole. Being the single most important political preoc-cupation for Arabs since World War II, the Palestinian question has been and continues to be in the minds of practically all Arabs as a cause, a symbol and a reality. Many Arab satellite channels have played an important role and have, in one way or another, adopted the struggle and plight of the Palestinians. The developments in Palestine have been covered by all Arab channels and virtually all media institutions in the Arab world have played a supporting role, often mobilizing Arab public opinion. This is a marked difference from the first intifada which, taking place in the pre-Arab satellite era (1987–94), was more of a political event than a media event. The second Palestinian intifada (or what is often called the Al Aqsa intifada, which erupted in September 2000 at the provocation of Ariel Sharon's visit to *Al Haram Al Sharif*) has been a "real laboratory" for Arab satellite channels,[1] putting their credibility and their professionalism to the test. Some of these channels have seized the opportunity to increase their popularity and widen their reach, covering the intifada and its repercussions with full intensity and providing news and analysis on the bloody clashes in the West Bank and the Gaza Strip. By and large, Arab satellite broadcasting has helped the Arab street mobilize its efforts to support the intifada. In some instances, telethons have been organized to raise money for the families of martyrs and victims of the intifada. Abbas El Tounsy summarizes some of the most visible effects of Arab satellite channels' coverage of the violence in Palestine:

> All the Arab satellite channels, although in varying degrees, have opened an unprecedented outlet for scenes of the ferocity of Israeli practices against the Palestinians. Pictures of the Al Aqsa Mosque and the Dome of the Rock appeared frequently in introductions to several programs. With the exception of the Saudi Satellite channel, songs about the intifada and Jerusalem have been repeatedly broadcast on all the Arab satellite channels. Even the Lebanese channels like Future TV, New TV, and MTV, which usually present light variety programs, have broadcast this type of song, with pictures and corpses of the victims in the background. Many Arab satellite channels, moreover, have broadcast nationalist movies reminiscent of the Arabs' dignity ... Arab satellite stations have designated a so-called "Open Day" to the intifada; such programs are being run under passionate slogans such as "The Massacre" on MBC, and "All of us are Palestine" on Abu Dhabi TV.[2]

More than any other channel, Al Jazeera has capitalized on the importance of the Palestinian question. It has not only provided instant coverage of the events and aired detailed reports on the latest developments, shedding an unpleasant light on the practices of Israel in the Middle East, airing raw footage and images of incursions, death and demolition in the West Bank and the Gaza Strip rarely displayed by Western media; it has also devoted many of its programs to supporting and serving the intifada, including debates, discussions and documentaries such as *The Missing Justice* and *Palestine under Siege*. These programs offer a history of the Palestinian people through a narrative of the resistance. The expulsion of the Palestinians from their lands in 1948, the 1967 Six Day War, and the October 1973 War are never far away as viewers are constantly reminded of these moments in the history of the Arab–Israeli conflict.

The network's on-the-ground coverage of the Palestinian uprising has made a great impact on news-hungry Arab viewers. With Al Jazeera, the Arab world follows events in the Occupied Territories at close range. The impact of images and footage of Palestinian cities and villages under the assault of the Israeli army with its helicopters and fighter jets is profound. Images of the brutality of the occupation, which had never been seen before in any significant way, directly touch the hearts of Arab viewers and shape Arab public opinion. As James Drummond put it, "the station's role in propelling the Palestinian uprising in the Arab public consciousness— and keeping it there—is considerable."[3] The images are indelible for the millions of viewers who are glued to their TVs watching the intifada unfold and the plight of Palestinians who are often subjected to collective punishment, especially during such times of crisis such as Operation Defensive Shield or the siege at the Church of the Nativity in Bethlehem. The coverage of the suffering of the Palestinians under the weight of the Israeli war machine has, in more than one way, intensified the feeling of solidarity among the Palestinian people. For David Makovsky, Al Jazeera has "helped revitalize the anti-Israel current in the Arab world ... Indeed, it has assisted in the evolution of a strong pan-Arab current of public opinion."[4]

The killing of Mohamed Al Durra is a case in point. Al Jazeera's repeated broadcasting of the pictures of the death of Mohamed Al Durra, the twelve-year-old Palestinian boy who was shot by Israeli soldiers and died in the arms of his father as the latter tried to shelter him from gunfire in the Gaza Strip, has inflamed passions and even become a rallying point as the Palestinian–Israeli conflict has intensified. The pictures depicting his death have even become part of a promo for the channel and were for some time the logo for its intifada coverage. Such media attention is not without consequences. For instance, partly because of the repeated airing of this high-profile shooting, Israeli authorities instituted an inquiry into the affair.[5] More importantly, the case suggests that Al Jazeera has the potential to shape Arab public opinion as the same images are viewed throughout the Arab world and responded to, often with a passive resentment, but occasionly with protests. Overall, the coverage of the conflict has fuelled the spirit of discontent among ordinary Arab men and women, some of whom have taken to the streets in support of the Palestinians. As Al Jazeera continues to broadcast images of the intifada across the Arab world and to stir up support for Palestinians, public support for the Palestinian cause is becoming more pronounced. The effect of the pictures and rhetoric of Al Jazeera can be observed in the numerous comments and viewpoints of frustrated callers who actively participate in such programs as *Under Siege* (*Taht al Hisar*) and *The Forum of Al Jazeera* (*Minbar Al Jazeera*), both of which are phone-in programs that encourage viewers to express their opinions on, and often give an outlet to their frustration about, the deteriorating situation in the Occupied Territories.

Al Jazeera's intense coverage of the intifada has not only fed Arab fury but also fostered anti-government behavior in the Arab world, making Arab governments vulnerable to charges and open to criticism that they have not sufficiently supported the Palestinians or decisively acted on the Palestinian cause. In this sense, Al Jazeera places itself as a counter-force to the official indifference towards the plight of the Palestinian people. Seen from this perspective, Al Jazeera's success is a symptom of the failure of Arab governments when it comes to Middle East politics. The Arab information ministers' attempt in August 2001 to formulate a media strategy to effectively publicize to the world the intifada to counterbalance biased Israeli coverage and to combat media deception amounted to little more than lip service. The initiative to persuade public opinion, particularly in the US, of the necessity of immediate action to contain the explosive situation in Palestine hides the very inability of Arab states to deal with the situation and the lack of a political will that can rise to the challenges the region is facing. Being at the forefront of Arab news channels, Al Jazeera has nonetheless helped shape the public context for Arab decision-making. In the words of David Makovsky, "Arab commentators are convinced that Al Jazeera's pan-Arab influence was a factor prompting Arab leaders, who have only rarely convened summits in the past decade, to hold two Arab summits during the seven months of the intifada."⁶ Many Arab governments have also become a bit more vocal in their effort to highlight the Palestinian problem, reflecting the public outrage at the suffering of Palestinians. The coverage of the Al Aqsa intifada is such that Arab governments can no longer ignore or brush aside its media effect; if anything, they are taking note of the changes brought about by the age of direct satellite television. The coverage of the intifada has gathered momentum and fueled passions in the street to an extent that some governments in the region have permitted public demonstrations and authorized fund-raising campaigns for the Palestinians.

Among Palestinians themselves, Al Jazeera is quite popular. In the West Bank and the Gaza Strip, Al Jazeera is a local channel. Because of the difficulties in communication caused by the curfews and sieges, many Palestinians watch Al Jazeera to see what is happening and follow what the reporters say. For these people, Al Jazeera is a convenient and reliable means to find out what is going on. The network receives statements from and features interviews with various political factions from Arafat's cabinet members to Hamas leaders. Al Jazeera's bureau in Palestine constantly receives tips about incidents and clashes and statements from various Palestinian political factions. Some Palestinians feel that "if Al Jazeera does not cover it, it simply did not happen," while others find in Al Jazeera a platform to expose the practices of Israel.

However, even those who admire what Al Jazeera is doing have reservations about the channel's coverage. Some believe that the effect of the coverage of the intifada is sometimes lost in the very act of reporting as this takes the form of a constant flow of information. Viewers are fed a constant stream of news which is often brief and dispersed. The reality is reported in a fragmented way. It is true that Al Jazeera covers the Palestinian intifada extensively, but the ensuing coverage is for the most part caught in events and develop-ments at the expense of a more profound treatment. The images of suffering and victimization, of blood and death become a daily staple for viewers who in turn become enmeshed media-wise in the details of the conflict and are hardly able to interact with the con-flict as a whole. The coverage of the intifada often comes down to material to be consumed by the frustrated masses to the point of being saturated with images. In some instances and during periods of heightened tension, whether it be an Israeli incursion in Ramallah or the bombing of a restaurant in Haifa, the same pictures are repeated over and over on news broadcasts as a guest speaker is commenting on the events via a satellite link. Half of the screen has the picture of the commentator and the second half shows a rerun of footage. At the beginning, the viewer is affected by the scenes and responds to them in varying degrees, but as these same images keep recurring, the viewer risks becoming numb as a result of experiencing "compassion fatigue"[7] which leaves him or her exhausted by the spectacle of violent events and reports about misery and suffering. He or she becomes accustomed to seeing graphic pictures and dreadful events to the point that the event loses its eventfulness in the daily routine screenings of violence. More than that, the images that are being fed are for the most part tragic and in that sense tend to sap the energies and hopes of the Arab viewer. The continuous or repeated airing of images of victims and victimization, of expulsion and demolition may incite the Arab masses, but it also tends to affect them negatively. Furthermore, the kind of passionate journalism some Al Jazeera reporters and anchors engage in often leads them to paint a black and white picture which pits two irreconcilables against each other—Sharon vs Arafat, armed incursions vs violent attacks, and so on. This black and white picture may reflect the international inertia and the absence of alternative visions to the stalemate between the Palestinians and the Israelis, but it leaves the "gray" in the Palestinian–Israeli question largely unexplored.

For John R. Bradley, Al Jazeera's coverage of the Palestinian issues gives it an ambiguous role in Middle Eastern politics:

> By emotionally charging the issue, the station is unwittingly supporting Arab regimes. It is doing this even more effectively than the government-appointed editors in chief across the region, who for decades have deflected public opinion from domestic issues by using the safety valve of the Palestinian issue. The Israeli–Palestinian conflict has contributed significantly to the democratic deficit in the Middle East by providing Arab governments with an excuse to divert resources to military spending.[8]

For other Western commentators, Al Jazeera's coverage of the intifada is dubious to say the least. According to Daniel Brumberg, Al Jazeera is manipulative:

> Over the past few years, especially since the collapse of the Oslo Peace Process, Arab young people have been fed a diet of horrific images of

Palestinian young people dying in the streets of Ramallah and Gaza. That these images are manipulated by pan-Arab satellite TV stations such as Al Jazeera to increase anti-Americanism, and/or by governments to detract attention away from their domestic shortcomings, is surely true.[9]

Similarly, Carol Rosemberg dismisses Al Jazeera's coverage as sheer propaganda and irresponsible journalism intended to rally support for the Palestinians. In her view, the network's stomach-turning broadcast of raw footage is nothing other than "a graphic commercial for the Palestinian cause."[10] On her part, Sharon Waxman finds fault with Al Jazeera for turning what she sarcastically calls "Israel's persecution of Palestinians" into "a constant litany of suffering and aggression."[11] Al Jazeera is further criticized for portraying the Arabs as helpless victims. Al Jazeera may concede to the fact that its coverage of the situation in the occupied territories is pro-Palestinian, but insists that "this is a matter of 'the field facts on the ground' rather than any propagandistic policy decision."[12] The situation in the Occupied Territories is tragic to say the least. According to the London-based newspaper *Al Hayat*, at the end of its fourth year, the Al Aqsa intifada left 3,334 Palestinians dead and thousands injured, many of whom were civilians.[13] To take the position of the detached observer or to claim objective neutrality when it comes to the Palestinian question is something that is hard to do for many Arab journalists partly because, as Schoemaker and Reese point out, factors intrinsic to the communicator—such as professional background, attitudes, values and beliefs, professional role and ethics— tend to influence media content.[14] Comparatively speaking, Matt Wells argues, "Al Jazeera reflects a certain cultural tradition: but only in the same ways that CNN approached stories from a Western perspective."[15]

The coverage of the intifada has also shaped the image of the United States. It is undisputed that there is a deep resentment towards America's—and in fact the West's—continued support of Israel in spite of its aggressions against the Palestinian people. There is a feeling, common among Arabs, that many Western media outlets tend to be partisan and that their coverage of Arabs and Muslims, and the Palestinian–Israeli conflict in particular, tends to be slanted. For example, American news does not often recognize or give due attention to the Palestinian perspective. Likewise, the Western media tends to resent the fact that the Israelis have been confronted by constant outbreaks of Palestinian violence but gives little attention to the Palestinian plight and provides little analysis about the roots of the problem. By and large, the perspective one gets in some Western media tends to criminalize the Palestinians. In "Worse than CNN?: BBC news and the Mideast," Paul de Rooij explores the charged meaning in the language of reports by the BBC on the Palestinian–Israeli conflict:

> Only when someone is killed is news obtained from the area. Unquestionably, Israeli deaths are deemed more important than Palestinian deaths; much more extended coverage is devoted to the suicide bombing casualties than to incidents where greater numbers of Palestinians are killed. Also, BBC *TeleText* and *Online* news refer to Israelis as having been "killed" thus denoting intent, whereas Palestinians invariably "die"; these media always enclose massacres and assassinations with quotation marks. Israeli killings and violent acts are always labeled "retaliation," thus justified. Increasingly, Palestinian violence has been labeled "terrorism"—it has never been labeled "resistance." Although the term "terrorism" is often applied to Palestinian violence, the term "state terrorism" is never applied to Israeli acts of aggression.[16]

Not surprisingly, Al Jazeera has been criticized for using the term "martyr" to describe Palestinians who die while fighting, regardless of whether they are victims of Israeli guns or so-called suicide bombers. When asked about Al Jazeera's tendency to use the word martyr for so-called suicide bombers, Ghida Fakhry—who used to cover the news for Al Jazeera in New York—replied:

> anyone you speak to in the Middle East will tell you American TV is definitely biased. You will never find the word "assassination" in the American press when it is about the Israeli policy of assassinating political activists. It is always called a targeted killing.[17]

Clearly, the issue here is far from being a linguistic one.

In some ways, Al Jazeera has been acting as a counter-force, albeit on a smaller scale and with a smaller audience, to the pro-Israel reporting on the intifada. Al Jazeera sees its contribution in introducing another dimension to the media, journalism and reporting, and in fact adding the Arab perspective which has been missing. For a long time, the Western perspective dominated. Given that Israel controls much of the media coverage about its conflict with the Palestinians[18] and given that the Western press relies to a large extent on the Israeli media, the Palestinian question has been largely framed through such borrowing. This should come as no surprise; most if not all press offices for Western media are based in West Jerusalem—which also serves as a regional hub for some major Western networks and media organizations. To write their reports, journalists visit the West Bank and the Gaza Strip but do not fully live the Palestinian experience; as it is, the Palestinian always remains the other. Adding to these shortcomings is the reality of press reporting in Palestine as it faces censure, bans and harassment from the Israeli side. There is a media containment on the part of Israel which is apparent not only during times of escalating violence, but also in the day-to-day reporting on events. Journalists cannot always get to the site of events or verify happenings as was the case during the Israeli siege of and alleged massacre in the city of Jenin and the refugee camp adjacent to it which impelled the UN to initiate a fact-finding mission only to be thwarted later.[19] Although in 2001, a year into the intifada, the Arab Information Ministers Council adopted a media strategy to publicize to the world the Arab and Palestinian view of the conflict and to combat media deception regarding the Palestinian issue, and although in 2002 the Council adopted an Arab media discourse aimed at counterbalancing the US and Israeli depiction of the Palestinian uprising against Israeli occupation as terrorism, these initiatives amounted to little. Neither in style nor in effect do they compare with the coverage of such pan-Arab channels as Abu Dhabi TV and Al Jazeera. The often live gruesome pictures Al Jazeera has been airing on the intifada, as in the case of the siege at the Church of the Nativity in Bethlehem, have provided a different perspective and even told a different story from the one aired by some non-Arab media. The images of Israeli practices in the Occupied Territories which the network is making instantly accessible and constantly updating on the airwaves are increasingly finding their way to the international community as the viewer base of Al Jazeera is expanding outside the Arab world, particularly in Europe. This is not without effects. Suffice it here to mention two developments which may not be direct consequences but are nonetheless noteworthy indicators that can help gauge the impact of Arab satellite television in general, and particularly Al Jazeera. The first pertains to the number and extent of demonstrations held in Europe in support of the Palestinian cause, not to mention the outcome of a poll conducted by the European community which ranks Israel as the leading threat to world peace. The second pertains to Israel's decision to launch an Arabic TV station to influence the thinking of Arab public opinion inflamed by its practices, to counter the effects of the plethora of Arabic channels which have sprung up recently and, more pointedly, to counter a channel like Al Jazeera which, given its exceptional attention to the Palestinian–Israeli conflict and the strong anti-Israel editorial line it is perceived to adopt, is popular among many Arabs.

In spite of Al Jazeera's claims to provide balanced coverage, some critics and viewers question the objectivity of the channel. Others criticize Al Jazeera on grounds that its coverage of the intifada has helped stoke the violence, incite Palestinians to riot, fuel Arab anger, and mobilize support for the Palestinians. Al Jazeera has also been rebuked for inflating the news, exaggerating events and spreading anti-Semitism. For Fouad Ajami, Al Jazeera's "unrelenting anti-Zionist reportage contributed to further alienation between Israelis and Palestinians."[20] For others, Al Jazeera's coverage of the intifada is slanted as many of the reporters, anchors and guests are themselves Palestinians. However, the network denies such allegations; it claims that it is virtually the only channel—although not the first one—to interview Israeli officials, including Shimon Peres, the former Israeli secretary of state, Ehud Barak, the former Israeli prime minister, and numerous spokespeople for the Israeli government. However, playing a *de facto* role of an interlocutor with Israel has often attracted harsh criticism. Al Jazeera has been frequently blasted for putting Israeli officials on the air and giving them much air time with fluent Arabic-speaking guests debating live the turbulent events during the intifada. Many Arabs argue that the Israeli media does not give the Palestinians the same opportunity to appear live on TV in order to present the Palestinian perspective and defend it; one does not find Palestinians or Arabs putting their points across as often and as freely as Israeli counterparts. By opening its airwaves to and holding interviews with Israeli spokespeople, Al Jazeera—which is often criticized for showing a map in its news bulletins with the word "Israel" on it at a time when other Arab channels refer to it as "the Zionist enemy"—has been perceived as a channel for normalizing relations or, at least, normalizing information and media ties with Israel—a move many, if not most, Arabs oppose. However, as Mohammed El Oifi explains, such a media rapprochement has not been all that bad; if anything, "it has made Israelis more human and, in fact, more vulnerable in the eyes of the public. They have been denuded of the aura that surrounds the myth of their invincibility."[21]

NOTES

1   "The intifada: a laboratory for Arab satellite channels," *Al Quds Al Arabi*, November 1, 2000.
2   Abbas El Tounsy, "Reflections on the Arab satellites, the Palestinian intifada and the Israeli war," *Transnational Broadcasting Studies*, No. 8 (Spring/Summer 2002), <http://www.tbsjournal.com/Archives/ Spring02/arab_satellites.html>.
3   James Drummond, "Qatari broadcaster emerges as key channel of communication," *Financial Times*, October 9, 2001, p. 4.
4   David Makovsky, "A voice from the heavens: Al Jazeera's satellite broadcasts inflame emotions across the Arab world," *US News & World Report*, May 14, 2001, pp. 26–8.
5   Harvey Morris, "Israel/Palestine meet the press," *Arabies Trends*, May 1, 2001.
6   Makovsky, "A voice from the heavens."
7   Keith Tester, *Compassion, Morality and the Media* (Buckingham: Open University Press, 2001), pp. 13–14.
8   John R. Bradley, "Will Al Jazeera bend?," *Prospect*, 97 (April 2004), p. 51.
9   Daniel Brumberg, "Arab public opinion and US foreign policy: a complex encounter," Testimony in front of the US House of Representatives Committee on Government Reform, Subcommittee on National Security, Veterans Affairs and International Relations, October 8, 2002.
10 Carol Rosemberg, "Qatar's maverick Al Jazeera TV news network causing major stir arena," *Knight Ridder Washington Bureau*, October 10, 2001. However, there is nothing that is specific to Al Jazeera in such a take. The criticism could equally be applied to a number of Arab channels, many of which refuse to refer to Israel by name and use the word "enemy" in their news bulletin because they do not acknowledge the existence of the the state of Israel in the first place.
11 Sharon Waxman, "Arab TV's strong signal: the Al Jazeera network offers news the Mideast never had before," *Washington Post*, December 4, 2001, p. C1.
12 See Dan Williams, "Al Jazeera ascends to World stage," *Washington Post*, October 12, 2001, p. 22A.
13 *Al Hayat*, September 28, 2004, p. 6. See also "Intifada: bilan," Health Development Information and Policy Institute, <http://www.solidarite-palestine.org/doc030.html>.
14 P.J. Schoemaker and D.S. Reese, *Mediating the Message: Theories of Influence on Mass Media Content* (White Plains: Longman, 1996), pp. 63–103.
15 Matt Wells, "How smart was this bomb?", *Guardian*, November 19, 2001, p. 8.
16 See Paul de Rooij, "Worse than CNN?: BBC news and the Mideast," *Counter Punch*, May 16, 2002, <http://www.counterpunch.org/rooij0516.html>.
17 See Joyce Wadler, "Public lives: television bureau chief leaves anonymity," *New York Times*, October 19, 2001, p. 2D.

18 See Edward Said, "Low point of powerlessness," *Al Ahram Weekly*, No. 605, September 26, 2002; Joss Dray and Denis Sieffert, *La guerre Israélienne de l'information* (Paris: La Découverte, 2002).

19 See "Report of the Secretary-General prepared pursuant to General Assembly resolution ES-10/10 (Report on Jenin)," <http://www.un. org/peace/jenin>.

20 Fouad Ajami, "What the Muslim world is watching," *New York Times*, November 18, 2001, p. 48.

21 Quoted in interview with Christophe Ayad, "For Al Jazeera, Bin Laden sells," *Libération*, October 12, 2001, <http://www.medea.be/files/ medea/ 3.doc>.

10
Al Jazeera and American Public Diplomacy: A Dance of Intercultural (Mis-)Communication

R.S. Zaharna

In the aftermath of the September 11 attacks, Americans were asking, "why do they hate us?" The attacks jolted the American psyche. Most Americans were blissfully unaware of how they were perceived in other parts of the world. To them, it was inconceivable that other people could harbor such animosity against America. In their search for an explanation, many Americans concluded that other peoples "don't understand us." American President George W. Bush echoed the sentiments of a stunned nation when he stated that "we have to do a better job of telling our story."

Americans felt it was particularly pressing to tell America's story to the Arab and Muslim world. There was a belief, common among many Americans, that America's message was most distorted in the Middle East—the region from which the hijackers originated.

Once attention turned to the Arab and Muslim world, the focus was on Al Jazeera as a channel to reach the Arab world. However, what looked like a promising relationship between Al Jazeera and American officials soon became plagued with misunderstandings. Each appeared to have unspoken assumptions about the other—its goals, audience, message, and even the way the other defined news. The more the two interacted, the more misunderstandings emerged. The frustration produced inevitable strains and tensions.

With the start of the American-led war in Iraq and Al Jazeera's intensive coverage of it, cultural misunderstandings have emerged once again. This time however, the relations between the Arab news network and American officials have become even more strained and the hostility against Al Jazeera has filtered down to the American media and public.

The cultural differences that plague the relationship between Al Jazeera and American public diplomacy officials relate to a hidden dance described by intercultural communication scholars John Condon and Fathi Yousef.[1] The dance occurs during a conversation between an Englishman named Mr Jones and a Mexican gentleman named Mr Lopez. Mr Jones prefers to stand at arm's length from his conversation partner, while Mr Lopez prefers to stand much closer. Neither is aware of each other's hidden cultural assumption about the "proper distance" one should observe while carrying on a conversation. So as they talk, a kind of dance ensues. As Mr Lopez steps forward to decrease the distance between himself and his interlocutor, Mr Jones steps back to increase the distance. Both feel awkward and uncomfortable, yet neither realizes why. In the end, Mr Lopez calls Mr Jones "aloof" and "cold," while Mr Jones complains that Mr Lopez is "pushy" and "aggressive."

Such is the nature of "miscommunication." As Condon and Yousef explain, "something is communicated, even though it is not what was intended and often it is not what was thought to have been communicated."[2]

In much the same way that the two gentlemen above dance around the hidden cultural assumptions that frustrate their communication, so too, Al Jazeera and American officials appear to be engaged in such a dance. At varying times, the two have gravitated toward each other with warm praise, only to recoil in confusion and frustration.

This chapter looks at the dance of intercultural miscommunication between Al Jazeera and American public diplomacy. The analogy may be a bit of a stretch, but hopefully it will help expose some of the intercultural dynamics that frustrate the efforts of American officials to effectively communicate with the Arab public using the Arab television medium Al Jazeera.

SEPTEMBER 11—SHALL WE DANCE?

Prior to September 11, Al Jazeera was, in essence, dancing alone. Few in the United States had heard of Al Jazeera—except that Osama bin Laden had appeared on the network to appeal to the Arab masses in his cause against America. For an American official to appear on the same network as a "known terrorist" was incongruent with American sensibilities. Not surprisingly, Al Jazeera's numerous requests for interviews with American officials went unanswered.[3]

After September 11, the relationship appeared to change dramatically between the network and the relatively new Bush administration.

If bin Laden could use Al Jazeera's airwaves to appeal to the Arab public, why couldn't the United States?

When America's War on Terrorism began, winning the information war became "an essential element of the military strategy."[4] In short order, one high-ranking American official after another began showing up for interviews at Al Jazeera's tiny studio in Washington. In September, US Secretary of State Colin Powell hastily granted an interview request that had been placed several months earlier. He was soon followed by the chairman of the Joint Chiefs of Staff, the Director of the Agency for International Development, the Assistant Secretary of State for the Near East, the White House National Security Advisor, then finally by the Secretary of Defense. Never before had so many senior American officials showed up at Al Jazeera's doorstep. In fact, more American officials granted interviews with Al Jazeera in the first two months after the attacks than in all of its previous three years in Washington.

The dance was on.

Yet, if Al Jazeera had been an ever willing dance partner, the Americans appeared more reluctant and ambivalent. On the one hand, most Americans associated Al Jazeera with the bin Laden videotapes. Still reeling from September 11, that association alone was enough for many Americans to tag Al Jazeera as the culprit in disseminating "hatred and misunderstanding" throughout the Arabic-speaking world. On the other hand, it was precisely because Al Jazeera could speak to the Arab world that the White House thought it would be "very constructive for members of the administration to do interviews with Al Jazeera."[5] In the need to take America's case directly to the Arab public, Al Jazeera soon became "the unofficial, two-way communications channel between the Arab and Western world."[6]

It appears that the rush of interviews with Al Jazeera was prompted more by necessity than choice. The interviews were a critical component in a concerted public diplomacy effort aimed at the Arab and Muslim world. Within a month of the attacks, the US State Department appointed Charlotte Beers, a former advertising executive with more than forty years of experience, as the new Undersecretary of State for Public Affairs and Public Diplomacy. Beers and other experts testified before Congress in a series of hearings on American public diplomacy. The prevailing conclusion reached during these hearings was that the world did not know and understand America. As the Chairman of the House International

Relations Committee wondered, "How is it that the country that invented Hollywood and Madison Avenue has such trouble promoting a positive image of itself overseas?"[7]

Undersecretary Beers outlined the goals of American public diplomacy in the Arab and Muslim worlds. The top priority of American public diplomacy was "to inform the international world swiftly and accurately about the policies of the US government" and to "re-present the values and beliefs of the people of America, which inform [US] policies and practices."[8]

The State Department compiled a booklet on the link between Al Qaeda and September 11, entitled "The Network of Terrorism," which quickly became its most widely disseminated brochure ever. It launched a new website and an Arabic-language radio station, Radio Sawa, featuring American and Arab pop music with short news broadcasts. It also retained an advertising firm to produce series of mini-documentaries on Muslim life in America. Beers even stated that she would consider buying advertising time on Al Jazeera if need be.[9]

The American administration and Congress had similarly intensified their efforts. The latter passed the new Freedom Promotion Act of 2002 which injected $497 million annually into the budget of public diplomacy. Both the Pentagon and the White House established special offices to help reach America's public diplomacy goals.

With such a concerted effort at the highest levels to "win the hearts and minds" of the Arabs and Muslims, American officials expected support and understanding to increase. Instead, after more than a year of intensive public diplomacy, anti-American sentiment in the Arab and Muslim world had grown further.[10]

Al Jazeera's interviews with American officials during that year stopped almost as quickly as they had started. "After about two or three weeks," said Al Jazeera Washington bureau chief, Hafez Al Mirazi, "the administration appeared to consider these interviews 'one shot' deals ... and we no longer found the same enthusiasm to give us such interviews after that."[11] One commentator complained that Al Jazeera had received a disproportionate amount of the administration's attention.[12] Another remarked that "in terms of content and impact, the interviews had fallen flat."[13] Some suggested that the administration had been burned by their experience with Al Jazeera, especially in the interview with the National Security Adviser, Condoleezza Rice.[14] For one reason or another, the interviews stopped, which according to Mirazi, meant that "Washington made the incorrect assumption that there was no longer any need to actively reach out to the Arab world."[15]

In February 2003, during a hearing before the Senate Foreign Relations Committee, Undersecretary Beers summed up the state of America's public diplomacy: "The gap between who we are and how we wish to be seen, and how we are in fact seen, is frighteningly wide."[16] In speaking specifically of the Arab and Muslim world, Beers was even more graphic:

> We are talking about millions of ordinary people, a huge number of whom have gravely distorted, but carefully cultivated images of us—images so negative, so weird, so hostile that I can assure you a young generation of terrorists is being created.[17]

Clearly, America's public diplomacy initiative backfired. The following week, Beers resigned her position, for health reasons. The relationship with Al Jazeera that had appeared so promising in the beginning proved neither satisfying nor enduring. American officials were perplexed, frustrated and even angry.

What went wrong?

HIDDEN ASSUMPTIONS ABOUT THE DANCE

From the outset, it appears that Al Jazeera and American officials had different assumptions about what dance they were dancing. In the dance, each side had self-images and goals. Additionally, each side expected the other to understand and help meet those goals and preserve those self-images. Unfortunately, the goals and expectations were buried in hidden cultural assumptions that neither side shared with the other. The resulting frustration was inevitable.

Al Jazeera's unstated goal rested on the pride of its unique and short history. As other scholars have pointed out in this collection and elsewhere, Al Jazeera broke with the tradition of Arab news media by offering differing views on controversial topics in an engaging manner. Its goal was not to be a "mouthpiece" for the Ministry of Information or government officials—in fact, the Ministry of Information, under which responsibility for censorship falls, was abolished altogether in Qatar as a *sine qua non* for launching such a channel. Al Jazeera's goal, as stated in its motto, is to present "the opinion and other opinion."

Al Jazeera's goal of not speaking on behalf of government officials was widely and vigorously applauded as a first step in a free and independent press in the Arab world. Some leading journalists and media organizations, especially in America, did not fail to take notice of the network. For instance, *Time Magazine* called it "the toast of Western media"[18] and *New York Times* reporter Thomas Friedman praised it as "not only the biggest media phenomenon to hit the Arab world since the advent of television, it also is the biggest political phenomenon."[19]

Al Jazeera's goal of not being a government voice but rather a voice that listens to and speaks to its audience fits well with America's own political goal of encouraging the development of civil society in the Arab region. One of the hallmarks of civil society is institutions that are independent of the government and that reflect the will of the people. America's goal of promoting independent journalism—independent of government control—and "freedom of the press" has been Al Jazeera's goal as well.

In pre-September 11 America, Al Jazeera's goals matched those of American journalists and politicians. Al Jazeera and American officials were dancing the dance of "free press in a civil society." Al Jazeera felt that it was mastering the steps with American encouragement and support.

In post-September 11 America, America's priorities changed overnight. The goal of a free and independent press became secondary to rallying support for America's "War on Terrorism." In wartime, all media become critically important as channels for a government to communicate with the people, and ultimately, as tools for rallying public support.

When America suddenly changed the dance to "we are at war," the hidden expectation of American officials for the media was to rally public support. Presumably, Al Jazeera's role was to rally support with the Arab public. When Al Jazeera did not follow suit, American administration officials strongly voiced their displeasure, thus exposing their hidden expectation of what the media should do in times of war.

Al Jazeera's airing of additional videos of bin Laden particularly distressed American officials. Secretary of State Colin Powell remarked on "an undue amount of time and attention to some of the most vitriolic, irresponsible kinds of statements."[20] Condoleezza Rice held a conference call with the editors of major television networks cautioning them not to air the videos because they might contain coded messages of further attacks against the United States. Both Vice President Dick Cheney and Powell sought to pressure Qatari officials to rein in Al Jazeera. The pressure was seen by some as censorship and by others as hypocrisy. As Daoud Kuttab put it, "I can see why [the Americans] are angry but it is not because Al Jazeera is not fair. On the contrary, I think they wish for Al Jazeera to be biased to the US."[21]

Al Jazeera was seen a journalistic success story for the Arab world primarily because it did not listen to Arab governments. However, when Al Jazeera did not listen to the American government during this time of crisis for America, Al Jazeera fell out of step. For the Americans, if not for Al Jazeera, the dance had changed.

ON OPPOSITE SIDES OF THE DANCE FLOOR

The dance became particularly awkward for both Al Jazeera and American public officials because of the hidden cultural assumptions of "us" and "them" in America's War on Terrorism. President Bush's pronouncement that "you are either with us or against us" reinforced an unstated cultural dividing line between Americans, on the one hand, and Arabs and Muslims, on the other hand.

For Americans, the unstated cultural assumption was that "us" meant Americans and the West. For Arabs, the unstated cultural assumption of "us" meant other Arabs and Muslims. These contrasting cultural assumptions of who is "us" are deep and enduring. When "us" became the "good guys" in the war against good and evil, "them" became the bad guys and even the enemy.

With this reversed and confused perspective, it was hardly surprising that American officials had repeatedly to reassure and explain who the war was against and who "the enemy" was. Many in the Arab and Muslim world felt that they were the target of America's war. America's targeting of primarily Muslim countries reinforced this perception. Try, as American officials may have, to say that the war was not against the Arabs or Islam, the confused, if not reversed, cultural assumptions of who was "us" and "them" persisted.

Inevitably, the media and journalists were caught in this cultural schism of "us" and "them." The unstated cultural assumption for the American media—as part and parcel of American culture—was that it was the voice of the "us" in the war against "them." While some American journalists struggled to maintain their objectivity and not become "co-opted" by the administration, few American journalists questioned the very notion that they were not part of the American cultural definition of "us."

For Arab media, the unstated cultural assumption was that it was part and parcel of Arab culture. The definition of "us" and "them" was less clear. Like its American media counterparts, Al Jazeera wanted to maintain its journalistic objectivity. However, it had difficulty putting itself in the "us" column when it and its viewing audience were clearly non-Americans. When Al Jazeera spoke to its audience from an Arab perspective, it was perceived as anti-American. Al Jazeera and the Arab media openly questioned the American administration's efforts to rally support for America's war against "them." America's insistence on Al Jazeera's aid to get America's message out to the Arab public was particularly awkward. What American officials were essentially asking Al Jazeera to do was to rally Arab support to fight Arabs, or for that matter Muslim support to fight Islam. This was clearly an intercultural misstep.

OUT OF TUNE

Not only were the two sides dancing different dances, they also appeared to be dancing to different music. Al Jazeera's music came from the "Arab street," a literal translation of the notion of Arab public opinion. American officials resonated with American public opinion and Washington political insiders. If Al Jazeera had problems convincing American officials that it could not rally the Arab public on behalf of the American government, American officials had problems responding to the voice of the Arab street.

In many ways, American officials appeared to be communicating with Al Jazeera's Arab audience as if it were the American public. The American interviews reflect the language and persuasive style that positively resonate with the American public, but negatively resonate with the Arab public. For example, virtually all American officials frequently state what America *will* or *will not* do in the future. Such a forceful and deliberate use of the word "will" can be particularly persuasive in the American culture because it underscores one's resolve or intention which fits well with the pioneering spirit that built America. In contrast, Arabs and Muslims tend to use the future tense more sparingly and more reverently. The frequently heard expression *"in shaa Allah"* is an admonition that only God knows what will happen. Knowledge of the unseen future is within the realm of God, not humankind. American officials' repeated insistence on what they will or will not do, especially in such a deliberate manner and forceful tone, could be perceived as naive at best or, at worst, profoundly arrogant.

Another cultural misstep in the interviews was American officials' vigorous efforts to present the "facts" or "evidence" to the Arab public. From the American perspective, facts are the critical ingredients of persuasive arguments. Hence, Americans tend to gather as many facts as possible and carefully construct their arguments. That the Arab public was clearly not convinced by the facts—and even believed the opposite—was an indication that the American officials were using the wrong persuasive tools. In Arab culture, metaphors and analogies that suggest important relationships are much more persuasive than impersonal "facts." American officials have been perplexed by how callously Al Jazeera's viewers dismiss the facts, yet many of Al Jazeera's audience were chagrined by how American officials are so myopically focused on the facts.

American officials also appear to miss important historical or religious cues that resonate strongly with Arab and Muslim listeners. Failure to acknowledge these cues represents missed opportunities for the American officials to connect with and persuade the audience whom they are trying to reach. One example in particular stands out. The interview Al Jazeera conducted with Condoleezza Rice showed a clear disconnection between the Arab-centered question and the American-centered response.[22]

Al Jazeera:	Dr Rice, I know your time is limited, and perhaps we just have a minute left, so I will move to the last question. But please take as much time as you need to answer. The perception of a post-war Iraq in the Arab world is one of foreign occupation forces returning to an Arab country, and to a city that used to be the capital of the Islamic caliphate. There is a fear of tearing Iraq apart between Kurds in the North and Shiites in the South, and a fear of intervention to change Arab regimes by force. How do you perceive a post-war Iraq?
Condoleezza Rice:	Well, Iraq is a special case because Iraq has been a serial abuser of UN Security Council resolutions. It is an outlaw regime that the Security Council has sanctioned many times. But let me be very clear, if we have to use military forces in Iraq, it is our intention to help the Iraqi

> people liberate themselves, to be there, as the President
> said, as long as we're needed but not one minute longer,
> and to very early on, put in place with Iraqis—from out-
> side the country and inside the country—an Iraqi
> authority that can administer and run the country.

Clearly, the interaction speaks of a cultural disconnection. First, the host of the program signals the importance of the question when he says "please take as much time as you need to answer," but fails to illicit a proportionate response. The guest's answer is in fact shorter than the question. Next he cues her to the historical signifi- cance of Iraq for Muslims and Arabs, referring to "a city that used to be the capital of the Islamic caliphate." She gets that "Iraq is a special case," but not in ways that connect her to her audience. Nor does she address the resentment, shared by many Arabs, about the attack on an Arab country which may be considered "a symbol of Islam's heritage," the fear that the use of military force may be the prelude to an American occupation or the speculation that such an intervention may tear Iraq apart. Her answer focuses solely on American concerns about ending the Iraqi regime. The reference to Iraq's violations of UN resolutions is particularly problematic because it is more likely to raise a red flag with Arab viewers who believe that Israel violated more resolutions and for far longer than Saddam Hussein had been in power.

Vocabulary is another area of cross-cultural contention. This is evident not only in the reporting of the war, but also in the Palestinian–Israeli conflict. Americans frequently cite Al Jazeera's use of the terms "martyrs" and "commando operations" instead of "terrorists" and "suicide bombings" as an indication of the net- work's biased coverage. Yet, American officials have also insisted on using a special vocabulary, without the label of being biased, to emphasize their perspective. In many instances, the differing vocab- ularies seem at cross-purposes. In much the same way that Al Jazeera's rhetoric can alienate American sensibilities, American rhetoric can alienate Arab sensibilities. By insisting on emotionally laden rhetoric to emphasize their point, American officials may have needlessly alienated an audience which might have been receptive to the underlying idea if it had been expressed in more neutral language. The deliberate use of such rhetoric on the part of the US can signal hostility and reinforce the Arab perception that American officials are out of touch with the region and its people.

Finally, the topic of the Palestinian–Israeli conflict and American policy is an area laden with miscommunication and disagreement. American officials appear impervious to how strongly the conflict resonates throughout the Arab world. In this context, American officials' focus and their condemnation of Al Jazeera's coverage of the conflict—instead of condemnation of the conflict itself—were alienating for Arab viewers causing them to align themselves even more with the network that represents their views than the American officials who condemn their perspective. When it comes to American policy, Stephen Blank called Washington "tone deaf, if not worse, throughout much of the Islamic world."[23] It is difficult, indeed, to dance if one cannot hear the music.

OFFBEAT

If American officials are out of tune with their verbal messages to the Arab public, they appeared conspicuously offbeat with their non-verbal behaviors, or on-screen television presence, during their Al Jazeera interviews. The non-verbal cues are often more important and more credible than the verbal message within one's own culture. In cross-cultural settings in which one may feel handicapped by language differences, non-verbal cues can carry even greater weight. American officials seem to be sending mixed messages or failing to use non-verbal behaviors to establish a relationship with Al Jazeera's Arab audiences. Again, there are hidden cultural assumptions and explanations.

To start with, the American officials' non-verbal behavior appears to be modeled after Walter Cronkite. The latter was the first news anchor to present the nightly news reports on the CBS broadcast network. He was a stoic figure with a low, authoritative and steady voice. His voice and image were the backdrop of news on the Vietnam War, the assassination of the young American president John F. Kennedy, the Civil Rights Movement and the Apollo space landing on the moon, among other important moments in American history. Through tragedy and triumph, Walter Cronkite maintained a calm demeanor. Not surprisingly, he became the "most trusted man in America."

What is important to note culturally is that many American officials over the age of forty grew up watching Walter Cronkite. Subliminally, Cronkite represented the ideal of credibility in the broadcast news context. It is an American ethnocentric model that reflects the hidden cultural assumption that news should be delivered the way Cronkite delivered it—calmly, objectively, factually and with minimum affect.

Not surprisingly, training for television broadcast interviews similarly reflects the Cronkite model. Interviewees are coached to maintain their composure even under fire from aggressive reporters. According to the American model, losing composure is the equivalent of losing objectivity. Losing objectivity makes one's argument and facts suspect and, ultimately, undermines one's credibility. Thus, to be an effective persuader in the American context, one should control the visual display of strong emotions. Rapid hand movement or animated facial expressions are discouraged. Instead, American officials tend to manipulate their voice tone or volume and language—either using sarcasm or understatement—to express anger.

Despite its BBC roots, Al Jazeera reflects more of a unique Arab television news style than an American model. As many observers have noted, Al Jazeera's news style and interview format are anything but calm or sedate. Interviewers as well as interviewees are highly vocal and emotionally expressive. The interplay between news and the human emotions it engenders is succinctly stated in the news philosophy of Ibrahim Helal, editor in chief of Al Jazeera. "Emotions are part of the story," says Helal, "The soul of the news lies in emotion. Emotion is the most important fact."[24]

There is an important caveat to mention in discussing the contrasting delivery styles of Americans and Arabs, and the differences in how most Americans and Arabs watch television. The two delivery styles appear to match the viewing styles.

Most Americans tend to have an intimate and somewhat private relationship with their televisions. Most Americans tend to watch television alone; homes often have multiple television sets with each person watching his or her "own TV program." The physical distance between the viewer and television set is normally about six feet—the distance between two people conversing. At this close distance, exaggerated body movement or vocal expression can be alienating for most Americans. Television close-ups can further magnify emotional impact several fold at this intimate distance. All of these factors tend to reinforce an American view of television as a McLuhan "hot medium," and hence the American preference for an on-screen demeanor that is emotionally cool or reserved.

In the Arab world, a variety of factors contribute to a preference for an emotionally expressive and engaging on-screen presence. First, because of the nature of Arab families and group social habits, television watching tends to be a group experience. It also tends to be an active experience, with the audience often commenting more than the television commentators. The physical distance between the viewers and television is not intimate but rather public, usually ten feet or more. Televisions in public settings, such as cafes, are common with a distance of up to twenty feet. Finally, compared with the dominant Anglo-American culture, the Arab culture is more emotionally expressive and more accepting of emotional expression. This combination of group viewing patterns, group interaction, physical distance and greater emotional expression tend to favor an on-screen presence that is emotionally engaging.

When one contrasts the emotionally engaging style characteristic of Arab television with the delivery style of American officials—who have been trained to be emotionally neutral—the American officials come across as wooden and stiff. When on TV, Americans speak in a formal and concise manner that is hard for Arab viewers to relate to. Void of human emotion, American officials fail to engage or persuade the Arab public.

In a comparative analysis, Jihad Fakhreddine highlights the power of emotion to capture and persuade the Arab audience in his contrasting descriptions of American ambassador Christopher Ross and the British Prime Minister, Tony Blair, during their interviews on Al Jazeera. Ambassador Ross, a fluent Arabic speaker, adeptly crossed the language hurdle. However, speaking Arabic is not the critical factor in connecting with the Arabic public:

> knowing fluent Arabic is not a sufficient and necessary condition for effective communication. Ross spoke exactly as a hesitant diplomat would, repeating many of his words and thoughts, without any passion for what he was stating. This performance has been very similar to that of every other US official who appeared on Arab TV channels.[25]

In contrast, Fakhreddine describes the persuasive power of Tony Blair, who knows no Arabic, but who had a passionate delivery:

> Blair was able to overcome this communication hurdle [of language] simply because he could overwhelm his Arab audiences with his passionate

delivery. Every facial, body and hand gesture Blair made with each word he uttered seemed to communicate genuine belief in what he had to say. His interview on Al Jazeera ... was an outstanding demonstration of successful British public diplomacy in the Arab region.[26]

While Ambassador Ross has received mixed reviews by other analysts, especially in a debate setting, Colin Powell's interview received the most positive feedback from viewers according to Al Jazeera.[27] Given that Powell knows no Arabic, one can conclude that the non-verbal element is more powerful than the verbal one. Success on Arab television appears to rest more on one's ability to connect non-verbally with the audience than on one's ability to speak Arabic.

Two final observations can be made about the power of non-verbal behaviors to shape the verbal message. First, the Americans believe that their verbal and non-verbal behaviors match; a verbal message focused on impersonal facts and rational arguments fits with a dispassionate delivery style. They believe that they are projecting an overall image of "objectivity" and credibility. In the Arab world, emotional neutrality, especially in an emotionally charged context, can be perceived as deceptive. In the minds of Arab viewers, if a person hides his or her own emotions, he or she can hide other things. Thus, the dispassionate delivery style erodes credibility.

Second, as scholars have noted, Americans have a tendency for understatement while Arabs have a tendency for overstatement.[28] In much the same way that Americans tend to view the Arabs' overstatement as exaggerating the situation—and thus less than truthful and not credible—Arabs tend to view the understatements of the Americans as not fully presenting the situation—and thus less than truthful and not credible. When American officials combine understatement with a dispassionate delivery they, in effect, completely undermine their credibility. Not only is the verbal message not credible, the non-verbal message reinforces that image of deception.

If Al Jazeera does not fit the American ethnocentric Cronkite-news model, neither do most American news programs today. However, people tend to be more accepting of variations within their own culture than within other alien cultures. Thus while Al Jazeera's interviews are often labeled as "sensational," similar examples in American media are called "hard-hitting." This apparent double standard happens often in intercultural communication; paradoxes within one's own culture are often overlooked while paradoxes within other cultures are glaringly obvious and demand explanation.

AND THE DANCE CONTINUES ...

With the start of the American-led war against Iraq the dance of miscommunication between Al Jazeera and American public diplomacy resumed again. There are several important features to note.

First, American officials once again rediscovered Al Jazeera—as both an opportunity and a concern. Before the war started, American political and military leaders were actively courting the Qatari network as part of their public diplomacy efforts. High-ranking administration officials began showing up at Al Jazeera's Washington studio. First Colin Powell, then Condoleezza Rice, then Donald Rumsfeld granted interviews in the days leading up to the military action. As Colin Powell told a congressional panel, "We have got to do all we can to change the tone in the world with respect to what we are doing ... We need to talk to ... the Arab public."[29]

The Pentagon was particularly vigorous in courting Al Jazeera. America's top brass were made available for interviews, while Al Jazeera reporters were provided choice positions as "embedded journalists" in the military's new media strategy of placing journalists with the American troops. As a "sign of how aggressively the Bush administration has embraced Al Jazeera," several media officials from the US Central Command attended a picnic hosted at the home of Al Jazeera's news director in Doha.[30]

These initial efforts to woo Al Jazeera by the Pentagon parallel those of the State Department earlier. This is hardly surprising. In many ways, the American military has become the new face of American public diplomacy, making the coverage of the American military operation in Iraq critical.

Second, Al Jazeera's ambivalent relationship with the Pentagon appears reminiscent of its earlier relationship with the State Department. Once again, American public diplomacy goals have run head-on into Al Jazeera's goal to remain independent and speak to its viewers. After what appeared to be a promising relationship between the American military and Al Jazeera, the relationship quickly turned sour in the first few days of the war when Al Jazeera aired footage of captured American soldiers. The Americans called this a violation of the Geneva Conventions and loudly voiced their outrage. Secretary of Defense Donald Rumsfeld, particularly incensed by the airing of pictures of captured American soldiers, called Al Jazeera "not a perfect instrument of communication" and "obviously, is part of Iraqi propaganda."[31] Days later, an American general refused to take a question from an Al Jazeera correspondent at a televised Central Command briefing.[32] Not long after that, Al Jazeera's office in Baghdad was hit, causing the death of one of its reporters.

Third, in what appears to be a new development, the displeasure of American officials with Al Jazeera has spread to the American public and American media. American officials are not the only ones in America who are upset with Al Jazeera. "In times like these," reads an editorial in The *New Jersey Star Ledger*, "Americans are concerned about the way the world is viewing us."[33] Many did not like the image they saw reflected in Al Jazeera's coverage. Wall Street kicked Al Jazeera off the floor of the New York Stock Exchange and NASDAQ, saying it would only accredit journalists from outlets that had "responsible business coverage."[34] In a similar move of disapproval, AOL, Yahoo and Reuters refused to carry Al Jazeera advertisements.[35]

If Al Jazeera was used to being at the apex of a media war, being the focus of a cyber war was new. After news broke of the footage of the America soldiers on Al Jazeera, Al Jazeera experienced a 2,000 per cent increase in site visits and "Al Jazeera" became the second most searched-for term on major search engines.[36] Although over 20,000 websites were defaced in the first week of the war in Iraq, "the most notable victim was Al Jazeera," according to Reuters. Both Al Jazeera's Arabic and new English-language websites were hacked with pro-American messages and visuals. The phrases "Let freedom ring" and "God bless our troops" were accompanied by a large American flag and the signature of the "Freedom Cyber Force Militia."[37] In the midst of this cyber war, Akamai Technologies abruptly cancelled its web server support to Al Jazeera,[38] leaving the websites even more vulnerable.

Finally, Al Jazeera has once again been in the American spotlight as the voice of and window to the Arab world through its coverage of Iraq. Numerous media analysts have noted that the difference between the American coverage and the Arab coverage of the events in Iraq is so dramatic that one gets the impression they are covering two different wars. As one writer commented, "while American media has focused on soldiers, tanks and sandstorms, Arab TV has seized on dramatic and visceral images of blown up houses and mangled bodies."[39] If some have called American media coverage "antiseptic" because of its aerial footage of the American military hitting its targets, others have described Al Jazeera's reporting as "grizzly" because of its close-ups of the after-effects of hitting those targets.

On the surface, the footage is very different; however, below the surface, both the American networks and Al Jazeera appear to share the same news philosophy and approach: cover the story from a local angle and the audience's perspective.

When it comes to presenting a "local angle" of the coverage in Iraq, Al Jazeera and the American media are literally and figuratively on opposite sides of the ocean. As many have noted, American media coverage of the war has focused on the American military and specifically the troops and weaponry. Not only do many Americans have their sons, daughters, fathers or friends among those troops, but in the patriotic spirit of war time, many Americans identify with the troops and their families. The focus is on the American military. On the opposite side of the airwaves, some of Al Jazeera's viewers also have family members in Iraq and they want to know what is happening to their loved ones on the ground. They are looking at the situation in Iraq from the personal, up close perspective. Thus, although it is one war, there are two perspectives and two local angles.

CONCLUSION

This chapter has explored the hidden cultural assumptions that have shaped the public diplomacy efforts of American officials to use an Arab television network, Al Jazeera, to communicate with the Arab public. The relationship between Al Jazeera and the American officials who have appeared for interviews has been plagued by misunderstandings, distrust and frustration—without anyone really understanding why. Such is the nature of culturally mediated behaviors. Mundane activities like "getting dressed," "eating breakfast" or even "watching the news" are familiar activities that Americans and Arabs engage in daily. Precisely because these activities are routine, they are often taken for granted. It is not until one begins exploring one's assumptions that one can expose the hidden cultural landmines that can explode into intercultural miscommunication.

In the first go around between Al Jazeera and the American officials, there were problems of differing goals, vocabulary and non-verbal delivery styles. These differences caused strains in their relationship and frustrated America's goal to use Al Jazeera as a medium for persuading the Arab public. American officials employed a verbal style that may have positively resonated with the American public but which negatively resonated with the Arab public. The non-verbal delivery style of the American officials lacked the emotional fortitude necessary for engaging and persuading the Arab public.

With the American-led military operation in Iraq, American officials have again sought the Arab television medium to communicate with the Arab public. This time, American officials are aiming for greater success in reaching the Arab public. The goal is to be more credible and more persuasive. What is interesting in the new approach by the American officials is that they are clearly trying to change and expand their media outlets—working with other Arab television networks—instead of exclusively with Al Jazeera. However, what is less clear is whether or not, and, if so, to what extent, they have changed their media style.

So far, it appears that American officials are still communicating with the Arab public in much the same way that they communicate with the American public. The problem is not switching Arab television channels, but recognizing the hidden cultural assumptions that undermined the American performance on Al Jazeera and adapting their style to fit the Arab audience. Changing the channel will not help as much as changing the perspective and approach. Until American officials are able to adapt their communication style to fit the Arab medium and Arab audience, their relationship with different Arab networks will probably be similar to that with Al Jazeera—a dance of intercultural miscommunication.

NOTES

1 J. Condon and F. Yousef, *Intercultural Communication* (Illinois: Bobbs Merrill, 1975), p. 15.
2 Ibid.
3 "Interview with Al Jazeera Washington bureau chief Hafez Al Mirazi," *Middle East Insight* (March/April 2002), <http://www.mideastinsight. org/03_02/arab.html>.
4 M. Gordon, "US tries to rally public support overseas," *New York Times*, November 6, 2001.
5 A. Fleischer, quoted in J. Hodgson, "Bush's security adviser to appear on Al Jazeera," *Guardian*, October 15, 2001.
6 "Window on the War," *News Hour* with Jim Lehrer, PBS, October 8, 2001.
7 H.J. Hyde, "The role of public diplomacy in support of the anti-terrorism campaign," Congressional Hearing, October 10, 2001.

8   C. Beers, "US public diplomacy in the Arab and Muslim worlds," Remarks at the Washington Institute for Near East Policy, Washington DC, May 7, 2002.

9   I. Teinowitz, "US considers advertising on Al Jazeera TV," October 15, 2001, <http://www.adage.com>.

10 Studies conducted by the Pew Research Center (2002), the German Marshall Fund and the Chicago Council on Foreign Relations (2002), and the University of Michigan (2002) all cite a precipitous drop in support for the United States around the globe, among traditional American allies as well as new adversaries. A British report on American values noted similar findings. See "Living with a superpower," *The Economist*, January 2, 2003.

11 "Interview with Hafez Al Mirazi," *Middle East Insight*.

12 F. Ajami, "What the Muslim world is watching," *New York Times*, November 18, 2001.

13 S. Sachs, "US appears to be losing public relations war so far," *New York Times*, October 28, 2001.

14 N. Abou El Magd, "Western officials finding it tough to reach Arabs, Muslims with message on war on terrorism," Associated Press, October 16, 2001, <http://multimedia.belointeractive.com/attack/perspective/1016aljazeera. html>.

15 "Interview with Hafez Al Mirazi," *Middle East Insight*.

16 C. Beers, "Hearing on American public diplomacy and Islam," US Senate Committee on Foreign Relations, February 27, 2003.

17 Ibid.

18 J. Reaves, "Prime time for the Arab CNN," *Time Magazine*, October 10, 2001.

19 T. Friedman, *The Lexus and the Olive Tree: Understanding Globalization* (New York: Farrar, Straus and Giroux, 2000).

20 Interview with Colin Powell, *The Early Show*, CBS, October 10, 2001.

21 D. Kuttab quoted in J. Campagna, "Between two words: Qatar's Al Jazeera satellite channel faces conflicting expectations," Committee to Protect Journalists Press Freedom Reports, October 20, 2001, <http://www.cpj.org/ Briefings/2000/Is_Pal_oct00/Is_Pal-oct00.html>.

22 Interview with Condoleezza Rice, Al Jazeera, Washington DC, March 14, 2003, <http://www.whitehouse.gov/news/releases/2003/03/20030314– 20. html>.

23 S. Blank, "Politics and war, Iraqi style," *Asia Times Online*, March 27, 2003, <http://www.atimes.com/atimes/Middle_East/EC27Ak03.html>.

24 Quoted in M. Dobbs, "America's Arab voice: Radio Sawa struggles to make itself heard," *Washington Post*, March 24, 2003.

25 J. Fakhreddine, "The US–Arab cross-communication exchange: a dialogue amongst mutes," *Transnational Broadcasting Studies*, No. 8 (Spring/Summer 2002), <http://www.tbsjournal.com/Archives/ Spring02/ fakhreddine.html>.

26 Ibid.

27 "Interview with Hafez Al Mirazi," *Middle East Insight*.

28 R.S. Zaharna, "Understanding cultural preferences of Arab communication patterns," *Public Relations Review*, Vol. 21 (1995), pp. 241–55.

29 C. Powell, "Testimony before the Subcommittee on Commerce, Justice, State, and Judiciary of House Appropriations Committee," March 26, 2003.

30 J. Perlez and J. Rutenberg, "Administration cozies up with Al Jazeera network," *New York Times*, March 20, 2003.

31 Interview with Donald Rumsfeld, *Face the Nation*, CBS, March 23, 2003.

32 H. Rosenberg, "Snippets of the unique Al Jazeera," *Los Angeles Times*, April 4, 2003.

33 A. Hoffman, "Language not the only barrier in foreign war news," *Star Ledger*, March 31, 2003.

34 I. Thomas, "Al Jazeera under attack from all sides," April 4, 2003, <http://www.vnunet.com/News/1139984>.

35 Ibid.

36 M. Geller, "Americans turn to online news in droves," *Internet Press Association*, March 31, 2003, <http://www.internet-press.net/newsevents_2003.htm>.

37 R. Lemos, "Pro-US message replaces Aljazzera.net," March 27, 2003, <http://www.zdnet.com.au/newstech/security/story/0,2000048600, 20273249,00.htm>. See also T. Bridis, "Hackers put US flag on Al Jazeera site," March 28, 2003, <http://www. siliconvalley.com/mld/siliconvalley/ 5500354.htm>.

38 S. Junnarkar, "Akamai ends Al Jazeera server support," April 4, 2003, <http://news.com.com/1200–1035–995546.html>.

39 B. Smith, "Powell goes on Arab TV to win minds of viewers," *Chicago Sun Times*, March 28, 2003.

Afterword—Arab Media Studies: Some Methodological Considerations

Jon B. Alterman

With all the ink that has been spilled over the phenomenon of Arab satellite television, our understanding of it—in both the West and in the Arab world—remains preliminary and incomplete. For an increasing number of people around the world, it is something that is seen, even if in glimpses. But even for those in the Arab world, it is something that is talked about far more than it is understood.

In order to understand the effects of the rise of satellite television on Arab societies, we need significantly more data along three lines of inquiry. The first is quantitative data, so that we can understand who is watching, what they are watching, and how much they are watching. The second is qualitative data, so that we can understand how such television affects peoples' lives. The last is comparative data, so that we can learn from experiences elsewhere in the world and distinguish what is distinctive in the Middle East from what is true elsewhere.

Until quite recently, most Western scholars systematically underestimated the effects of satellite television on the Middle East. Westerners had only a dim sense of the high interest with which Arab audiences followed the Al Aqsa intifada in its early months, and Arab-produced images of the violence rarely reached Western television screens. In many ways, it was two other conflicts, the US wars in Afghanistan and Iraq, that demonstrated the presence of an alternative source of news and images, produced at a highly professional level for a global audience.

For many Americans, Arab satellite television comes down in its entirety to Al Jazeera. It is the brand name they know (and sometimes struggle to pronounce), and for many it is the enemy. Millions who have not watched Al Jazeera complain about its attitude, about its bias, and about its incitement of Arab populations. Overall, its role in the Arab world, or in the broader Arab media scene, is only dimly understood.

In the United States, in particular, satellite television is a far more marginal technology and generally requires a subscription fee. In the Middle East, however, satellite television tends to be free-to-air, meaning no subscription fees are required, and the one-time cost of a locally manufactured dish antenna can dip below $100. Combine the relatively low cost of watching satellite television, an interface that people already know how to use, and programming that can unite people by transcending borders, and you may be looking at a hugely important force in the region in the next several decades.

As a first principle, we need to free our studies of new media and technology in the Middle East from the straitjacket of the Western experience. We need to be more sensitive to how identical technologies can have vastly different impacts in different regions. Once we have done that, we need to think about developing data along three lines: quantitative, qualitative, and comparative. Unless we make progress on all three fronts, our ability to understand the future of the Middle East will be severely impaired.

QUANTITATIVE DATA

Some market research firms have conducted surveys on media and technology related use in the Middle East. For the most part, these efforts have concentrated on the wealthier countries of the Persian Gulf, where incomes are higher, consumption is higher, and brand advertising is more developed. However, the Arabs of the Gulf are atypical of much of the Arab world. Likewise, there are great disparities between different countries of the region. Per capita income across the Middle East and North Africa region is scarcely more than $2,000, but is more than ten times that amount in Kuwait.[1] Demographics differ from country to country as well. Although populations throughout the Middle East and North Africa tend to be young, the younger age cohorts are especially large in Saudi Arabia and Iran, and somewhat smaller in Lebanon.[2]

We need data on three aspects of media and technology use. The first addresses the question of precisely who the users are, especially outside the Gulf Cooperation Council (GCC) countries. Data tend to be developed for marketing studies, and thus concentrate on wealthier populations and remain proprietary. For that reason, scholars and public policy officials often lack access to the data that is theoretically available. In addition, many of the wealthier Arab countries have high numbers of expatriate workers. Yet, no study on media and technology use appears to separate out expatriates from nationals.

Also with regard to users, we need better data on usage patterns than is currently available. There is some proprietary evidence from market research firms which suggests that the Gulf audience for the Qatar-based Al Jazeera, for example, tends to be older and male, while the audience for the Lebanese Broadcasting Corporation (LBC) is younger and more evenly balanced between males and females.

Other lines of analysis come to mind: When people watch television, what are they watching? What Western programs do people watch, and how does viewership of Western programs compare with Arab programming? Are younger people watching significantly different programs than older people? Do Gulf viewers watch significantly different programming than, say, Egyptian viewers, and is there more national variation in viewing habits among older people than among younger people? All of these are significant and researchable questions, yet ones to which we do not yet know the answers.

It is important to note that none of these queries is static. For example, costs for dishes may come down, but digital encoding may raise costs. Efforts to curtail the widespread counterfeiting of digital decoders could raise prices and curtail audiences in a matter of months. Any research needs to take account of the shifting dynamics of regional media consumption, and keep an eye out for developing trends.

QUALITATIVE DATA

We need a better sense of how people see communications technology and the media affecting their own lives, and on their own terms. How do people watch satellite television, and what do they take away from it? Does "channel surfing" mean people catch more highlights, or are they left with an undifferentiated blur of images. How do these effects differ among different national population groups and among different age cohorts? Are young Jordanians affected in the same ways as young Emiratis, or older Moroccans? Are effects (both in nature and degree) different between male and female viewers, or between urban and rural viewers?

On the qualitative side, there has been very little content analysis of the Arab media of any stripe. There are several issues of interest here. One is how the satellite television stations cover news, how their coverage compares with that of terrestrial stations, and how coverage has changed over time. While anecdotally viewers report that the local news is becoming both livelier and more comprehensive, such a claim is difficult to prove. Equally significantly, how will the current migration of regional television stations to the Middle East affect their news coverage and entertainment programming?

Given the pervasiveness of the phenomenon, there have been remarkably few studies on the effects of videotapes, foreign television programming and foreign films in the Middle East.[3] What do people watch, why do they watch it and how does it affect their lives? Programming can be full of explicit and implicit messages, and some of them may differ from that intended by the maker of the program. Videotapes (and also television programs) can be important tools for political or religious mobilization. To what extent are people watching videotapes with explicitly political or religious content, and to what extent are they watching Western-style entertainment (which has its own implicit messages)?

On a different level, how does foreign programming affect Arabs' ideas about the non-Arab world, Arabs' ideas about their own societies, and Arabs' sense of their own identity? Global media, in some respects, make it impossible for Arabs not to see themselves as Arabs (if only because of language), but it may also make some aspire to different social and political conditions than those under which they currently live.

COMPARATIVE DATA

There have been very few studies of the new media in the Middle East, but there have been even fewer that have explicitly compared the creation of a regional media market with other areas of the world. Comparisons could yield quite interesting results. For example, Latin America is the only other region of the world in which so many countries are united by language but divided by political borders. In Latin America as well, there are significant regional powers with populations that do not speak the same language as the majority of the region. A number of trends would be fascinating to compare. One is the rise of a regional identity. Another is the possible emergence of regional information markets that transcend national borders or, better yet, the degree of business integration across the region. Yet another is how greater unification among countries that speak the same language (Spanish and Arabic) affects interactions with countries in those regions that speak different languages (Portuguese, Hebrew, Turkish, and Farsi).

CONCLUSION

In order to understand what is happening in the Middle East today, and to have any sense at all of what will happen in the future, we need far more data than we currently have. As the Arab world gets more deeply enmeshed in satellite television, we know shockingly little about what the people of the Middle East watch, and how they interpret that information. We also need to pursue efforts to compare the Middle East with other regions of the world. Eventually, we could see television uniting the region in a way that has not been envisioned for decades—although we may witness a new Middle East united through commerce or we may see a new Arabism emerge which comes from the grassroots up rather than from the top down.

For sure, satellite television is a new force in the Arab world and Al Jazeera has so far succeeded in acquiring a prominent position. In the longer run, Al Jazeera's impact may turn out to have little to do with its news coverage. Rather, Al Jazeera may turn out to be the pioneer of experimental, risk-taking and audience-driven programming that drives a range of changes within and between Arab states. Al Jazeera may reinvent itself to even better serve its audience, or it may prove unable to adapt to a more competitive media market. The channel's audience may prove to be a moving target, as well. Staying fresh and relevant may prove an increasingly difficult challenge, especially if popular attitudes begin to shift or fragment. Changes could partly be brought on by Al Jazeera itself, as the channel and its competitors introduce new ideas and new formats in a struggle to retain the attention of their audiences.

NOTES

1 Country income data is available at <http://www.worldbank.org/data/countrydata/countrydata.html>.
2 International demographic data is available at <http://www.census.gov/ipc/www/idbsum.html>.
3 Foreign can mean two things in this case. It can refer to what is external to the region, and thus to American or European content. But foreign

can also refer to intraregional differences. Thus, differences in mores between the Persian Gulf and the Mashriq can affect both societies. Anecdotally, we hear reports of Egyptian-produced dramas respecting Gulf sensibilities on male–female relations, and we see a huge audience for the flirtatious style of Lebanese programming in the more conservative Gulf.

Select Bibliography

Abou Amoud, Mohamed Saad. 2002. "The changing dynamics between media and politics: developing Arab media." *Arab Affairs*, 112: 90–105.

Ajami, Fouad. 2001. "What the Muslim world is watching." *New York Times*, November 18.

Al Ghreibi, Habib, Ismail, F., Al Kasim, F., and Zayani, M. 2003. "Arab satellite channels and the coverage of the war against Iraq." *Al Mustaqbal Al Arabi*, 295 (September): 117–52.

Al Kasim, Faisal. 1999. "*Crossfire*: the Arab version." *Harvard International Journal of Press/Politics*, 4 (3): 93–7.

Al Shammari, Suleiman. 1998. *The Opposite Direction: An Academic Study*. Doha: Dar Al Sharq.

——. 1999. *The Arab Nationalist Dimension in Al Jazeera Satellite Channel: A Case Study of the Opposite Direction*. Doha: Dar Al Sharq.

Alterman, Jon B. 1998. *New Media, New Politics: From Satellite Television to the Internet in the Arab World*. Washington DC: The Washington Institute for Near East Policy.

Anderson, Jon, and Eickelman, D.F. 1999. "Media convergence and its consequences." *Middle East Insight*, 14 (2): 59–61.

Ayish, Muhammad I. 2002. "Political communication on Arab world television: evolving patterns." *Political Communication*, 19: 137–54.

——. 2004. *Arab World Television in the Age of Globalization: An Analysis of Emerging Political, Economic, Cultural and Technological Patterns*. Hamburg: Deutsches Orient-Institut.

Bahry, Louay Y. 2001. "The new Arab media phenomenon: Qatar's Al Jazeera." *Middle East Policy*, 8 (2): 88–99.

Bodi, Faisal. 2004. "Al Jazeera's war." In David Miller (ed.), *Tell me Lies: Propaganda and Media Distortion in the Attack on Iraq*. London: Pluto Press, 243–50.

Bradley, John R. 2004. "Will Al Jazeera bend?" *Prospect*, 97 (April): 46–51.

Bukholder, Richard. 2002. "Arabs favor Al Jazeera over state-run channels for world news." *Gallup Tuesday Briefing*, November 12.

Da Lage, Olivier. 2000. "La diplomatie de Doha: deux yeux plus gros que le ventre." *Arabies* (May). <http://mapage.noos.fr/odalage/autres/qat.html>.

Eickelman, Dale, and Anderson, J. (eds). 1999. *New Media in the Muslim World: The Emerging Public Sphere*. Bloomington: Indiana University Press.

El-Nawawy, Mohamed, and Farag, A.I. 2002. *Al Jazeera: How the Free Arab News Network Scooped the World and Changed the Middle East*. Boulder: Westview Press.

Fandy, M. 2000. "Information technology, trust, and social change in the Arab world." *Middle East Journal*, 54 (3): 378–94.

Ghadbian, Najib. 2002. "Contesting the state media monopoly: Syria on Al Jazeera television." *Middle East Review of International Affairs*, 5 (2). <http://www.biu.ac.il/SOC/besa.meria/journal/2001/issue2/jv5n2a7.html>.

Gher, Leo A., and Amin H.Y. (eds). 2000. *Civic Discourse and Digital Age Communication in the Middle East.* Stamford, CT: Ablex Publishing Corporation.

Hafez, Kai (ed.). 2000. *Islam and the West in the Mass Media: Fragmented Images in a Globalizing World.* Cresskill: Hampton Press.

——. (ed.) 2001. *Mass Media, Politics, and Society in the Middle East.* Cresskill: Hampton Press.

Hirst, David. 2001. "Qatar calling: Al Jazeera, the Arab TV channel that dares to shock." *Le Monde Diplomatique,* August 8.

The Information Revolution and the Arab World: Its Impact on State and Society. 1998. Abu Dhabi: The Emirates Center for Strategic Studies and Research.

Kraidy, Marwan. 2003. "Arab satellite television between regionalization and globalization." *Global Media Journal,* 2 (2). <http://lass.calumet.purdue.edu/cca/gmj/SubmittedDocuments/Kraidy.htm>.

Lynch, Marc. 2003. "Taking Arabs seriously." *Foreign Affairs,* 82 (6).

Lamloum, Olfa (ed.). 2003. *Irak: les medias en guerre.* Paris: Sindbad/Actes Sud.

——. 2004. *Al Jazira, miroir rebelle et ambigu du monde arabe.* Paris: La Decouverte.

Mermier, Frank (ed.). 2001. *Mondialization et nouveaux medias dans l'espace Arabe.* Paris: Maison Neuve & Larose.

Miles, Hugh. 2005. *Al Jazeera: How Arab TV News Challenges America.* New York: Grove Press.

Saad, Lydia. 2002. "Al Jazeera: Arabs rate its objectivity." *Gallup Poll Tuesday Briefing,* April 23.

Sakr, Naomi. 2001. *Satellite Realms: Transnational Television, Globalization and the Middle East.* London: I.B. Tauris.

Sreberny-Mohammadi, Annabelle. 1998. "The media and democratization in the Middle East: the strange case of television." In Vicky Randall (ed.), *Democratization and the Media.* London: Frank Cass, 179–99.

Tabar, Mary-Denise. 2002. "Printing press to satellite: a historical case study of media and the Arab state." <http://cct.georgetown.edu/thesis/MaryDeniseTabar.pdf>.

Wu, Steven. 1999. "This just in: Qatar satellite channel." *Harvard International Review,* 21 (4): 14–15.

Zayani, Mohamed. 2004. *Arab Satellite Television and Politics in the Middle East.* Abu Dhabi: The Emirates Center for Strategic Studies and Research.

Zubeidi, Moufeed. 2003. *Al Jazeera Channel: Breaking Taboos in Arab Media.* Beirut: Dar Atalia'a.

Notes on Contributors

Jon Alterman is Director of the Middle East Program at the Center for Strategic and International Studies in Washington, DC. He holds a Ph.D. in history from Harvard University. He is the author of *New Media, New Politics: From Satellite Television to the Internet in the Arab World* and numerous scholarly articles.

Faisal Al Kasim is a journalist and the host of a talk show program on Al Jazeera Satellite Channel called *The Opposite Direction*. After earning his Ph.D. in literature, he worked for the BBC Arabic Service as a broadcast journalist, producer and announcer for seven years. Then he moved to BBC Arabic television to work as a presenter of the main news rounds and anchor of panel discussions for nearly two years. He joined Al Jazeera in 1996.

Muhammad I. Ayish is acting Dean of the College of Communication at the University of Sharjah, UAE. He holds a Ph.D. in broadcasting from the University of Minnesota-Twin Cities. He is the author of *Arab World Television in the Age of Globalization* and several articles in Arabic and English in leading international journals. His research interests include Arab world broadcasting, new media technologies, media and politics and media and social change.

Gloria Awad is a journalist and a writer. She has a doctorate in information science from Paris. Currently she teaches at the University of Artois in France. She is the author of *Du sensationnel: les media dans le collimateur*. Her main research interests include media and mediation, communication and internationalization, and media and identity.

Ehab Yassir Bessaiso is a Ph.D. candidate in the Department of Journalism, Media and Cultural Studies at the University of Wales, where he is teaching and conducting research on propaganda and political communication. His early graduate work is on Al Jazeera after September 11. Currently, he is working on the Palestinian media strategy in addressing Western societies.

Olivier Da Lage is a journalist with Radio France Internationale specializing in the Middle East. He is the author of *Géopolitique de l'Arabie Saoudite* and *Obtenir sa carte de presse et la conserver*, and co-author of *Golfe: le jeu des six familles*. He is also a frequent contributor to *Le Monde diplomatique, Ouest-France* and *Science et vie*. Since 1982, he has been in charge of the economic and social Prospectus which is published by *Le Monde* on the countries of the Arab Peninsula.

Mohammed El Oifi is Associate Professor of international relations and political science at the Institut d'Études Politiques de Paris. His research focuses on Arab media and the evolution of political debates in the Arab world. His most recent publications include "L'opinion publique arabe et la guerre en Iraq" (in *RAMSES*) and "L'effet Al Jazira" (in *Revue Politique Etrangère*).

Naomi Sakr is a lecturer on the political economy of communication and communication policy and development at the University of Westminster, UK. She is the author of *Satellite Realms: Transnational Television, Globalization and the Middle East* and editor of *Women and the Media in the Middle East*. She writes on issues of media development and governance in the Middle East and North Africa for academic journals and various international organizations, including the London-based NGO Article XIX, and the Human Development Report Office of the United Nations Development Program.

R.S. Zaharna is Director of the Graduate Program for Professionals in the School of Communication at the American University in Washington, DC. She has a Ph.D. in communication from Columbia University. She has written and lectured extensively on international public relations and specializes in communication issues affecting Arab–American relations. During the past three decades, she has served as a media advisor and communciation consultant for international corporations, non-governmental organizations, and diplomatic missions, including the United Nations, the World Bank, and USAID.

Mohamed Zayani is an Associate Professor of critical theory at the American University of Sharjah, UAE. He received his Ph.D. from Indiana University in Bloomington. Since then, he has taught at several universities both in the United States and in the Middle East. He is the author of *Reading the Symptom* and *Arab Satellite Television and Politics in the Middle East*. Currently, he is working on a Social Science Research Council collaborative research project on media in the Arab world.

Index

Compiled by Auriol Griffith-Jones

Note: Page numbers in **bold** refer to Tables; those in *italic* refer to Figures. Notes are indexed only where there is substantial additional information.